Routledge Revivals

The Novels of Virginia Woolf

This is a reissue of a critical introduction to the novels of Virginia Woolf, first published in 1977. It makes close, illuminating readings of her nine novels, placing Woolf in her literary context and providing an accessible, clear and valuable guide for students starting out on a study of Woolf as a novelist, and for general readers seeking a fresh, helpful entry-point to the challenge of reading Woolf. Twenty years later, Hermione Lee wrote a prize-winning and acclaimed biography of Virginia Woolf: this critical study represented an early stage in this biographer-critic's life-long interest and involvement with Woolf's life and work.

The Novels of Virginia Woolf

Hermione Lee

This edition includes a new
Introduction by the author

Routledge
Taylor & Francis Group

First published in 1977
by Methuen & Co. Ltd

This edition first published in 2010 by Routledge
4 Park Square, Milton Park, Abingdon, Oxon OX14 4RN
605 Third Avenue, New York, NY 10017

Routledge is an imprint of the Taylor & Francis Group, an informa business

Publisher's Note
The publisher has gone to great lengths to ensure the quality of this
reprint but points out that some imperfections in the original copies may
be apparent.

Disclaimer
The publisher has made every effort to trace copyright holders and
welcomes correspondence from those they have been unable to contact.

ISBN 13: 978-0-415-56242-3 (hbk)
ISBN 13: 978-0-415-56800-5 (pbk)

Foreword to 2010 edition

This was my first book. I wrote it – instead of writing a doctoral thesis – in my late twenties, while teaching at Liverpool University in the 1970s. It was commissioned by Helen Fraser at Methuen, who was then, like me, at the beginning of her career. Personally, it came out of a very early, private, intense and uncritical passion for Woolf's work, which, during my time in the 1960s as an undergraduate and graduate student at Oxford, had run up against two ways of thinking about her, completely at odds with each other, both of which I found difficult to deal with. One was a haughty, rationalist dismissal of her work by male critics and teachers, as over-sensitive, "feminine", impressionistic, precious, and negligible. This attitude, which I encountered in force at Oxford, had been going strong since the 1930s. (It still thrives in Britain, and never ceases to amaze her critics and readers in America or Europe). If Woolf was praised at all by this camp, it would be for her essays, which were often used as a tool for disparaging the novels.

The opposite way of thinking about her came out of the feminist revolution of the late 1960s – which I was slow to understand or learn from – which had begun to construct Woolf as a feminist heroine, and the beginnings of Bloomsbury-mania, fuelled by the on-going publication of her biography and her letters in the 1970s. Both these schools of thought about Woolf inhibited me. I was sufficiently under the influence of Oxford's then very male-dominated academic environment (as Woolf herself felt inhibited, at the start of her writing life, in the company of her public-school educated, Cambridge rationalist friends) to be anxious in this book not to express my own strong feelings about her work, not to say "I", and not to relax into colloquial, simple prose from what I thought should be the formal language of scholarly criticism. (I remember being mortified when someone, meeting me soon after he had looked at this book, said, "Oh, I thought you'd be much older, from your prose style".)

At the same time, I felt the need to resist what seemed to me a sentimentalising or sensationalising of Woolf's life by her fans.

Hence the stiff, gloomy and puritanical tone of my first paragraph, and my reluctance to grant her the status of a "major" novelist, which now read to me as comical and embarrassing hostages to fortune. On the other hand, the publisher's need for a clear, useful introduction to the novels for students and general readers, and my own desire to look closely at the language and structure and meanings of each novel and to try and see how they worked, freed me up to write directly and carefully about the books, without reference to other critics. The book got better as it went on, I think, and it makes a few points which still seem fresh and original, like the comparisons with Stevie Smith, or the account of the fairy-tale in *To the Lighthouse*, or the analysis of speech patterns in *The Waves,* or of language in *Between the Acts*.

Twenty years later, looking back on my literary relationship with Virginia Woolf at the end of my 1996 biography of her, I briefly traced her critical history. The paragraph is worth quoting here, since this book plays a small part in the story it tells. "In the mid-1960s ... she was not studied in my Oxford English course. At graduate level, she was described to me by my tutor as a minor modernist, not to be classed with Joyce, Eliot or Lawrence, and this was how I thought of her for some years. While I was a student, Leonard Woolf's collections of her essays began to come out, but it was not until the 1970s that Quentin Bell's biography (1972), the edition of the *Letters* (beginning in 1975), the *Diary* (beginning in 1977), *Moments of Being* (1975) and the first of the edited manuscripts (*The Pargiters*, 1977) were being published. The edited essays would not follow for another ten years ... I published a short introduction to Virginia Woolf's novels, in 1977, which the publishers thought useful for novice readers of difficult modernist works, "whose interest has been aroused by the continuing publication of biographical material". In the twenty years since, I have been reading a Virginia Woolf who has greatly changed. She has changed from the Virginia Woolf who died in 1941, or the Virginia Woolf whose *Writer's Diary* in 1953 seemed so aesthetically intense, so painfully serious and driven, or the Virginia Woolf of Quentin Bell's biography, eccentric genius, brilliant comic aunt, enchanting friend ... Posthumously, it feels as if she has generously, abundantly opened herself up to such retellings ... Virginia Woolf's story is reformulated by each generation."

I'm glad, looking back, that I ended this little book by quoting the vaguely prophetic words of Mrs Swithin in *Between the Acts* – "but we have other lives, I think, I hope" – as suggesting "the impersonal achievement of the writer, whose immortality is words", and whose posthumous life continues to change and evolve as those words are re-read.

The Novels of
VIRGINIA
WOOLF

HERMIONE LEE

The Novels of
VIRGINIA
WOOLF

Methuen & Co Ltd
LONDON

First published in 1977
by Methuen & Co Ltd
11 *New Fetter Lane London* EC4P 4EE
Printed in Great Britain
by Butler & Tanner Ltd
Frome and London
© 1977 *Hermione Lee*

ISBN 0 416 8 28604 (*hardbound*)
ISBN 0 416 8 28701 (*paperback*)

to my parents

Contents

Acknowledgements

My thanks are due to Joan Welford, Secretary in the Department of English at Liverpool, for typing the manuscript. I am also grateful to students, colleagues and friends for inspiration, encouragement and advice, in particular to Nick Grene and Nick Shrimpton in the Department of English at Liverpool, Tom Heacox in the Department of English at the College of William and Mary, Williamsburg, and Jenny Uglow.

The author and publishers wish to thank the Virginia Woolf Literary Estate, the Hogarth Press and Harcourt Brace Jovanovich, Inc., for permission to reproduce extracts from Virginia Woolf's writings; Faber and Faber Ltd for permission to reproduce an extract from *The Whitsun Weddings* by Philip Larkin; Alfred A. Knopf, Inc., and Faber and Faber Ltd for permission to reproduce extracts from *The Palm at the End of the Mind*; and James Mac-Gibbon, the Stevie Smith Estate executor, for permission to reproduce an extract from *The Collected Poems of Stevie Smith* (Allen Lane).

A note on the text

REFERENCES to Virginia Woolf's novels and short stories, and to *A Room Of One's Own*, are to the Penguin Modern Classics editions. References to *Flush*, *Roger Fry* and *Three Guineas* are to the Hogarth Press editions.

In Chapters 1–9 page references to the novel under discussion are found in brackets after the quotations. All other references are in the footnotes.

Omissions I have made in quotations from Virginia Woolf are indicated thus, [. . .], to distinguish them from Virginia Woolf's own use of a series of periods, which are indicated thus, . . .

The following abbreviations have been used:

AWD	*A Writer's Diary: Being Extracts from the Diary of Virginia Woolf*, ed. Leonard Woolf (London, Hogarth Press, 1953)
Bell	Quentin Bell, *Virginia Woolf: A Biography* (London, Hogarth Press, 1972)
I:	Volume I: *Virginia Stephen 1882–1912*
II:	Volume II: *Mrs Woolf 1912–1941*
CE I–IV	Virginia Woolf, *Collected Essays*, ed. Leonard Woolf, 4 vols (London, Chatto and Windus, 1966–7)

The Novels of
VIRGINIA
WOOLF

Introduction

Tʜɪs is not a book about Bloomsbury, lesbianism, madness or suicide. It does not deal with Virginia Woolf as a feminist, as an owner of the Hogarth Press, as a critic and essayist, or as a biographer. It is a literary criticism of her nine novels, written in the hope of turning attention back from the life to the fictional work, but in the belief that the interest which has been aroused by Quentin Bell's biography, and which continues to be serviced by the publication of Virginia Woolf's letters and by an aggregation of Bloomsburiana, makes this an appropriate time for another study of her achievement as a novelist.

The criticism of Virginia Woolf has gone through several phases. The enthusiasm and admiration she aroused in the twenties (in France as much as in England) was offset in the thirties by hostile attacks from the 'Scrutineers', J. F. Holms, Muriel Bradbrook, Q. D. Leavis and W. H. Mellers, and from American critics such as William Troy and J. W. Beach.[1] Wyndham Lewis, an enemy of Bloomsbury, struck the most aggressive note in *Men without Art* (1934), where he accused Virginia Woolf of inheriting the worst of the Paterian 'reaction against Victorian manners', and of perpetuating the 'suffocating atmosphere' of 'a very dim Venusberg indeed: but Venus has become an introverted matriarch,

---

[1] Details of the critical books and articles referred to in this Introduction will be found in the Bibliography.

brooding over a subterraneous "stream of consciousness" – a feminine phenomenon after all . . .'[1] Lewis's attack has since been supported by, among others, F. R. Leavis, who summed up the 'Scrutineers'' position with his dismissal in 1942 of her 'sophisticated aestheticism'; by D. S. Savage, who complained of the lack of any 'positively dynamic spiritual affirmation' in her work; by Graham Greene in his expression of dislike for Mrs Dalloway's whimsical subjectivity; and by Barbara Hardy in her attack on Mrs Ramsay for being too like Mrs Dale and not enough like The Wife of Bath or Molly Bloom. More sympathetic English criticism reached a high level in the forties with David Daiches's and Joan Bennett's excellent books, and the fifties produced two very different studies which have both had considerable influence. One was the chapter in Auerbach's *Mimesis* (translated into English in 1953), which arrived at an understanding of Virginia Woolf's significance through the analysis of a passage from *To the Lighthouse*, and the other was J. K. Johnstone's book *The Bloomsbury Group* (1954), in which a close relationship is established between the philosophy of G. E. Moore and the work of Virginia Woolf, E. M. Forster and Lytton Strachey. But, although the publication of *A Writer's Diary* in 1953 enlarged the perspective of Virginia Woolf's critics, interest seemed to lapse in the late fifties and early sixties, apart from a short but impressive reappraisal by A. D. Moody in 1963 (which contains, in its final chapter, a splendid demolition of the 'Scrutineers'' critical line). It was not until the latter part of the sixties, well after the publication of Leonard Woolf's *Autobiography*, that the fascination with Bloomsbury and with Virginia Woolf began to grow, in America as well as in England. It was fed by the publication of Holroyd's biography of Lytton Strachey (1967–8), E. M. Forster's *Maurice* (1971) and Bell's biography of Virginia Woolf (1972). The spate of biographical and critical works culminated, in 1973, in the publication of four full-length studies of Virginia Woolf (three of them American), a new collection of her short stories, and Nigel Nicolson's *Portrait of a Marriage*.

The activities of biography and criticism are reciprocal: Virginia

[1] Wyndham Lewis, *Men without Art* (London, Cassell, 1934), Ch. V, pp. 158–71.

Woolf's novels seem to have become more interesting, and are more widely read, because of the vogue for Bloomsbury. But what makes Bloomsbury intriguing has not, perhaps, really very much to do with what makes Virginia Woolf an important novelist.

Bloomsbury follows the tendency of many English intellectuals and artists to form themselves, however loosely, into groups. In the last century alone, the Lake Poets, the Oxford Movement, the Clapham Sect and the Pre-Raphaelite Brotherhood provide widely differing examples of the same process. Interest in such groups is usually partly historical, partly intellectual and partly sexual. There is obviously a comparison to be drawn between the vogue for the PRB and for Bloomsbury, which is the latest of such groups to have become sufficiently distant in time to bear analysis and commentary. It is entertaining to discover who was sleeping with whom and what they said about it, in a group of more or less talented, intelligent and malicious people, which ranged (taking 'Bloomsbury' in its very widest sense) from the aristocratic goings-on of Ottoline Morrell and Vita Sackville-West to the bohemian life of the Slade. The perspective of the seventies on the interbellum years has the advantage of a recently acquired historical aloofness. Those sexual permutations out of which Michael Holroyd, Nigel Nicolson and others make such lively capital win our interest (and even our applause) as particularly clear manifestations of a reaction against Victorian manners, in a circle which largely drew its antecedents from the intellectual aristocracy of the nineteenth century. Bloomsbury's selfconscious ideal of a sexual revolution (perhaps more talked about than practised) is summed up by Lytton Strachey (of course), in a characteristic piece of Bloomsburian bravado:

> Obviously Victorianism had incapacitated him [Henry Sidgwick]. 'What an appalling time to have lived!' Lytton exclaimed in horror. 'It was the Glass Case Age. Themselves as well as their ornaments, were left under glass cases. Their refusal to face any fundamental question fairly – either about people or God – looks at first sight like cowardice; but I believe it was simply the result of an innate incapacity for penetration – for getting either out of themselves or into anything or anybody else. They were enclosed in glass. How

intolerable! Have you noticed, too, that they were nearly all physically impotent? – Sidgwick himself, Matthew Arnold, Jowett, Leighton, Ruskin, Watts. It's damned difficult to copulate through a glass case.'[1]

Copulation as an expression of liberation from Victorian hypocrisy took predominantly homosexual forms, from Lytton Strachey's or Vita Sackville-West's outspoken pursuits of their ideal passions, to Forster's or Virginia Woolf's more tentative and reticent emotional preferences. At the same time, Bloomsbury developed strongly matriarchal characteristics. The masculine ambience of Cambridge in which it had its origins was much changed by the London influence of the Stephen sisters. Vanessa Bell at Charleston, Carrington at the Mill House and at Ham Spray, and Ottoline Morrell 'murmuring on buggery'[2] at Bedford Square or at Garsington, created an atmosphere in which their friends and lovers (who included many of the most important intellectual figures of the time) could thrive. Bloomsbury has not for this reason been hailed as a precursor of the woman's movement, but there is nevertheless a link between the interest in its sexual and social organization, and the recent enshrinement of Virginia Woolf, not only as a leading member of the Bloomsbury Group, but also as a dedicated feminist.

This byway in the criticism of her works has been pursued, following Herbert Marder's lively book *Feminism and Art* (1968), in three recent critical studies. James Naremore, Nancy Topping Bazin and Alice van Buren Kelley concentrate on the dichotomy expressed in Virginia Woolf's work between two kinds of life. Naremore (much the best of the three critics) defines these as the masculine, ego-ridden, assertive, factual world of the self and the amorphous, creative, feminine, intuitive world without a self. Bazin, in a book called *Virginia Woolf and the Androgynous Vision*, distinguishes more crudely between the masculine and feminine type of experience and relates them to the two stages of Virginia Woolf's mental illnesses, mania (feminine) and depression (masculine). She suggests that the experiences Virginia Woolf underwent in her 'manic' phases were

[1] Lytton Strachey to Maynard Keynes, 1906, quoted Michael Holroyd, *Lytton Strachey: A Biography* (Harmondsworth, Penguin, 1971), p. 312.

[2] Ibid. p. 627.

creatively productive. Kelley describes the conflict in the novels between 'fact and vision' – between, again, the masculine and the feminine point of view.

Following this type of criticism, a table might be drawn up to categorize the dualities in Virginia Woolf's novels, thus:

Masculine	*Feminine*
Intellect	Intuition
Fact	Vision
Day	Night
Waking	Dreaming
Words	Silence
Society	Solitude
Clock time	Consciousness time
Realism	Impressionism
Opaqueness	Transparency
Land	Water

and so on – the elements in the two columns being fused in the androgynous mind. This does to some extent describe the business of the novels. But to centre a criticism of Virginia Woolf entirely on these dualities provides a rather narrow perspective. Taken to extremes, criticism of Virginia Woolf which is emphatically feminist cannot get very far with any of the fiction, except perhaps *Orlando*. Kate Millett's attempt at criticism, for example, gives up uneasily, betraying a lack of sympathy for the tone and content of the novels:

> Virginia Woolf glorified two housewives, Mrs Dalloway and Mrs Ramsay, recorded the suicidal misery of Rhoda in *The Waves* without ever explaining its causes, and was argumentative yet somehow unsuccessful, perhaps because unconvinced, in conveying the frustrations of the woman artist in Lily Briscoe. Only in *A Room of One's Own*, essay rather than fiction, could she describe what she knew.[1]

The reasons for reading Virginia Woolf do not make themselves felt in that critique. As fuel for the women's movement, or as

[1] Kate Millett, *Sexual Politics* (London, Hart-Davis, 1971; Abacus, 1972), pp. 139–40.

fictionalized versions of the ethics of Bloomsbury, her novels are of very limited significance, though, paradoxically, their recent popularity arises largely from those two centres of interest.

It is not enough to judge Virginia Woolf's work in terms of its affinity with Bloomsbury's atmosphere and attitudes, if only for the reason that such an emphasis leaves out of count the important positive influence of Leslie Stephen. The sense of moral responsibility which characterizes her achievement owes as much to her father as it does to Bloomsbury. In fact, as Noel Annan points out in his fine book on Stephen, there is some similarity between Bloomsbury's aesthetic revolution against Victorianism and Stephen's rationalist departure from Evangelicism. Both set themselves courageously and honestly against the traditions in which they had been brought up; but both were influenced by the idea of Election, though grace, in their eyes, came through reason rather than faith. Both used the eighteenth century as a model; and both were engaged in the pursuit of the true. In Leslie Stephen's philosophical, biographical and critical work there is a sense of duty which forges a link between the beliefs of the Clapham Sect and the ideals of Bloomsbury and Virginia Woolf:

> Unable to remould the scheme of things nearer to his heart's desire, the rationalist labours on, now in this vineyard and in that, striving to bring order into one small corner of the chaos which surrounds him and to which he inescapably belongs. The belief that order can be created, and the realisation that his own efforts will change little in the world, are the two central facts in his experience that dignify and ennoble him.[1]

The mixture of desolation and effort which Annan characterizes here, though it reminds us of the absurd side of Mr Ramsay, also has relevance for Virginia Woolf's own achievements. She was, it is true, in revolt against her father's personal characteristics – his male aggression and tyranny, his violent opposition to the morbid and the effeminate, and his idealization of the domesticated woman. Her discomfort under those pressures and assumptions went on being expressed in her fictional and non-fictional works long after

[1] Noel Annan, *Leslie Stephen: His Thought and Character in Relation to his Time* (London, MacGibbon and Kee, 1951), p. 284.

Leslie Stephen's death. The stifling oppressiveness of the patriarchal Victorian family life (which she so often summed up by the image of a certain sort of room) had to be escaped from over and over again. In that reiterated rejection itself there is evidence of Leslie Stephen's influence on the material of her novels. Though Lytton Strachey's portrait is drawn several times, most obviously in her first novel, and *Night and Day* is said by Bell to be inspired by Vanessa Bell's life at Wissett with Duncan Grant,[1] the later novels found far more potent sources in her memories of her family, childhood and adolescence. And, though there can be no doubt that Mr Ramsay is in many ways a hostile portrait, it also expresses admiration and respect. Virginia Woolf was intellectually in debt to her father as much as she was emotionally oppressed by him. Not only were his friends – Thomas Hardy, George Meredith, Henry James – some of the most important of the nineteenth-century English writers; not only had he married into Thackeray's family; he also provided a generous literary education, which consisted of 'allowing a girl of fifteen the free run of a large and quite unexpurgated library'.[2]

And more than this, his interest in the character of an age as an essential part of the biography of individuals, the humour and elegance of much of his literary criticism, and the scrupulousness of his literary judgements, have a great deal in common, both in attitudes and methods, with Virginia Woolf's critical and theoretical work.

> Literature represents all the reasonings and feelings and passions of civilized men in all ages. . . . To select any particular variety as best for all is as absurd to say that every man ought to be a priest or that every man ought to be a soldier. But this I may say, Take hold anywhere, read what you really like and not what someone tells you that you ought to like; let your reading be part of your lives.[3]

> After all, what laws can be laid down about books? [. . .] To admit authorities, however heavily furred and gowned, into

---

[1] See p. 62 below, note 1.   [2] 'Leslie Stephen' (1932), *CE* IV, p. 79.

[3] Leslie Stephen, 'The Study of English Literature' (1887), *Men, Books and Mountains: Essays by Leslie Stephen,* collected S. O. Ullmann (London, Hogarth Press, 1956), p. 43.

our libraries and let them tell us how to read, what to read, what value to place upon what we read, is to destroy the spirit of freedom which is the breath of those sanctuaries.[1]

Her faith in enlightened independent judgement is evidently an inherited one. Similarly, Virginia Woolf's attempts to empathize with the characteristics of a historical period or a literary personality in order to understand them owe a good deal to Leslie Stephen's biographical and critical methods:

> No human being was ever more acutely sensitive to the opinions of the day than Pope . . . *The Rape of the Lock*, the *Dunciad* . . . first take their true colouring when you know the people for whom they were written; when you have a clear vision of Queen Anne 'taking sometimes counsel and sometimes tea' at Hampton Court, quarrelling with the Duchess of Marlborough, and going to meet Harley at Mrs Masham's; when you can elect yourself a member of Addison's 'little senate', where Steele, listening reverentially over his cups, and Budgell and Tickell and namby-pamby Philips are sitting around in rapt admiration, or follow the great man to Holland House and watch him writing a *Spectator* and revolving round two foci, each marked by a bottle of port . . . or drive over with Pope himself in a chariot to sit with Bolingbroke under a haystack and talk bad metaphysics in a pasture painted with spades and rakes; or let his waterman row you up from Westminster stairs to see his garden and present a crystal for his grotto, and talk to Gay and Swift till your host says, 'Gentlemen, I leave you to your wine,' and leaves three of you to finish the pint from which he has deducted two glasses.[2]

That lively, undemanding, impressionistic piece is quite close in character to Virginia Woolf's whimsical and fantastic review (in the form of a conversation) of the *Recollections of Lady Georgiana Peel*:

> Lord and Lady John were resting under an oak tree in Richmond Park when Lord John remarked how pleasant it

---

[1] 'How Should One Read a Book?' (1926), *CE* II, p. 1.

[2] Leslie Stephen, op. cit., p. 30.

would be to live in that white house behind the palings for the rest of their lives. No sooner said than the owner falls ill and dies. The Queen, with that unfailing insight, etc., sends for Lord John, etc., and offers him the lodge for life, etc., etc., etc. I mean they lived happily ever after, though as time went by, a factory chimney somewhat spoilt the view. *Judith:* And Lady Georgiana? *Ann:* Well, there's not much about Lady Georgiana. She saw the Queen having her hair brushed, and she went to stay at Woburn. And what d'you think they did there? They threw mutton chops out of the window 'for whoever cared to pick them up.' And each guest had a piece of paper by his plate 'in which to wrap up an eatable for the people waiting outside.' *Judith:* Mutton chops! People waiting outside! *Ann:* Ah, now the charm begins to work.[1]

The point of departure, as well as the points of comparison, make themselves felt. Virginia Woolf's passage is also trying to get 'under the skin' of the period, but it picks out for emphasis the odd, the unexpected and the grotesque, instead of the central and the decorative, in pursuance of her belief that we should not assume 'that life exists more fully in what is commonly thought big than what is commonly thought small'.[2] The sense of fun and the spirited, easy tone which are on display in 'A Talk about Memoirs' distinguish her critical work from her father's, which has a more authoritative and conventional tone. Here the influence of Bloomsbury does make itself felt, however peripheral it may be in her novels. In her journalism and her essays it is important. She shares a tone of voice, part conversational, part erudite, but never quite without the saving grace (or, in some cases, the fatal irresoluteness) of irony, which can be found in works as various as Strachey's *Eminent Victorians* (1918), Roger Fry's *Vision and Design* (1920) and Forster's essay 'What I Believe' (1939). The tone is used to set, without aggression, a civilized, liberated personal judgement against prevailing conventions which seem to the writers outmoded, hypocritical or repressive. It is informed, but not laborious; humorous, but not

---

[1] 'A Talk about Memoirs' (1920), *CE* IV, p. 217.
[2] 'Modern Fiction' (1919), *CE* II, p. 107.

trivial. Practised at an inferior level, as in Clive Bell's *Civilization*, it is extremely smug and offensive:

> To point the road is the task of the few. Neither guides nor lecturers these, the highly civilized, will merely live their lives; and living will be seen to have pleasures and desires . . . different from those of the busy multitude. By living passively they become the active promoters of good. For when it begins to appear that the few have discovered intense and satisfying delights which have escaped the notice of the less inquisitive and less gifted pleasure-seekers, the many will begin to wonder. They will wonder whether there may not be pleasures better than their own. Can art and thought, the play of wit and fancy, and the subtler personal relations really mean more to these odd people than racing, yachting, hunting, football, cinemas and whisky?[1]

That is Bloomsbury at its very worst. But those easy manners, used for more interesting ends, were nevertheless a perfect tool for Virginia Woolf's essays, particularly when she is being humorous.

> You who come of a younger and happier generation may not have heard of her – you may not know what I mean by The Angel in the House. I will describe her as shortly as I can. She was intensely sympathetic. She was immensely charming. She was utterly unselfish. She excelled in the difficult arts of family life. She sacrificed herself daily. If there was chicken, she took the leg; if there was a draught she sat in it – in short she was so constituted that she never had a mind or a wish of her own, but preferred to sympathize always with the minds and wishes of others. Above all – I need not say it – she was pure. Her purity was supposed to be her chief virtue – her blushes, her great grace. In those days – the last of Queen Victoria – every house had its Angel. And when I came to write I encountered her with the very first words.[2]

Still, the memory of talking about Marivaux to George Eliot on a Sunday afternoon was not a romantic memory. It

[1] Clive Bell, *Civilization* (London, Chatto and Windus, 1928), pp. 209–10.
[2] 'Professions for Women' (1931), *CE* II, p. 285.

had faded with the passage of years. It had not become picturesque.[1]

> In short, the only place in the mansion of literature that is assigned her [Mrs Browning] is downstairs in the servants' quarters, where, in company with Mrs Hemans, Eliza Cook, Jean Ingelow, Alexander Smith, Edwin Arnold, and Robert Montgomery, she bangs the crockery about and eats vast handfuls of peas on the point of her knife.[2]

That witty and irreverent tone is characteristic of Bloomsbury, and in Virginia Woolf's case, as in Forster's and Strachey's, it is misleading. The fun is for a purpose. Strachey's refashioning of historical biography and Forster's morality of personal relationships are serious matters, made acceptable to their audience by a deceptively agreeable, light presentation. Virginia Woolf is a very good literary critic, erudite, perceptive and thoughtful, particularly in her criticism of English, French and Russian novelists. If she had written no novels, she would have a place in twentieth-century letters as a considerable essayist. The fun at the expense of those who talk solemnly about George Eliot or Mrs Browning is the froth on the surface of a sound and wide-ranging literary judgement. And, though her non-fictional work amalgamates the high standards of Leslie Stephen with the ease and wit of Bloomsbury, it is at the same time idiosyncratic and distinctive. Her most valuable literary judgements work through images, which link the technique of the essays to those of the novels, as in this commentary on *Mansfield Park*:

> Here is nothing out of the way; it is midday in Northamptonshire; a dull young man is talking to rather a weakly young woman on the stairs as they go up to dress for dinner, with housemaids passing. But, from triviality, from commonplace, their words become suddenly full of meaning, and the moment for both one of the most memorable in their lives. It fills itself; it shines; it glows; it hangs before us, deep, trembling, serene for a second; next, the housemaid passes, and this drop, in

[1] 'George Eliot' (1919), *CE* I, p. 196.
[2] '*Aurora Leigh*' (1931), *CE* I, pp. 209–10.

which all the happiness of life has collected, gently subsides again to become part of the ebb and flow of ordinary existence.[1]

The passage reveals the difference between Leslie Stephen's nineteenth-century rational discursiveness and Virginia Woolf's modernist effort to encapsulate truth in figures of speech.

Virginia Woolf's contribution to modernism is an important one. The term is most easily defined through examples, as by Frank Kermode in 'The Modern' when he says that 'on the whole, everybody knows what is meant by modern literature, modern art, modern music. The words suggest Joyce, Picasso, Schoenberg, or Stravinsky – the experiments of two or more generations back.'[2] Elsewhere in the same essay Kermode fixes the 'peak period' of the modernist 'movement' as 'somewhere around 1910–1925'.[3] A similar kind of definition through example occurs in an article by Richard Wasson, who describes 'the literature we call modern' as 'the literature represented in English by Yeats, Eliot, and Joyce, in French by Proust, in German by Hesse'.[4] Other names – Lawrence, Kafka, Gide, Musil, Pound, Stein – might be invoked. But such descriptions of modernism, though suggestive rather than definitive, do imply that the 'movement' has some recognizable common denominators. It is associated with the first third of this century. It applies to different art forms. It is experimental. And it is international – one of the marked characteristics of modernism being its crossing of cultural boundaries, for instance in the exodus of writers from America to France and England.

---

[1] 'Jane Austen' (1923), *CE* I, pp. 150–1.

[2] Frank Kermode, 'The Modern' (1956), reprinted in *Modern Essays* (London, Collins, 1971), pp. 65–6. For further definition, discussion and examples of modernism, see Richard Ellmann and Charles Fiedelson (eds), *The Modern Tradition* (Oxford University Press, 1965), and Cyril Connolly (ed.), *One Hundred Key Books from England, France and America 1880–1950* (London, André Deutsch and Hamish Hamilton, 1965).

[3] Kermode, op. cit. p. 42.

[4] Richard Wasson, 'Notes on a New Sensibility', *Partisan Review*, Vol. XXXVI (1969), pp. 460–77. Quoted by William A. Johnsen in 'Towards a Re-definition of Modernism', *Boundary 2*, Vol. II, No. 3 (Spring 1974), p. 542.

Definitions of literary modernism (particularly when the modern is being contrasted with the avant-garde or the contemporary) very often emphasize the two aspects with which Virginia Woolf herself was most concerned in her comments on modern fiction. First, modernism is usually described as a response to an era whose political and social developments invited nihilism, scepticism and despair; an era thus described in 1929:

> The structures which are variously known as mythology, religion, and philosophy, and which are alike in that each has as its function the interpretation of experience in terms which have human values, have collapsed under the force of successive attacks and shown themselves utterly incapable of assimilating the new stores of experience which have been dumped upon the world. With increasing completeness science maps out the pattern of nature, but the latter has no relation to the pattern of human needs and feelings.[1]

If modernism has 'a persistent world-view', Kermode writes, 'it is one we should have to call apocalyptic'.[2] Modern literature is, then, an attempt to create in an environment hostile to order and faith – and, it seemed after 1914, to life itself. Second, it is often pointed out that there is an intimate relationship between the 'apocalyptic' world view of modernism and the *form* of its repeated efforts to 'make it new'. The experiments of the modernists were very largely (and very minutely) concerned with form, as though, by an intensive ordering process of a kind not before attempted, the chaotic universe might be mastered. Thus Kermode finds 'a kind of formal desperation' in the 'great experimental novels of early modernism'.[3] Through elaborate structuring, through allusion and literary references – the fusion of 'tradition and the individual talent' – through images and through myths, the modern writer expressed 'a yearning to pierce through the messy phenomenal world to some perfect and necessary form and order'.[4]

[1] Joseph Wood Krutch, *The Modern Temper* (New York, Harcourt Brace and World, 1929; Harvest Books, 1956), p. 9.
[2] Kermode, op. cit. p. 40.   [3] Ibid. p. 48.
[4] William A. Johnsen, op. cit. pp. 541–2. Johnsen is here paraphrasing Iris Murdoch's criticism of modern literature, in 'The Sublime and the Beautiful Revisited', *Yale Review*, Vol. XLIX (1959), pp. 247–71.

Virginia Woolf is a remarkable, though not a major figure in this 'movement'. None of her novels has the stature or scope of Proust or of Conrad, of Joyce's *Ulysses* or of Lawrence's *The Rainbow*. She is, with Forster, in the second rank of twentieth-century novelists. Her imaginative territory is strictly demarcated by her social environment, her intellectual inheritance, her mental instability[1] and her sexual reserve. Yet no other English novelist of the period combined the theoretical analysis of the requirements for the modern novel with a continuing attempt, in every new work, to match her vision of reality with its appropriate form.

That she is aware of herself as being part of a movement is clear from her brilliant statements on the future of the modern novel (found essentially in 'Modern Fiction' (1925), 'Mr Bennett and Mrs Brown' (1924) and 'The Narrow Bridge of Art' (1927)) which dominate her reputation as an essayist. The most frequently quoted paragraph of her writing is reinvoked not only as an illustration of her own methods but as a central comment on modernism:

> Examine for a moment an ordinary mind on an ordinary day. The mind receives a myriad impressions – trivial, fantastic, evanescent, or engraved with the sharpness of steel. From all sides they come, an incessant shower of innumerable atoms; and as they fall, as they shape themselves into the life of Monday or Tuesday, the accent falls differently from of old; the moment of importance came not here but there; so that, if a writer were a free man and not a slave, if he could write what he chose, not what he must, if he could base his work upon his own feeling and not upon convention, there would be no plot, no comedy, no tragedy, no love interest or catastrophe in the accepted style, and perhaps not a single button sewn on as the Bond Street tailors would have it. Life is not a series of gig-lamps symmetrically arranged; life is a luminous halo, a semi-transparent envelope surrounding us from the beginning of consciousness to the end. Is it not the task of the novelist to convey this varying, this unknown and uncircumscribed spirit . . .[2]

---

[1] See p. 95–6 below.

[2] 'Modern Fiction' *CE* II, p. 106.

The passage has suffered from being too much quoted. Out of its historical context it does not seem a very convincing definition of what the novel should do; nor is it an entirely accurate summing up of her own achievements and intentions. In spite of the fluid structure of the novels, which creates the movement of intangible consciousnesses rather than of visible appearances or large-scale destinies, there is nevertheless a foundation of 'plot', 'comedy' and 'tragedy' which unites, in her best work, solidity with the 'luminous'. But for all this the message of 'Modern Fiction' was apt and useful in 1919, expressing exactly the Bergsonian[1] feeling of the time, in arts and in letters, that to think in terms of a fixed identity and of a common reality was no longer possible. The images with which she expresses this idea do double duty. They establish her idea of true reality; but in doing so they also reject, by implication, a whole tradition of literature. The lamps of a horse-drawn carriage and the buttons sewn by the Bond Street tailor suggest the material as well as the methods of the Victorian and Edwardian novel. The images that replace those figures of realism are cunningly chosen so as to have an air of scientific modernity, and, also, so as to seem intangible: the atoms, the luminous halo and the semi-transparent envelope are visual references which have, however, a vague and shapeless quality.

The antithesis in 'Modern Fiction' between representational scenes and amorphous shapes bears a marked resemblance to Roger Fry's theories of art. His preference for post-impressionist painters over a realist such as Sargent is analogous to Virginia Woolf's rejection of Bennett, Galsworthy and Wells in favour of the 'Georgians' – Forster, Lawrence, Joyce, Strachey, Eliot, Dorothy Richardson. In her biography of Roger Fry (1940) she quotes his description of Sargent's portrait of the Duke of Portland, which anticipates the distinction she makes in *Between the Acts* between portraits and pictures:

'First the collie dog which the Duke caresses has one lock of very white hair; secondly the Duke's boots are so polished that they glitter; thirdly the Duke's collar is very large and very stiffly starched; fourthly the Duke was when he stood for his

[1] See further, p. 111, n. 3, below.

portrait sunburnt. After that we might come to the Duke himself.' But by the time he came to the Duke himself [he] is so 'deadened by the fizz and crackle of Mr Sargent's brush work that (he) can see nothing'.[1]

The grounds for dislike are exactly the same as in Virginia Woolf's criticism of how Mr Bennett would treat Mrs Brown:

> Mr Bennett, alone of the Edwardians, would keep his eyes in the carriage. He, indeed, would observe every detail with immense care. He would notice the advertisements; the pictures of Swanage and Portsmouth; the way in which the cushion bulged between the buttons; how Mrs Brown wore a brooch which had cost three-and-ten-three at Whitworth's bazaar; and had mended both gloves – indeed the thumb of the left-hand glove had been replaced.[2]

What is to be set against this engrossment in 'childish problems of photographic representation'? (The phrase is Fry's.)[3] Fry and Virginia Woolf have the same answer: not illusion, but another reality; not imitation, but equivalence. The work of art must create, through form, its own terms for truth. Roger Fry tries to explain this in his Introduction to the catalogue of the second Post-Impressionist exhibition of 1912 (which contained works by Cézanne, Matisse, Picasso, Lhôte, Braque, and the English artists Duncan Grant, Vanessa Bell, Spencer Gore, Eric Gill and Wyndham Lewis):

> These artists [. . .] do not seek to give what can, after all, be but a pale reflex of actual appearance, but to arouse the conviction of a new and definite reality. They do not seek to imitate form, but to create form, not to imitate life, but to find an equivalent for life. By that I mean that they wish to make images which by the clearness of their logical structure, and by their closely-knit unity of texture, shall appeal to our disinterested and contemplative imagination with something of the same vividness as the things of actual life appeal to our

---

[1] Virginia Woolf, *Roger Fry* (1940), pp. 110–11.
[2] 'Mr Bennett and Mrs Brown' (1924), *CE* I, p. 328.
[3] *Roger Fry*, p. 164.

practical activities. In fact they aim not at illusion but at reality. [1]

He expands the argument in a letter written in 1913 to P. J. Atkins, a Leicester water-colourist:

The reality of a picture is immensely greater if the spectator is not referred back by illusion to a possible exterior reality (which is stronger and more real) but is held within the reality of the artistic creation by its sheer necessity and intensity of unity. [2]

It is no accident, then, that Virginia Woolf dated the change in 'human character' which called for a new kind of literature as taking place in December 1910 – the date of Roger Fry's first Post-Impressionist exhibition – nor that in her thoughts on literature she frequently employs analogies with painting. [3] But Virginia Woolf goes further than Roger Fry when she relates modernism in the arts to the emotional, social and intellectual climate of the 1910s. The need for the creation of a new reality, not through 'photographic representation' but through 'necessitated form', [4] is a need created by the conditions of existence. When she talks of a change taking place in December 1910 she is talking about a change in life rather than in art, as she makes humorously clear:

In life one can see the change, if I may use a homely illustration, in the character of one's cook. The Victorian cook lived like a leviathan in the lower depths, formidable, silent, obscure, inscrutable; the Georgian cook is a creature of sunshine and fresh air; in and out of the drawing-room, now to borrow the *Daily Herald*, now to ask advice about a hat. [5]

This may seem too bland and cosy to be taken seriously. But it presents the lighthearted side of the difficult and unsettling nature

[1] Ibid. pp. 177–8.
[2] *Letters of Roger Fry*, ed. Denys Sutton (London, Chatto and Windus, 1972), Vol. I, p. 364.
[3] See Chapter 4, pp. 92–3 below, for her correspondence with the painter Jacques Raverat; see 'Walter Sickert' (1933), *CE* II, pp. 233–44; and see Lily Briscoe in *To the Lighthouse*.
[4] *Letters of Roger Fry*, p. 364.
[5] 'Mr Bennett and Mrs Brown', *CE* I, p. 320.

of twentieth-century life, which must be taken seriously, and for which the artist has a public duty to find some fitting expression:

> The mind is full of monstrous, hybrid, unmanageable emotions. That the age of the earth is 3,000,000,000 years; that human life lasts but a second; that the capacity of the human mind is nevertheless boundless; that life is infinitely beautiful yet repulsive; that one's fellow creatures are adorable but disgusting; that science and religion have between them destroyed belief; that all bonds of union seem broken, yet somehow control must exist – it is in this atmosphere of doubt and conflict that writers have now to create [. . .][1]

The old confidence in a general, recognizable perspective on life and character has vanished. There is indeed some envy and wistfulness in the tone in which Virginia Woolf looks back on the literature of an empiricist universe:

> In both [Scott and Jane Austen] there is the same natural conviction that life is of a certain quality. They have their judgment of conduct. They know the relations of human beings towards each other and towards the universe [. . .] Certainty of that kind is the condition which makes it possible to write. To believe that your impressions hold good for others is to be released from the cramp and confinement of personality.[2]

But there should be no pretending that that comfortable perspective remains. The idea of life and character presented in the Edwardian novel is, according to Virginia Woolf, a fraudulent attempt to sustain a fixed idea of reality under inappropriate conditions. Paradoxical though it may seem to call her a more realistic novelist than H. G. Wells, that is the response she demands. Her idea of modernism was that it must pursue the expression of a reality more true to post-war sensibilities. A settled point of view, chronological continuity, and the idea that one can say of anyone

---

1 'The Narrow Bridge of Art' (1927), *CE* II, p. 219.
2 'How it Strikes a Contemporary' (1923), *CE* II, p. 159.

'that they were this or were that'[1] will no longer do. 'Georgian' writers have already learned – from Sterne, from Meredith, from the Russian novelists and above all from Proust – that the soul is 'streaked, variegated, all of a mixture',[2] and that if it is to be accurately 'translated' into literature, we must learn to 'tolerate the spasmodic, the obscure, the fragmentary, the failure'.[3]

I use the word 'translated' because it is the word which Proust uses in the antithesis drawn in *Time Regained* between photographic realism and true reality.

> If reality were indeed a sort of waste product of experience, more or less identical for each one of us, since when we speak of bad weather, a war, a taxi rank, a brightly lit restaurant, a garden full of flowers, everybody knows what we mean, if reality were no more than this, no doubt a sort of cinematograph film of these things would be sufficient and the 'style', the 'literature' that departed from the simple data that they provide would be superfluous and artificial. But was it true that reality was no more than this? If I tried to understand what actually happens at the moment when a thing makes some particular impression upon me – on the day, for instance, when as I crossed the bridge over the Vivonne the shadow of a cloud upon the water had made me cry: 'Damn!' and jump for joy; or the occasion when, hearing a phrase of Bergotte's, all that I had disengaged from my impression was the not specially relevant remark: 'How splendid!'; or the words I had once heard Bloch use in exasperation at some piece of bad behaviour, words quite inappropriate to a very commonplace incident, 'I must say that that sort of conduct seems to me absolutely fffantastic!'; or that evening when, flattered at the politeness which the Guermantes had shown to me as their guest and also a little intoxicated by the wines which I had drunk in their house, I could not help saying to myself half aloud as I came away alone: 'They really are delightful people

[1] *Mrs Dalloway*, p. 10.
[2] 'Street Haunting' (1927), *CE* IV, p. 161. (Dated in *CE* 1930, but first printed *Yale Review*, October 1927.)
[3] 'Mr Bennett and Mrs Brown', *CE* I, p. 337.

and I should be happy to see them every day of my life' – I
realised that the words in each case were a long way removed
from the impressions that I or Bloch had in fact received. So
that the essential, the only true book, though in the ordinary
sense of the word it does not have to be 'invented' by a great
writer – for it exists already in each one of us – has to be
translated by him. The function and the task of a writer are
those of a translator.[1]

Though it is complex, humorous and analytical of social experience
in a manner foreign to Virginia Woolf, the passage can nevertheless
be compared to the flimsier, more abstract statement of a similar
idea in 'Street Haunting':

But what could be more absurd? It is, in fact, on the stroke of
six; it is a winter's evening; we are walking to the Strand to
buy a pencil. How, then, are we also on a balcony, wearing
pearls in June? What could be more absurd? Yet it is nature's
folly, not ours. When she set about her chief masterpiece, the
making of man, she should have thought of one thing only.
Instead, turning her head, looking over her shoulder, into
each one of us she let creep instincts and desires which are
utterly at variance with his main being, so that we are streaked,
variegated, all of a mixture; the colours have run. Is the true
self this which stands on the pavement in January, or that
which bends over the balcony in June?[2]

Virginia Woolf is describing the coexistence of different states of
mind inhabiting an apparently fixed personality; Proust is describing
the imbalance between response and actuality. But both imply that
reality is not fixed; it is not the same to each person, nor does each
person partake of that sameness and fixedness. Though Virginia
Woolf (however much in debt to Proust) may not have been
directly influenced by that passage from *Time Regained*, it does,
however, become clear from the comparison that she was, and felt
herself to be, part of a movement. Two excellent critics, one

---

[1] Marcel Proust (translated Andreas Mayor), *Time Regained*, Vol. 12 of
Remembrance of Things Past (London, Chatto and Windus, 1970), p. 255
(first published as *Le Temps retrouvé* in 1927).

[2] 'Street Haunting', *CE* IV, p. 161.

writing on Virginia Woolf and one on Proust, have useful comments here:

> A shift in emphasis followed; and now many writers present minor happenings, which are insignificant as exterior factors in a person's destiny, for their own sake or rather as points of departure for the development of motifs ... This shift in emphasis expresses something that we might call a transfer of confidence: the great exterior turning points and blows of fate are granted less importance; they are credited with less power of yielding decisive information concerning the subject; on the other hand there is confidence that in any random fragment plucked from the course of a life at any time the totality of its fate is contained and can be portrayed.[1]

> As the novel form has developed beyond the description of a deterministic environment towards the inner reality of the self, it has necessarily shifted its techniques of presentation. The fetish of point of view in fiction corresponds to an awareness of the self as the source of meaning, of significance in experience. The style of writing known as stream of consciousness consists in pure point of view, no other order than that of the self struggling to reach the core of feeling (or to escape from it) in each successive moment.[2]

The comparison with Proust, and these two general statements about the modern novel, show that Virginia Woolf was not working alone. Even Lawrence, who was not at all in sympathy with anything that came out of Bloomsbury, shared some of Virginia Woolf's ideas about life and the novel:

> The universe is like Father Ocean; a stream of all things slowly moving. We move, and the rock of ages moves. And since we move and move for ever, in no discernible direction, there is no centre to the movement, to us. To us, the centre shifts at every moment ... *Allons!* there is no road before us!

[1] Erich Auerbach, *Mimesis* (1946), translated Willard Trask (Princeton, NJ, Princeton University Press, 1953; New York, Anchor Books, 1957), pp. 483–4.

[2] Roger Shattuck, *Proust's Binoculars* (London, Chatto and Windus, 1964), p. 68.

> There is nothing to do but to maintain a true relationship
> to the things we move with and amongst and against.[1]

The novel, he feels, must change to accommodate this Bergsonian
sense of flux.

> 'You can put anything you like in a novel. So why do people
> *always* go on putting the same thing? Why is the *vol au vent*
> always chicken!' So wrote Lawrence in 1925 ... 'Tell
> Arnold Bennett,' he once wrote to his literary agent, 'that all
> rules of construction hold good only for novels that are copies
> of other novels.' [2]

These statements illuminate Virginia Woolf's otherwise rather
surprising feeling about Lawrence, that 'he and I have too much
in common'.[3] Nevertheless she found his novels hard to read. In
fact she was not entirely in sympathy with the 'crashing and
destruction'[4] being carried out by any of the other 'Georgian'
modernists. *A Portrait of the Artist as a Young Man* (1917) and the
early chapters of *Ulysses* had a very powerful influence on Virginia
Woolf, and their appearance coincided with the major change in
her style between 1919 and 1922. She felt that Joyce's concern 'at
all costs to reveal the flickerings of that innermost flame which
flashes its messages through the brain'[5] marked an extremely
important development in fiction. But, in spite of her belief that
'any method is right, every method is right, that expresses what we
wish to express, if we are writers',[6] Joyce made her uneasy. She
found him distasteful – she was 'irritated and disillusioned by a
queasy undergraduate scratching his pimples'[7] – and she felt that
his narrative method was too self-regarding. It 'never embraces or
creates what is outside itself and beyond',[8] leaving one inside the

---

[1] D. H. Lawrence, 'Art and Morality', *Phoenix*, ed. E. D. MacDonald (London,
Heinemann, 1936; reprinted 1961), p. 525.
[2] David Daiches, *The Novel and the Modern World* (University of Chicago
Press, 1960), p. 140.
[3] *AWD*, 2 October 1932, pp. 187–8.
[4] 'Mr Bennett and Mrs Brown', *CE* I, p. 334.
[5] 'Modern Fiction', *CE* II, p. 107.   [6] Ibid. p. 108.
[7] *AWD*, 16 August 1922, p. 47.   [8] 'Modern Fiction', p. 108.

'damned egotistical self'.[1] Again, in considering Dorothy Richardson's gargantuan stream of consciousness novel, *Pilgrimage*, she is disappointed, because, when we are given up to the consciousness of Miriam Henderson, 'we should perceive in the helter-skelter of flying fragments some unity, significance, or design' but instead 'Things look much the same as ever.'[2]

By the 1930s she was faced with a different sort of difficulty. Her experimentation seemed to have outlasted the period with which it had most in common. The 'Georgian' movement had petered out, and, as Bell remarks, the adversaries and the collaborators she had cited in 1924 had (with the exception of H. G. Wells) either stopped living or stopped writing:

> The English novelists of roughly her own generation were Compton Mackenzie, Aldous Huxley, J. B. Priestley, Hugh Walpole, David Garnett and Rose Macaulay; they none of them seemed to be carrying forward the revolution which, in 1924, she had believed to be imminent. Having lost both her adversaries and her collaborators she stood very much alone.[3]

But her sense of isolation did not prevent her from continuing to carry out what she felt to be the task of the modern novelist. Though her novels move from the treatment of youth to middle age, and then from individuals to society, and though they experiment with a wide variety of techniques – *The Waves* being as different from *To the Lighthouse* as *Between the Acts* is from *Night and Day* – they perpetually make an attempt to formulate and express a true reality. In every novel we find a consistent and energetic presentation of perception and experience, which invites analogies between the conditions under which her characters feel and live, and their creator's idea of the nature of fiction. But the mirror which allows manner to reflect matter, form to reflect content, does not frame an aesthetic paradise. Her continual, self-conscious struggle for an accurate rendering of life as she perceived it is a struggle for mastery over the intractable and the chaotic, both inside and outside the mind. These forces are never excluded:

[1] *AWD*, 26 January 1920, p. 23.
[2] Review of 'The Tunnel' (1919), *Contemporary Writers* (London, Hogarth Press, 1965), pp. 140–1.   [3] Bell II, p. 185.

the characters, like the narrator, are always dealing with them. Both are engaged in 'an exacting form of intercourse'.[1] Virginia Woolf is often praised for sensitivity and lyricism and criticized for ineffectuality and preciousness. There is truth on both sides, but such praise and blame sidestep equally the determined pursuit of control and authenticity which invigorates even the slightest of her work, and makes her major achievements solid with integrity and rich with inventiveness.

The nature of the achievement can be usefully defined by a minor piece of work, a passage from a wartime short story called 'The Searchlight', published for the first time in *A Haunted House and Other Stories* in 1944.

> In the half light, they could see that Mrs Ivimey was leaning over the balcony, with her chin propped on her hands, as if she were looking out over the moors from the top of a tower.
>
> 'Nothing but moor and sky, moor and sky, for ever and ever,' she murmured.
>
> Then she made a movement, as if she swung something into position.
>
> 'But what did the earth look like through the telescope?' she asked.
>
> She made another quick little movement with her fingers as if she were twirling something.
>
> 'He focussed it,' she said. 'He focussed it upon the earth. He focussed it upon a dark mass of wood upon the horizon. He focussed it so that he could see . . . each tree . . . each tree separate . . . and the birds . . . rising and falling . . . and a stem of smoke . . . there . . . in the midst of the trees . . . And then . . . lower . . . lower . . . (she lowered her eyes) . . . there was a house . . . a house among the trees . . . a farm-house . . . every brick showed . . . and the tubs on either side of the door . . . with flowers in them blue, pink, hydrangeas, perhaps . . .' She paused . . . 'And then a girl came out of the house . . . wearing something blue upon her head . . . and stood there . . . feeding birds . . . pigeons . . . they came flut-

---

[1] *To the Lighthouse*, p. 180.

tering round her . . . And then . . . look . . . A man . . . A man! He came round the corner. He seized her in his arms! They kissed . . . they kissed.'

Mrs Ivimey opened her arms and closed them as if she were kissing someone.

'It was the first time he had seen a man kiss a woman – in his telescope – miles and miles away across the moors!'

She thrust something from her – the telescope presumably. She sat upright.

'So he ran down the stairs. He ran through the fields. He ran down lanes, out upon the high road, through woods. He ran for miles and miles, and just when the stars were showing above the trees he reached the house . . . covered with dust, streaming with sweat . . .'

She stopped, as if she saw him.

'And then, and then . . . what did he do then? What did he say? And the girl . . .' they pressed her.

A shaft of light fell upon Mrs Ivimey as if someone had focussed the lens of a telescope upon her. (It was the air force, looking for enemy aircraft.) She had risen. She had something blue on her head. She had raised her hand, as if she stood in a doorway, amazed.

'Oh, the girl . . . She was my –' she hesitated, as if she were about to say 'myself.' But she remembered; and corrected herself. 'She was my great-grandmother,' she said.

She turned to look for her cloak. It was on a chair behind her.

'But tell us – what about the other man, the man who came round the corner?' they asked.

'That man? Oh, that man,' Mrs Ivimey murmured, stooping to fumble with her cloak (the searchlight had left the balcony), 'he, I suppose, vanished.'

'The light,' she added, gathering her things about her, 'only falls here and there.'

Though not an outstanding achievement, the passage is characteristic, in that it deals, by means of concentrating on two 'spots of time', with the interplay between past and present in the human consciousness. On a grander scale, *Mrs Dalloway*, *To the Lighthouse* and *The Waves* concern themselves with that interplay, providing various but consistent answers to the question

> What composed the present moment? If you are young, the future lies upon the present like a piece of glass, making it tremble and quiver. If you are old, the past lies upon the present, like a thick glass, making it waver, distorting it. All the same, everybody believes that the present is something, seeks out the different elements in this situation in order to compose the truth of it, the whole of it.[1]

'In order to compose the truth of it.' The narrator of 'The Searchlight' orders and selects, shaping her sentences to resemble the action of looking through a telescope, contrasting Mrs Ivimey's hesitating, fragmented recollections with the curt details of her present actions, and creating a relationship betwen the past and the present by slight emphases on, for instance, the colour blue. Within the story there are three activities analogous to the narrator's. There is the ray of the searchlight, which, though impersonal and haphazard, and associated with the harsh reality of the present, is still ironically comparable to the other 'rays' in the story: Mrs Ivimey's thoughts, which concentrate on and select from her great-grandfather's experience in order to understand his life and his love; and his view through the telescope, which shapes the blank, undifferentiated waste of 'moors and sky' into a rich selection of 'real' detail, making every brick show.

Mrs Ivimey's narrative method is like the author's, in that it refuses to accommodate the 'low atavistic' response 'And then?', which Forster, unlike Virginia Woolf, believes resignedly to be at the back of all fiction.[2] Virginia Woolf – and Mrs Ivimey – attempt

[1] 'The Moment: Summer's Night' (*CE* II, p. 293), published in *The Moment and Other Essays* (London, Hogarth Press, 1947). The date is unknown, but Guiguet finds affinities between this sketch and *The Waves*, and suggests that they date from the same period (Jean Guiguet, *Virginia Woolf and Her Works*, translated Jean Stewart (London, Hogarth Press, 1965), p. 289, note 415).

[2] Yes – oh dear yes – the novel tells a story . . . The primitive audience was an audience of shock-heads, gaping round the camp-fire, fatigued with contending against the mammoth or the woolly rhinoceros, and only

to channel that primitive response into an aesthetic interest. The story tells of the way Mrs Ivimey is telling the story – not of what will happen to her great-grandfather. But human action makes itself felt through the aesthetic experience. The man in the story sees life through the telescope and then rushes out to possess it, so becoming merged with it. Mrs Ivimey's train of thought is also an action. She goes out of herself in order to empathize with the man's experience (re-enacting, incidentally, Virginia Woolf's procedures as a literary critic as well as a novelist). The giving up of the personality, which enables her by the end of the story to be at one with the figures in her imagination, is seen as a positive action, and again suggests an analogy between content and narrative form. Perception and empathy come through the intuition, not the intellect – though the intellect must play its part. Clarissa Dalloway's relation to Septimus Smith and Lily Briscoe's to Mrs Ramsay (which particularly investigates the interplay between aesthetic selection and human action) provide the most important treatments of this idea. But it is not only found within the fictions. 'How should one read a book?' Virginia Woolf asks.

> Wait for the dust of reading to settle; for the conflict and the questioning to die down; walk, talk, pull the dead petals from a rose, or fall asleep. Then suddenly without your willing it, for it is thus that Nature undertakes these transitions, the book will return, but differently. It will float to the top of the mind as a whole.[1]

How does the writer 'compose'?

> After a hard day's work, trudging round, seeing all he can, feeling all he can, taking in the book of his mind innumerable notes, the writer becomes – if he can – unconscious. In fact, his under-mind works at top speed while his upper-mind

kept awake by suspense. What would happen next? The novelist droned on, and as soon as the audience guessed what happened next, they either fell asleep or killed him.

(E. M. Forster, *Aspects of the Novel* (London, Edward Arnold, 1951; Harmondsworth, Penguin, 1965), p. 34).

[1] 'How Should One Read a Book?' *CE* II, p. 8.

drowses. Then, after a pause the veil lifts; and there is the thing – the thing he wants to write about – simplified, composed. Do we strain Wordsworth's famous saying about emotion recollected in tranquillity when we infer that by tranquillity he meant that the writer needs to become unconscious before he can create?[1]

The reference to Wordsworth (Leslie Stephen's favourite poet) is illuminating – though it is as much Keats who springs to mind here:

When Man has arrived at a certain ripeness in intellect any one grand and spiritual passage serves him as a starting post towards all 'the two-and thirty Pallaces'. How happy is such a 'voyage of conception,' what delicious diligent Indolence! A doze upon a Sofa does not hinder it, and a nap upon Clover engenders ethereal finger-pointings . . . let us open our leaves like a flower and be passive and receptive . . .[2]

Clearly Virginia Woolf inherits something of the Romantic idea of the potency of the imagination, working at a depth below the conscious mind. And there is a further echo of Wordsworth in her idea of a creative relationship between the imagination and the natural world, though she is not interested in the moral effect of nature on man, nor does she actually write *about* nature. But she can find no other way to express the truth of life and character than through natural images and physical perceptions. In 'The Searchlight', as in *To the Lighthouse*, the dominant figure of a beam of light draws the story together. But what the light picks out are also visual images, and emotion is engendered in both the great-grandfather and Mrs Ivimey, through the physical reaction to those images. The essay on 'The Moment', quoted above, continues its definition of 'the present situation' thus: 'To begin with: it is largely composed of visual and of sense impressions.'[3]

---

[1] 'The Leaning Tower' (1940), *CE* II, p. 166.

[2] Keats to Reynolds, 19 February 1818, *Letters of John Keats*, selected Robert Gittings (Oxford University Paperbacks, 1970), pp. 65–6. Gittings's note for the 'Pallaces' reads – 'of Buddhist doctrine'.

[3] 'The Moment: Summer's Night', *CE* II, p. 293.

'The Searchlight' corroborates this statement, and so, on a larger scale, do all Virginia Woolf's novels. Objects, colours and physical sensations express the life of the mind. But were this all, the accusation levelled against Virginia Woolf by Muriel Bradbrook (among others) would be a damning one: 'Emotions are reduced to a description of their physical accompaniment. . . . Mrs Woolf never . . . attempts to reproduce the process of thinking.' [1] But the translation of mental states into physical images is not reductive. The process is the natural expression of her concept of existence, not a superficial, decorative technique. Virginia Woolf not only felt that the expression of the life of the mind through physical images was the most accurate equivalent that art can make for reality; she also believed in the relationship between people and non-human objects as being life-enhancing. The Wordsworthian idea of the consolatory and educative function of nature is too joyful for her; her novels are melancholy and uncertain. But they do express a secular faith in the value of the seen and felt – a faith more usually expressed in the twentieth century in poetry. These two examples, one from the twenties and one from the sixties, express in different ways the belief, shared by Virginia Woolf, in the objects of the mortal world as the most significant metaphors of, and vehicles for, our spiritual life:

> We live in an old chaos of the sun,
> Or old dependency of day and night,
> Or island solitude, unsponsored, free,
> Of that wide water, inescapable.
> Deer walk upon our mountains, and the quail
> Whistle about us their spontaneous cries;
> Sweet berries ripen in the wilderness;
> And, in the isolation of the sky,
> At evening, casual flocks of pigeons make
> Ambiguous undulations as they sink,
> Downward to darkness, on extended wings.[2]

---

[1] 'Notes on the Style of Mrs Woolf', *Scrutiny*, Vol. 1, No. 1 (May 1932), pp. 36–7.

[2] Wallace Stevens, 'Sunday Morning', *Harmonium* (1923); collected in *The Palm at the End of the Mind*, ed. Holly Stevens (New York, Knopf, 1971), p. 8.

The grass is green
The tulip is red
A ginger cat walks over
The pink almond petals on the flower bed.
Enough has been said to show
It is life we are talking about. Oh
Grateful colours, bright looks: Well, to go
On. Fabricated things too – front doors and gates,
Bricks, slates, paving stones – are coloured
And as it has been raining and is sunny now
They shine. Only that puddle
Which, reflecting the height of the sky
Quite gives one a feeling of vertigo, shows
No colour, is a negative. Men!
Seize colours quick, heap them up while you can.
But perhaps it is a false tale that says
The landscape of the dead
Is colourless.[1]

[1] Stevie Smith, 'Oh grateful colours, bright looks!', *Scorpion* (London, Longman, 1972), p. 35.

I

The Voyage Out

1915

LYTTON Strachey praised *The Voyage Out* for being 'very, very unvictorian'.[1] Virginia Woolf's first novel is not revolutionary, but it is unsparingly satirical of the restrictions on freedom and truth that she and Strachey both associated with Victorianism. And, within its deceptively traditional form, it undertakes a theme sufficiently abstract and methods sufficiently impressionistic to make it, as she herself allowed, 'a gallant and inspiring spectacle'.[2]

The 'unvictorian' quality is suggested by its first working title, *Melymbrosia*, which romantically evokes the ethics of a pastoral Greek antiquity, as opposed to those of nineteenth-century England. The flowery, sentimental name points, ironically, to the humorous triumph of enlightenment over conventionality enacted, for instance, by St John Hirst (who is modelled on Strachey) in his selfconscious reading of Sappho during the British community's Church of England service.

> 'Sappho,' he replied. 'The one Swinburne did – the best thing that's ever been written.'
> Mrs Flushing could not resist such an opportunity.

[1] *Virginia Woolf and Lytton Strachey: Letters*, ed. Leonard Woolf and James Strachey (London, Hogarth Press, 1956), Lytton Strachey to Virginia Woolf, 25 February 1916, p. 56.
[2] *AWD*, 4 February 1920, p. 24.

> She gulped down the Ode to Aphrodite during the litany [. . .]
> (p. 233)

Melymbrosia (which might itself be the title of a translation by Swinburne) was abandoned, however, during the many revisions of the novel (seven, according to Leonard Woolf, between 1907 and 1913). But the Greek allusion was retained in the name of the ship, the *Euphrosyne*.[1] The change of title from a name to a phrase descriptive of time and space (like the later changes from *The Pargiters* to *The Years* and from *Pointz Hall* to *Between the Acts*) was cunning and discreet. Like the title *To the Lighthouse*, *The Voyage Out* can be literally interpreted, but is at the same time suggestive of further significance. Even at a literal level the title does double duty, in that it covers both the journey from England to South America on the *Euphrosyne*, and the river journey from Santa Marina into the native wilderness. And it lends itself flexibly to other possible meanings; Rachel's journey into maturity, her discovery of love, her approach to death (and, retrospectively, Virginia Woolf's own embarkation as a novelist). We are frequently encouraged to think of the voyage as a metaphor:

> She [the ship] was a bride going forth to her husband, a virgin unknown of men. (p. 28)

> She [Helen] was working at a great design of a tropical river running through a tropical forest. (p. 28)

> Visions of a great river [. . .] beset her. Helen promised a river. (p. 84)

> On the bank grew those trees which Helen had said it was worth the voyage out merely to see. (p. 172)

In these passages the journey takes on a predestined quality, and the objects described seem as much symbols of Rachel's inner development as real objects. Helen appears as the designer of Rachel's fate

---

[1] The name was a private joke. In 1909 she was calling the ship the *Mary Jane* and the heroine Cynthia, a name that dissatisfied her. Clive and Vanessa Bell suggested, among alternatives, Barcelona, Apricot and Euphrosyne (Bell I, p. 137) – the last being the name of an ephemeral book of poems, much ridiculed by Virginia, which Clive Bell, Leonard Woolf and others of her friends published in 1905 (Bell I, pp. 98, 205–6).

(anticipating Mrs Ramsay's mythic, even sinister, qualities in *To the Lighthouse*). But Helen is also a human being. Rachel's journeys do take place; there is a real ship and a real river. We are prepared by the title[1] for a continuous shifting from the literal to the metaphorical, which gives, as Virginia Stephen hoped it would, 'the feel of running water'.[2]

The novel's hazy, fluid interplay between the material and the metaphoric is well illustrated by the account of Santa Marina's history, information which 'died within' poor Mr Pepper but which the reader, not Rachel, acquires. We learn that, when the country was still 'a virgin land behind a veil' (p. 86), it was colonized by Elizabethan settlers, but that 'the English dwindled away', for want of leaders like Richard Dalloway, in the face of threats from land and sea. Not much advanced since those days, it has recently become a rather popular holiday spot for the English. The description establishes Santa Marina realistically, but it also reminds us of other things: of the *Euphrosyne*, travelling like 'a virgin unknown of men' 'with veils drawn before her and behind' (p. 28), and of Rachel, 'her mind' 'in the state of an intelligent man's in the beginning of the reign of Queen Elizabeth' (p. 30). The analogies are not firmly drawn. We are not being forced to think of Santa Marina as symbolic of Rachel's virginal state of mind, liable to be impressed by the political and physical onslaught of a man like Dalloway. Nor do we have to imagine Rachel as a naïve, adventurous Elizabethan settler. But some such suggestions are lightly made by the fluid link between the vestal ship, the doomed Elizabethan colony and the girl's mind, encouraging us to look for metaphorical possibilities in other 'real' things such as the villa and the hotel. Such possibilities allow the book to work both as a literal, satirical account of Rachel's development and as an abstract argument about existence, underlying, and related to, the level of realism.

> It seemed dreadful that the town should blaze for ever in the same spot; dreadful at least to people going away to adventures

[1] It was a mistake to render *The Voyage Out*, as the French translator Savitzky did, as *La Traversée des Apparences*, which destroys the title's flexibility by reducing it to an abstract concept.

[2] Bell I, p. 211.

> upon the sea, and beholding it as a circumscribed mound, eternally burnt, eternally scarred. From the deck of the ship the great city appeared a crouched and cowardly figure, a sedentary miser. (p. 13)

From this first Conradian description of the *Euphrosyne's* voyage out of London, it looks as though the journey is to be a liberating one. We imagine that it will provide opportunities for the twenty-four-year-old Rachel Vinrace to move away, at last, from the sheltered background provided by her aunts and her ship-owning father Willoughby, and to discover, under the protection of her aunt Helen Ambrose, adventure and self-fulfilment. But the structure of the book turns out not to be a simple drawing away from English civilization towards an exotic, enfranchising world. Both on the ship and in Santa Marina, Rachel's development takes place within a microcosm of the upper-middle-class conventional English way of life which has ensured her ignorance and her inexperience. In a remote, exotic setting, that civilization can be sharply ridiculed, and a contrast established between personal susceptibility to the grandeur and dangers of the landscape, and a social group ludicrously protecting itself against strangeness.

> Mrs Parry's drawing-room, though thousands of miles away, behind a vast curve of water on a tiny piece of earth, came before their eyes. They who had had no solidity or anchorage before seemed to be attached to it somehow [. . .] But [. . .] there was no time to enjoy the fruits of the discovery. The donkeys were advancing, and it was advisable to begin the descent immediately, for the night fell so quickly that it would be dark before they were home again. (p. 145)

The exotic setting, which might seem rather perversely chosen[1] and was certainly not to be characteristic, provides the basis for a satirical contrast between Rachel's private needs and the public

---

[1] Virginia Woolf had not been to South America. The setting is drawn from her experience of Portugal and Greece, and from Leonard Woolf's accounts of Ceylon, fictionalized in his novel *The Village in the Jungle* (London, Hogarth Press, 1913).

world she must inhabit. In Virginia Woolf's later works, the romantic, exotic life of love or solitude is incorporated into the 'circumscribed mound', the England which *The Voyage Out* leaves behind in order to make its point. In *Night and Day* the heroine's search for self-fulfilment takes place in London and county settings, her exotic jungles are in her own mind. After *Night and Day*, the characters are increasingly enabled to create a balance between the demands of an ordinary external landscape and the sensations of their inner lives. It is left for a character such as Rhoda in *The Waves*, a refugee from the conditions of real life, to create exotic mental landscapes reminiscent of Santa Marina.

Far from being left behind, the image of the 'circumscribed mound' is reinvoked in the little hunched figures which suggest the sexual oppression of women:

> Rachel again shut her eyes, and found herself walking through a tunnel under the Thames, where there were little deformed women sitting in archways playing cards [. . .] (p. 336)

It is an image of nightmare and fever, suggesting a horror of sex. And although the principal point of the novel is not really that 'Rachel discovers sex in the jungles of Latin America',[1] it is significant that when she first tries to define to Hewet the 'terrors and agonies' of being a young woman, she formulates it as 'Men kissing one' (p. 217). Since she has only been once kissed, by the 'pompous and sentimental' Richard Dalloway, we are allowed to laugh at her exaggeration here. But the implication is a serious one: that girls of Rachel's (and Virginia Stephen's) age and class are both overprotected from, and the victims of, a system which exploits women intellectually, sexually and socially. Rachel's ignorance about sex and her lack of proper education, described by Helen as her confusion between politics and kissing politicians, stem from the same social assumption that she is to be subservient in a masculine world. Her teachers, who 'would as soon have forced her to go through one piece of drudgery thoroughly as they would have told her that her hands were dirty' (p. 29); her aunts, who disapprove of Rachel's spoiling her arms playing the piano as 'then

---

[1] James Naremore, *The World Without a Self* (New Haven and London, Yale University Press, 1973), p. 22.

one won't marry' (p. 16); her father, who assumes that Rachel can be turned into a 'Tory hostess' (p. 84) – all further the acceptance of 'an ideal scale of things where the life of one person was absolutely more important than the life of another' (p. 216). The Dalloways, who, in this book, support the scale by word and deed, impress Rachel immensely when they irrupt into the life of the *Euphrosyne*. Both seem perfectly adapted to their functions in life. Both convince Rachel, temporarily, of the value of being a dominated wife or an anti-intellectual politician, very much as Helen Schlegel, at the beginning of *Howards End* (1910), is temporarily convinced by 'the energy of the Wilcoxes' and 'liked being told that . . . Art and Literature, except when conducive to strengthening the character, [were] nonsense'.[1] When Richard says that he is prouder of his factory reforms than of 'writing Keats and Shelley', 'It became painful to Rachel to be one of those who write Keats and Shelley' (p. 62). Rachel's attraction towards philistinism is given a check, however, when Richard kisses her. The action makes her violently aware of her ignorance and fear of sex, but it also has an intellectual effect. Both Virginia Woolf and E. M. Forster felt that brutal sexual hypocrisy was the corollary to the energetic chauvinism of men like Richard Dalloway or Henry Wilcox. Rachel's eyes are opened to this, and in reaction she swings towards Helen, whose influence is from now on to be of increasing importance.

The narrator satirizes the Dalloways in a tone of voice rather like Helen's, whose free and rational mind and pessimistic, passionate nature sets an ethical standard in the book, though not an absolute one. Helen embodies some aspects of Julia Stephen, Virginia's mother. But we may assume that Helen's morality also reflects the ambience into which Virginia Stephen moved, in moving from Hyde Park to Gordon Square, during the gestation of *The Voyage Out*. The book is not autobiographical, but it is importantly personal in ways which one would expect from a first novel. Rachel's incoherence and fealty to the masculine world suggest Virginia Stephen's youth; Helen's proffered alternatives are those of Bloomsbury. She is cynically aware that the conventionally religious society in which she lives is an enemy to the artist and a trivializer of relationships. She has brought her children up to 'think of God

[1] E. M. Forster, *Howards End*, Ch. 4.

as a kind of walrus' (p. 23); in contrast to the Dalloways, 'it seemed to her as wrong to keep sailors as to keep a zoo' (p. 66), and her medicine for Rachel is talk – 'talk about everything, talk that was free, unguarded, and as candid as a habit of talking with men made natural in her own case' (p. 122).

Helen begins her education of Rachel by setting at naught an object which Virginia Woolf was fond of using as an image of a male-dominated society: a volume of *Who's Who*. Rachel, trying to express her interest in people who inhabit a larger world than her own, becomes absorbed in its lists of public figures. Helen, who is encouraging her to be discriminating, enables her to set the volume aside:

> 'I can be m-m-myself,' she stammered, 'in spite of you, in spite of the Dalloways, and Mr Pepper, and Father, and my Aunts, in spite of these?' She swept her hand across a whole page of statesmen and soldiers.
> 'In spite of them all,' said Helen gravely. (p. 81)

Helen makes Rachel more definite, but her influence is only a groundwork for the diversity of new experience which Rachel encounters at Santa Marina. And, though Helen's intellectual influence is liberating and beneficial, at the book's underlying, abstract level she has an almost sinister role to play. In weaving her design of a tropical river she does lure Rachel to her death. In encouraging her to think of life cynically, even pessimistically, she does, as will be seen, make it harder for Rachel to find union with another person.

At the book's realistic, satirical level, however, Helen prepares Rachel for Santa Marina. Already made aware of different approaches to life by the contrast between the Ambroses and the Dalloways, Rachel now encounters further varieties of characters and attitudes. The lives in the 'little boxlike squares' (p. 101) of the hotel rooms enable Rachel to create new categories. Looking in from the dark garden, Helen and Rachel, trespassers from the more personal, intimate life of the villa, can see how 'each window revealed a different section of the life of the hotel' (p. 98). Entertainment is provided by these 'sections', but of a cold and superficial variety. Most of them display, for Rachel's benefit, the different kinds of existence available to women who are part of a conventional and philistine society. But childless, fussy Mrs Elliott, absentminded Mrs Thornbury, bovine Susan Warrington and her tyrannical old aunt, and the would-be liberated flirt, Evelyn M., are callous caricatures. There is little warmth even in the treatment of the kind academic spinster, Miss Allan, or of the jolly, eccentric Mrs Flushing. The tone for the presentation of the minor characters is feebly satirical.[1]

> It was close on twenty years now since Mrs Paley had been able to lace her own shoes or even to see them, the disappearance of her feet having coincided more or less accurately with the death of her husband [. . .] (p. 178)

The men to whom these women are subservient are, of course, equally ludicrous, though it seems as if Virginia Stephen did respond to Clive Bell's criticism of the novel in 1909:

> To draw such sharp and marked contrasts between the subtle, sensitive, tactful, gracious, delicately perceptive, and perspicacious women, and the obtuse, vulgar, blind, florid, rude, tactless, emphatic, indelicate, vain, tyrannical, stupid men, is not only rather absurd, but rather bad art, I think.[2]

Although there is still a marked difference in stature between Helen Ambrose and her husband (an absentminded Greek professor who is a first draft for Mr Ramsay), the dichotomy between the sexes had been largely transferred, by 1915, to a division between serious 'major' characters and ludicrous 'minor 'ones. These 'human beings' (p. 133) are frequently ridiculed by being compared to animals. Helen and Rachel look into the hotel:

> Through the open window came an uneven humming sound like that which rises from a flock of sheep pent within hurdles at dusk. (p. 99)

---

[1] Virginia Woolf looked back with embarrassment on these attempts to amuse: 'I [. . .] must go down to posterity the author of cheap witticisms, smart satires, that will never cease to rankle in the grave'. (*AWD*, 4 February 1920, p. 24).

[2] Clive Bell to Virginia Stephen, 25 February 1909, Bell I, Appendix D, p. 209.

Susan Warrington's breathing in sleep is described:

> With its profoundly peaceful sighs and hesitations it resembled that of a cow standing up to its knees all night through in the long grass. (p. 103)

The hotel guests reading their letters 'prompted Hirst to make the caustic remark that the animals had been fed' (p. 175). During the church service animal imagery turns to vegetable in Rachel's mind: she hears 'the patter of baaing inexpressive human voices falling round her like damp leaves'. That the imagery of sheep should be used in the context of the religious service is obviously apt. Rachel is in retreat from a society which comforts itself with hypocritical formulae; she has suddenly found herself able to despise those 'innumerable men and women, not seeing clearly, who finally gave up the effort to see, and relapsed tamely into praise and acquiescence' (p. 231).

Clearly Virginia Woolf shares her 'major' characters' disdain for commonplace minds. There is a rigid distinction between the heroine's love affair and the courtship of Susan Warrington and Arthur Venning (though in fact the two love scenes have points of resemblance). There is no analogy drawn between silly Evelyn's cravings for feminine equality and Rachel's vague approach to a sense of freedom. And it is never in any doubt that the commonplace minds will try to destroy the outstanding, and that therefore they are not to be tolerated. The hero of the novel, Terence Hewet, is the spokesman for this belief.

> 'They are not satisfactory; they are ignoble,' he thought. [. . .] Amiable and modest, respectable in many ways, lovable even [. . .] how mediocre they all were and capable of what insipid cruelty to one another! [. . .] these were the people with money, and to them rather than to others was given the management of the world. Put among them some one more vital, who cared for life or for beauty, and what an agony, what a waste would they inflict on him if he tried to share with them and not to scourge!
> 'There's Hirst,' he concluded [. . .] (pp. 132–3)

The conclusion to this passage of romantic disdain is appropriate, since in the mutual hostility which exists between the brilliant St John Hirst and the inmates of the hotel lies the clearest indication of the community's conventionality and philistinism. Their encounters are satirically presented – the knife cutting both ways – with reference to animals again being used for comic effect.

> Hirst [. . .] observed: 'Oh, but we're all agreed [. . .] that nature's a mistake [. . .] I once met a cow in a field by night. The creature looked at me. I assure you it turned my hair grey. It's a disgrace that the animals should be allowed to go at large.' 'And what did the cow think of *him*?' Venning mumbled to Susan, who immediately decided in her own mind that Mr Hirst was a dreadful young man. (p. 119)

If Hirst is meant to be one of the three cleverest men in England the reader must feel some disappointment with his conversation (though Virginia Woolf was always to find a difficulty in telling us what her clever characters actually say). However, he is evidently portrayed as the interesting and sympathetic character in this exchange. Hirst is the first of a number of misogynist or homosexual academics in the novels who come from highly privileged social backgrounds and who suffer from their ugliness or loneliness: William Rodney, Bonamy, Charles Tansley (whose relationship with Mrs Ramsay is a development from Hirst's with Helen), Neville and William Dodge are alike. It was a type very well known to Virginia Woolf and in the relationship between Hirst and Rachel she may well have been drawing on her early feelings about Lytton Strachey.[1]

Hirst brings home to Rachel the gap between men and women, a gap resulting largely from education, which he makes her feel is impassable: 'It's no good; we should live separate; we cannot understand each other; we only bring out what's worst' (p. 154). Rachel feels outraged by him because he has patronizingly assumed that she won't be able to understand Gibbon; Hewet consoles her by pointing out the ludicrous side of Hirst's character. Rachel was as much outraged by Dalloway's kiss, and Helen had to undercut

[1] 'She found him, I suspect, very frightening . . . it was not until later that she was to discover how kind and sympathetic he could be.' (Bell I, p. 102.)

the impression it made. These upsetting encounters with two absolutely different kinds of superior males are laughed off by a woman or by a man sympathetic to women. But they remain as indications to Rachel of the unassailable male fortresses, politics and scholarship, and of the male assumptions of privilege and domination in sexuality and in intellect. She can only set against these assumptions something impersonal, rather than feminine: her musicianship; satire; or an indefinable quality in her which Hewet calls 'the extraordinary freedom with which she [...] spoke as she felt' (p. 247).

Both Richard Dalloway and St John Hirst advise Rachel to read writers whom Virginia Woolf thought of as very much part of the male tradition.[1] It is highly characteristic of the novel that the impact of the two men should be summed up by their recommending Burke and Gibbon, for Rachel's development is to some extent marked out in literary stages. *The Voyage Out* is full of quotations and references, and is evidently written by a well-read essayist turning her hand to fiction. The mass of undigested literary allusions in *The Voyage Out* compares badly with their more integrated use in the later novels; the quotation from *Cymbeline* running through *Mrs Dalloway* and from Cowper's 'The Castaway' in *To the Lighthouse* are, by contrast, literary allusions firmly woven into their context. But there are interesting anticipations of such devices in the first novel. Sophocles' *Antigone*, which was to be of great importance as a motif for the oppression of women in *The Years* and *Three Guineas*, is used here (in Greek) for its reference to a sea voyage (p. 41):

> Many the wonders but nothing walks stranger than man.
> This thing crosses the sea in the winter's storm,
> Making his path through the roaring waves.[2]

But the allusion also calls to mind the fate of the heroine, the woman buried alive, as in Rachel's dream of the hunched figures in

---

[1] 'That is a man's sentence; behind it one can see Johnson, Gibbon, and the rest.' (*A Room of One's Own*, p. 77.)

[2] Sophocles, *Antigone*, ll. 322–37, translated Elizabeth Wyckoff in *Greek Tragedies*, Vol. I, ed. David Grene and Richard Lattimore (Chicago, University of Chicago Press, 1960).

the tunnel. Rachel, who is frequently identified with sea creatures, is listening to the address to Sabrina from *Comus* when she falls ill. The quotation is full of coolness, beauty and shade, in contrast to Rachel's feverish state. But it also suggests that Rachel is like Sabrina – a water nymph, virginal and elusive – and gives poetic form to the feeling in the whole novel of the strangeness of water, the element creative of life, death and change.

> While all her tormentors thought she was dead, she was not dead, but curled up at the bottom of the sea. There she lay, sometimes seeing darkness, sometimes light, while every now and then someone turned her over at the bottom of the sea. (p. 346)

Sabrina is still at the back of our minds, but fused with other impressions: again, the crouched figures of women from Rachel's nightmares; or Lycidas, even, visiting 'the bottom of the monstrous world'.

Literature is used as a conscious, inner part of Rachel's development, as well as providing external images for her fate. She is as susceptible to people's literary suggestions as she is to their characters, and is almost as shocked at being told by Hewet that Thackeray is a second-rate writer as she was at being kissed by Dalloway. Indeed, we are meant to think of literary preferences as indications of personality. Clarissa's patriotic taste for *Henry V* and Jane Austen is as revealing as Hirst's admiration for Gibbon and Sappho, Helen's reading of G. E. Moore[1] and recommendation of Defoe and Maupassant, and Ridley Ambrose's dedication to Pindar. Rachel progresses from Cowper's letters to Meredith, Ibsen and modern feminist novels. (Meanwhile, in the hotel, Miss Allan is writing her History of English Literature, which she finishes just before Rachel dies.) But when Rachel falls in love with Hewet she finds that 'none of the books she read [. . .] suggested from their analysis of love that what their heroines felt was what she was feeling now' (pp. 226–7).

---

[1] Richard Dalloway picks up her book and reads 'Good, then, is indefinable' (p. 71). The quotation is from *Principia Ethica* (Cambridge University Press, 1903; reprinted 1960), Ch. 1, Section 14, p. 17.

Before falling in love with Terence, when Rachel is still in the process of discovering that she can have a separate, unmergeable existence, she sometimes falls into peculiar states of impersonality.

> Inextricably mixed in dreamy confusion, her mind seemed to enter into communion, to be delightfully expanded and combined with the spirit of [. . .] the sea, with the spirit of Beethoven Op. 112,[1] even with the spirit of poor William Cowper [. . .] (p. 33)

> Her dissolution became so complete that she could not raise her finger any more, and sat perfectly still, listening and looking always at the same spot [. . .] She forgot that she had any fingers to raise . . . The things that existed were so immense and so desolate . . . She continued to be conscious of these vast masses of substance for a long stretch of time [. . .] (p. 123)

The style used for these trance-like states begins to predominate from the time of the journey up the river, when Hewet and Rachel declare their love, and culminates in the descriptions of Rachel's delirium. After her death we are returned to the external world of personalities and activity. As in *Night and Day*, the experience of love removes the characters, and the narrative, further from daylit realism. There is a hint of a trite romantic dichotomy between the caricatured tedium of unimpassioned everyday life and the intense private happiness of love. To some extent *The Voyage Out* and *Night and Day* do fall into this trap, but in both books the effect is complicated by the fears and difficulties the lovers encounter. Rachel and Terence's love scene in the jungle, their most private and intense moment of communication, is 'terrible' and exhausting; the scene is described in sinister and unreal tones:

[1] Though one might suspect Virginia Woolf of making a musical error here, since Rachel, being a pianist, would be more likely to have the last piano sonata, Op. 111, in her mind, Op. 112 is in fact an appropriate choice, since it is the Cantata 'Meeresstille und glückliche Fahrt' ('Calm Sea and Happy Voyage'), dedicated to Goethe and published in 1823.

Rachel followed him, stopping where he stopped, turning
where he turned, ignorant of the way, ignorant why he stopped
or why he turned.

'I don't want to be late,' he said, 'because –' He put a flower
into her hand and her fingers closed upon it quietly. 'We're
so late – so horribly late,' he repeated as if he were talking in
his sleep. 'Ah – this is right. We turn here.' (p. 276)

The sense of helpless dread may be meant to anticipate Rachel's
death. But this is not really its main function. Our strongest
reaction to it is to be aghast at the terrifying idea of falling in love.
It is a perilous experiment, threatened by the stultifying effect of
intimacy, which Terence has earlier pictured to himself in the image
of 'married couples [. . .] walled up in a warm firelit room' (p. 244),
by the public trivialization of the relationship by well-wishers,
'mouths gaping for blood' (p. 314), and by the impossibility of
absolute union, so that when they most wish to be indivisible they
are 'really very small and separate' (p. 308).

There is dread, too, in the idea of sexual desire, suggesting a
profound inhibition which extends from the author to her heroine.
Though Rachel's fear and ignorance are not explicitly mentioned
again after the Dalloway episode, the delirious recurrence of her
nightmare vision of hunched figures implies that her sexual fears
have not been quieted; and she wriggles out of her game with
Terence – a kind of playing at sex – by pretending to be a mermaid
(p. 302). Their erotic relationship is eerily dominated by Helen.

A hand dropped abrupt as iron on Rachel's shoulder; it might
have been a bolt from heaven. She fell beneath it, and the grass
whipped across her eyes and filled her mouth and ears.
Through the waving stems she saw a figure, large and shapeless against the sky. Helen was upon her. Rolled this way and
that [. . .] she was speechless and almost without sense. At
last she lay still, all the grasses shaken round her and before
her by her panting. Over her loomed two great heads, the
heads of a man and woman, of Terence and Helen.

Both were flushed, both laughing, and the lips were moving;
they came together and kissed in the air above her [. . .]

> Raising herself and sitting up, she too realized Helen's soft
> body, the strong and hospitable arms, and happiness swelling
> and breaking in one vast wave. (pp. 287–8)

This extraordinary passage is the first of several in the novels which
describe a moment of emotion in terms of a physical orgasm.[1]
Helen, who sets in motion Rachel's maturing process, here takes part
in what reads as a sexual initiation. The description is alarming and
dreamlike, mainly because the characters seem to be depersonalized.
It is this, in fact, which gives love its importance. Like music,
it enables the difficult approach to a more impersonal plane of
existence, in which divisions of character cease to oppress:

> Although they sat so close together, they had ceased to be
> little separate bodies; they had ceased to struggle and desire
> one another. There seemed to be peace between them. It might
> be love, but it was not the love of man for woman. (p. 320)

There is, inevitably, a conflict between the impersonal achievements of solitude, music or love, and the personal emphasis of society.
To an extent the conflict makes for an artistic failure. There is an
imbalance in the novel between satire and abstraction, and it is
hard for Virginia Woolf to express the difficult and obscure argument which really interests her before she has evolved a fictional
structure that can deal both with the material of life and with a
vision of life. *The Voyage Out* does not have an integrated structure;
it moves about in a hazy and ramshackle manner, wishing away its
own plot in the interests of its central argument, and then, as if
guiltily, returning itself to people and things. For much of the
time it pretends to be a novel about women in society or, even more
convincingly, about Rachel's development. But it is really a novel
which presents the question of whether existence entails division
or unification, and, as such, cannot be considered as being of a
different species from Virginia Woolf's later work, in which the
fusion of the abstract and the material is more masterfully achieved.
The abstract question lies behind the different narrative styles of
the book; it dominates most of the descriptions of sea or landscape;

---

[1] See *Mrs Dalloway* (p. 36) and *To the Lighthouse* (pp. 75–6).

it is the basis of people's literary tastes; and it is the key which unlocks all the 'important' characters.

Rachel learns from Helen on the *Euphrosyne* the possibility of being an 'unmergeable' personality. Helen is witty, cynical, pessimistic and divisive; though maternal, she has a masculine attitude (which enables her to get on well with St John Hirst).[1] But we are tempted to feel that Helen's separatist view of existence is not conclusive when we move from the *Euphrosyne* to the conversation between Hirst and Hewet in the hotel. Hirst presents a satirical and divisive view. He draws chalk circles round people, partitions them and disdains them. Hewet's opposition to this view suggests that of the two men it will be he who most affects Rachel; she has already learnt what Hirst believes. By falling in love with Hewet, she moves towards his view of life as not divisive, but as always merging and confused, a matter of overlapping bubbles rather than chalk circles. Unlike Hirst, who judges entirely by the mind, Hewet resists characterization in favour of a more intuitive sympathy for human beings:

'We don't care for people because of their qualities,' [he tells Evelyn] 'It's just them that we care for' – he struck a match – 'just that,' he said, pointing to the flames. (pp. 190–1)

Hewet anticipates the ways in which Virginia Woolf wanted fiction to reflect the nature of existence. And Hewet is himself a novelist, planning to write a novel about 'Silence', 'the things people don't say' (p. 218). But, though this is frequently quoted as an indication of what is to come in Virginia Woolf's work, neither she nor her character is able to opt entirely for the merging, unifying, 'feminine' approach. Hewet is also writing another novel, not at all about Silence, but about a would-be gentleman with a worn-out suit who carries off the Lady Theo Bingham Bingley to a 'snug little villa outside Croydon' (p. 220). His style for describing this social comedy is quite unlike the style in which he talks of streaked and

---

[1] Sexual characteristics, here and elsewhere in Virginia Woolf (see, particularly, *Orlando*), are in the mind rather than in the body. Hirst, who is homosexual, and Helen, who is feminine and maternal have 'masculine', analytical, divisive minds; Hewet, who is virile, has a feminine, unifying world view.

merging bubbles: it is the witty public style familiar to readers of Virginia Woolf's essays and reviews. Hewet's two novels illustrate the choice of narrative techniques which Virginia Woolf saw before her, as well as the two world views which *The Voyage Out* is examining. Just as Hewet is writing the two novels at once, so Virginia Woolf, in the style and content of *The Voyage Out*, is vacillating between the satirical, divisive view of existence and the merging, unifying view.

The two approaches to life create a running battle between Rachel and Terence. Superficially this expresses itself in her reluctance, and his eagerness, to share their secret lives with other people. Answering the letters of congratulation, Rachel feels an absurd dichotomy to exist between the words of communication and her aloof sense of reality:

> She stopped writing and looked up; looked at Terence deep in the armchair, looked at the different pieces of furniture, at her bed [. . .] at the window-pane [. . .] heard the clock ticking, and was amazed at the gulf which lay between all that and her sheet of paper. Would there ever be a time when the world was one and indivisible? (p. 301)

Her reluctance to write letters or to visit the hotel indicates her position in the argument: in her efforts to create a definite personality for herself, she has become a divisive person. She feels no intuitive sympathy for human beings; at best she can achieve a sense of unity only on an impersonal plane, through the trance-like states in which she goes outside herself, through her music and at times through love. Terence attempts to change her view; it is the beginning of what would have been a long struggle. (When we meet it again in *To the Lighthouse*, the positions have been reversed: the woman has become the unifier, the man has the divisive view.)

> According to him, [. . .] there was an order, a pattern which made life reasonable [. . .] Nor were people so solitary and uncommunicative as she believed. She should look for vanity [. . .] and she would find it in ten people out of every twelve she met; and once linked together by one such tie she would find them not separate and formidable, but practically indistinguishable, and she would come to love them when she

found that they were like herself. If she denied this, she must
defend her belief that human beings were as various as the
beasts at the Zoo [. . .] (p. 304)

The reference to the zoo throws more light on the unpleasant tone
of the satire on the minor characters. The animal imagery was not
simply intended to belittle them. It placed them, as Rachel is said
by Hewet to place them, in a universe where satire is applicable
because human beings are 'separate and small'. The unsatisfactoriness
of *The Voyage Out* arises from the inconsistent application of its
argument by the narrator, who treats some of the characters as
though Hewet's unified world were a possibility, and others – the
'minor' characters – as though satire and division were the only
possible perspectives.

Rachel would like to be convinced by Terence, but is not; she
continues, though unhappily, to apply the divisive view of life to
the landscape, as well as to the people in it:

'What's so detestable in this country,' she exclaimed, 'is the
blue – always blue sky and blue sea. It's like a curtain – all the
things one wants are on the other side of that. I want to know
what's going on behind it. I hate these divisions, don't you,
Terence? One person all in the dark about another person.'
(pp. 306–7)

Repeated colours in landscape are to be used again, particularly in
Between the Acts, as fearsome indications of a divisive universe.
The Voyage Out frequently uses landscape as part of the book's
abstract argument. Just as people are different if seen from a satirical
or from a unifying point of view, so natural scenes, and the objects
in them, are subjected to different perspectives. We are continually
made aware of the change in attitude which distance ironically
creates. The image quoted earlier of London seen as a 'circumscribed mound' from the ship (p. 13) is the first of several shifts
in perspective, which enable the onlooker to take an aloof, depersonalized view of scenes in which detail is suppressed by distance. As the ship moves further and further away from England,
land and sea dwellers have less and less sense of each other's detailed
reality. Those on land are satirically described as thinking themselves unique, but as all being part of a unified pattern:

Innumerable parties of picnickers coming home at sunset cried, 'Was there ever such a day as this?' 'It's you,' the young men whispered; 'Oh, it's you,' the young women replied. (p. 27)

Gradually, distance eradicates even this amount of detail. To the land dwellers, the ship passes out of mind entirely, 'like snow on water'; and likewise, 'when the ship was out of sight of land, it became plain that the people of England were completely mute' (p. 28). By contrast with the silenced land dwellers, the ship becomes ennobled by her solitary journey and her union with the sea.

Again, when other ships sight the *Euphrosyne*, they regard her as the *Euphrosyne* regarded England: at first satirically (Mr Pepper is 'mistaken for a cormorant and then, as unjustly, transformed into a cow' (p. 85)) and then, at night, when only the lights can be seen, as 'mysterious and impressive', 'an emblem of the loneliness of human life' (p. 85). All point of view is relative: Rachel, later, can block out the whole town of Santa Marina with her hand from the distant hill above (p. 128), or can turn her eyes from 'the great size of the view' to an 'inch of the soil of South America' made 'into a world where she was endowed with the supreme power' (p. 139). All these shifts in perspective contribute to the central argument. Distance merges and unifies and invests the object perceived with dignity, while the perceiver acquires an impersonal aloofness which does not allow for satire. The antithesis between division and unity is not a comforting one. The 'distant', unifying view is no more warm or humane than the 'close-up' satirical, divisive view. It simply annihilates the familiar distinctions provided by details in landscape or by characteristics in human beings.

The book culminates in a final shift of perspective, from health to sickness and from life to death. Rachel's divisive view of the universe has not been corrected by Terence's intuitive sympathy for human beings. Now she voyages even further out, creating her own universe in her fever just as she did when blocking out Santa Marina with her hand. In the extraordinary and brilliant Chapter 25, which describes the fever, there is a strong ironic emphasis on the different perspectives of Rachel and of those who surround her. Of course we are not surprised, in the description of a fever, to come across such phrases as

> The world [. . .] appeared distinctly further off (p. 334)

> She was completely cut off, and unable to communicate with the rest of the world (p. 335)

> She [. . .] made an effort to remember certain facts from the world that was so many millions of miles away (p. 337)

> She did not wish to remember; it troubled her when people tried to disturb her loneliness (p. 352)

But these phrases are also reminders of the journey of the *Euphrosyne* away from England, and of the trance-like states into which Rachel has fallen earlier in the novel. The fever and the death are the furthest points on the voyage through and out of experience, a voyage which has had three stages. On the *Euphrosyne* and in the early stages of her stay at Santa Marina Rachel finds herself in possession of a discrete identity. On the journey up the river she attempts to merge and unify herself with another; through fever and death she withdraws entirely from the claims of personality into an impersonal mystery.

Presumably Rachel's death is intended from the start of the novel, though the reader sometimes feels, with Strachey, as though he has read 'only the beginning of an enormous novel, which had been – almost accidentally – cut short by the death of Rachel.'[1] If one shares this feeling, then the death could be seen as the arbitrary stroke of a force dooming Rachel's chances of happiness, rather than as the inevitable climax to the themes of the book. That there should be a difficulty in deciding whether the death is inevitable or arbitrary suggests a weakness in the book; Daiches was perhaps right in wishing that the death had been definitely anticipated throughout.[2] Of course there are clues, provided not only by sinister or ominous moments such as Rachel's dream or the parting

---

[1] *Virginia Woolf and Lytton Strachey: Letters*, ed. Leonard Woolf and James Strachey (London, Hogarth Press, 1956), Lytton Strachey to Virginia Woolf, 25 February 1916, p. 56.

[2] David Daiches, *Virginia Woolf* (Norfolk, Conn.: New Directions, 1942; London, Nicholson and Watson, Editions Poetry, 1945), p. 20.

from the Dalloways ('so, too, would they be forgotten' (p. 76)) but also by more particular, even comic, anticipations. Mr Pepper leaves the villa for the better-cooked vegetables of the hotel, saying 'If you all die of typhoid I won't be responsible!' (p. 91). Hewet, as a joke against Evelyn, pretends to be dead:

> 'Now,' he murmured in an even, monotonous voice, 'I shall never, never, never move again.' His body, lying flat among them, did for a moment suggest death. (p. 144)

But if these moments are meant to be clues, their effect is diminished by the diffuse structure of the book and by the abruptness with which Rachel is made to fall ill. It does not seem convincing to treat the illness as the *outcome* of Rachel's emotional experiences – as a flight from sex or from the unsatisfactoriness of love. It is not the fault of her attitude to life that she falls ill. At the level of plot and character development, the death is arbitrary.

At the more abstract level below the plot, the death feels conclusive, as being the furthest point of the voyage. Yet it has a baffling and paradoxical effect. Rachel's death allows her to achieve an ultimately remote perspective on the world. But that absolute impersonality mysteriously, and momentarily, creates a sense of unification.

> They had now what they had always wanted to have, the union which had been impossible while they lived [. . .] It seemed to him that their complete union and happiness filled the room with rings eddying more and more widely. (p. 358–9)

The conflict between Terence and Rachel as to whether human beings must be separate from each other is fleetingly solved by her death. If the personality is relinquished altogether, it can no longer be a barrier to unification. But, for all that, death is loss. The book's ending is problematical, and answers uncertainly the question that was to be asked again in *Jacob's Room*, in *To the Lighthouse* and in *The Waves*: is there any consolation for the apparently meaningless death of the loved person?[1] After Rachel's death we return to

---

[1] The death of Virginia's brother Thoby Stephen, of typhoid fever in 1906, is particularly the subject of this book and of *Jacob's Room* and *The Waves*. See p. 73, n. 1.

the satirized world of the hotel, and the death itself becomes
material for the humour associated with that world:

> 'Miss Vinrace is dead,' he said very distinctly. Mrs Paley
> merely bent a little towards him and asked, 'Eh?'
>
> 'Miss Vinrace is dead,' he repeated. It was only by stiffening
> all the muscles round his mouth that he could prevent himself
> from bursting into laughter [. . .] Mrs Paley [. . .] sat vaguely
> for at least a minute before she realized what Arthur meant.
>
> 'Dead?' she said vaguely. 'Miss Vinrace dead? Dear me . . .
> that's very sad. But I don't at the moment remember which
> she was. We seem to have made so many new acquaintances
> here.' (pp. 366–7)

Relief is brilliantly provided here from the intensity of the previous
chapter. But the suggestion the comedy appears to make – that
the importance of Rachel's existence has been irrecoverably lost
in the trivia of commonplace life – is qualified by the very end of
the book. For Hirst, the most satirical proponent of the divisive
view of the universe, comes back to the hotel and is consoled, not
disheartened, by its continuance:

> All these voices sounded gratefully in St John's ears as he lay
> half-asleep, and yet vividly conscious of everything around
> him. Across his eyes passed a procession of objects, black and
> indistinct, the figures of people picking up their books, their
> cards, their balls of wool, their work-baskets, and passing him
> one after another on their way to bed. (p. 380)

The erstwhile comic figures achieve impersonality: they are 'black
and indistinct', 'a procession of objects', moving inevitably on their
nightward voyage. A consolation, though a dark and tentative one,
is offered for Rachel's death. Though pointless and tragic in itself,
it sheds its impersonal mystery on others, lending them, even in the
eyes of a satirist, an unprecedented dignity.

2

Night and Day

1919

A s its title implies, the novel concerns two kinds of experience: the private and the social, the silent and the communicable. It is a daylit comedy: in spite of obstacles and
misunderstandings, the younger generation achieve integrity and
enlightenment, and some get married. But it is also a 'melancholy'[1]
exploration of the mind's obscure search for an intangible vision
which can only be described tentatively and impressionistically.

There are then similarities between the first two novels, even
though *The Voyage Out* ends as a tragedy. Both explore the possibilities for individual happiness within a restrictive society, and
suggest that such happiness can be achieved only by going beyond
relationships to more impersonal areas of existence. But *Night and
Day* encourages the hope that some link can be forged between its
silent and its communicable worlds. It makes a claim for the unification of 'little separate bodies' within the conditions of everyday
life. Although the increased emphasis towards the end of both
novels on the abstract and the metaphorical is at odds with their
traditional mould, *Night and Day*, like its heroine, is more en-
cumbered by the exigencies of convention. Plot and characters
are assiduously manipulated, and, with the exception of the last
chapter, the obscure haziness of *The Voyage Out* is suppressed in the
interests of comedy. After Rachel's delirium, Virginia Woolf has
come up for air: a process she was frequently to repeat, turning,

---

[1] *AWD*, 27 March 1919, p. 10.

for instance, from *To the Lighthouse* to *Orlando*, and from *The Waves* to *Flush*.

Night and Day takes its tone from established comic models. It is the only one of Virginia Woolf's novels to imitate the techniques of dramatic farce. The book is full of scenes of ridiculous confusion, abrupt exits and entrances, coincidental meetings, secrets, conversations at cross-purposes, and unwelcome interruptions from absurd figures like Katharine Hilbery's stage-comedy aunts:

> I come from Woking, Mr Popham. You may well ask me, why Woking? and to that I answer, for perhaps the hundredth time, because of the sunsets. We went there for the sunsets, but that was five-and-twenty years ago. (pp. 137–8)

Cassandra Otway is introduced into the novel with extraordinary abruptness in order to provide a suitable match for William Rodney, and makes entrances like a *dea ex machina*:

> 'You're right,' he exclaimed [. . .] 'I love Cassandra.'
> As he said this, the curtains hanging at the door of the little room parted, and Cassandra herself stepped forth.
> 'I have overheard every word!' she exclaimed. (p. 383)

Such dramatic techniques permeate the whole of *Night and Day*, and a debt is explicitly acknowledged to Shakespearian comedy. The heroine is associated with Rosalind (pp. 162, 285), but it is her mother, Mrs Hilbery, who, 'benevolent and sarcastic' (p. 304), embodies the spirit of comedy and herself enacts the role of the wise Shakespearian fool, in her erratic mixture of whimsical optimism and canny perception.[1] She plays a double part, being also (like Mr Emerson in Forster's *A Room with a View* (1910)), a resolver of muddle. She returns from a visit to Shakespeare's tomb to stage-manage a happy ending, as if she were Hymen in *As You Like It*:

> Peace, Ho! I bar confusion,
> Tis I must make conclusion
> Of these most strange events.[2]

---

[1] Mrs Hilbery is based on Lady Ritchie, 'Aunt Anny', whose dottiness is neatly summed up by the anecdote in 'Leslie Stephen' (1932), *CE* IV, p. 77. See also Bell I, p. 11.

[2] *As You Like It*, V. iv. 125–7.

Mrs Hilbery draws attention to the dramatic models for the novel, but it is as much indebted to Jane Austen, sharing the same idea of the ethics of comedy. As in Jane Austen's novels, understanding and right action only come through pain. Katharine has to struggle free of her mistaken idea of marrying William before she can come to terms with her truer, more important feelings for Ralph. The pattern of development is reminiscent of Emma's or of Elizabeth Bennet's. Both writers, too, create a link between emotional development and seasonal growth. Like *Emma*, *Mansfield Park* and *Persuasion*, *Night and Day* progresses from a gloomy autumn to the suggestion of summer. The change from dead to living season – the basis of comedy – provides both Jane Austen and Virginia Woolf with a satisfying frame for the transformation of tangled love affairs into marriages. More particularly, *Night and Day* evokes *Pride and Prejudice*. Katharine's reaction to Aunt Celia's interference in her life suggests Elizabeth Bennet's reaction to Lady Catherine, and Katharine's scene with her father, when she first tells him she is no longer engaged to William, is markedly reminiscent of Elizabeth's two conversations with Mr Bennet about Darcy, the first arising from Mr Collins's warning letter, the second from Darcy's proposal. Both fathers are slow to understand their daughters, largely because of their literary and peace-loving habits which have kept them aloof. Both have been warned about their daughters' behaviour by officious spokesmen for conventional morality, and both expect their daughters to be amused by these warnings:

> Elizabeth tried to join in her father's pleasantry, but could only force one most reluctant smile. Never had his wit been directed in a manner so little agreeable to her.
>
> 'Are you not diverted?'
> 'Oh yes. Pray read on.'[1]

Mr Hilbery was [. . .] secretly amused at the thought of the interview [with Aunt Celia], although he could not licence such irreverence outwardly.

> 'Very good. Then you authorize me to tell her that [. . .] there was nothing but a little fun in it? [. . .]'

[1] Jane Austen, *Pride and Prejudice*, Ch. 58.

> She did not respond, as he had hoped, with any affectionate or humorous reply. (p. 432)

There is more to this than a resemblance of situation; the language of the passages is also comparable. *Night and Day* sustains a rather formal, preponderantly Latinate diction which allows for a satirical tone to colour the presentation of all the characters, not just the comic turns like Katharine's aunts, the irascible Sir Francis Otway, or the enthusiastic Mrs Seal, the White Queen of the suffragette office. Though the complexities of the major characters may involve a more lyrical and intimate tone, such comic weaknesses as they display – William Rodney's fussy, fastidious inhibitions, Mary Datchet's self-conscious fluctuations of mood about Ralph and her work, Katharine's absentmindedness and Ralph's pride and resentments – are rendered in a dry, hard language which makes no concessions to the obscure, incommunicable areas of the personality:

> He was roused by a creak upon the stair. With a guilty start he composed himself, frowned, and looked intently at the fifty-sixth page of his volume. A step paused outside his door, and he knew that the person, whoever it might be, was considering the placard, and debating whether to honour its decree or not. Certainly, policy advised him to sit still in autocratic silence, for no custom can take root in a family unless every breach of it is punished severely for the first six months or so. But Ralph was conscious of a distinct wish to be interrupted, and his disappointment was perceptible when he heard the creaking sound rather farther down the stairs, as if his visitor had decided to withdraw. He rose, opened the door with unnecessary abruptness, and waited on the landing. (p. 25)

The narrator, formal, omniscient and ironic, sets us down in the room with Ralph and shows us his endearing mixture of silliness and self-pity. He takes himself seriously, while we are encouraged to laugh at him by the mock-heroic pomposity of the Latinisms which describe his efforts at dignity, combined with the clichés – 'a guilty start', 'a distinct wish' – which give away his real feelings. The authorial voice (much given to aphorisms and commentary in *Night and Day*) will never again present itself in such a direct, traditional manner, though it will never be made to disappear entirely.

With such uncharacteristically straightforward presentation of character is found a very large amount of vivid, naturalistic dialogue. Much use of dialogue will be made in *The Years* and *Between the Acts*, but no other of her novels presents it with the air of direct representation. There is none of the later uncertainty as to whether a person is speaking aloud, or to himself, or even speaking at all. Here the speech of the characters is quite unambiguous, and, though this style was to be abandoned, often brilliantly achieved:

> 'No one enjoys being made a fool of before other people,' he blurted out [...] 'That refers to me, I suppose,' she said calmly.
>
> 'Every day since we've been here you've done something to make me appear ridiculous,' he went on. 'Of course, so long as it amuses you, you're welcome; but we have to remember that we are going to spend our lives together. I asked you, only this morning, for example, to come out and take a turn with me in the garden. I was waiting for you ten minutes, and you never came. Every one saw me waiting. The stable-boys saw me. I was so ashamed that I went in. Then, on the drive you hardly spoke to me. Henry noticed it. Every one notices it ... You find no difficulty in talking to Henry, though.' [...]
>
> 'None of these things seem to me to matter,' she said.
>
> 'Very well, then. I may as well hold my tongue,' he replied.
>
> 'In themselves they don't seem to me to matter; if they hurt you, of course they matter.' (p. 221)

In isolation, the interplay in this passage between William's nervous, exasperated iteration and Katharine's unimpassioned comments is extremely impressive. But the effect of the dialogue is rather lessened, in context, by there being so much of it. The reader may well be tired of such conversations by the end of 'that interminable *Night and Day*'.[1] Though it is far more elaborately plotted than *The Voyage Out*, which, after the arrival at Santa

[1] Bell II, p. 42.

Marina, is loosely structured along the path of Rachel's development without leading up to any necessary moment for her death,
Night and Day nevertheless gives the effect of unwieldy shapeless-
ness. 'It's so long and so tahsome,' Katherine Mansfield tartly
remarked;[1] and Virginia Woolf (who was taking time off from the
novel to write such short sketches as 'Kew Gardens' and 'The Mark
on the Wall') expressed her impatience with it in 'Modern Fiction'
(1919):

> We go on perseveringly, conscientiously, constructing our
> two and thirty chapters after a design which more and more
> ceased to resemble the vision in our minds.[2]

The organization of the novel reflects the pointless and repetitive
quality of its upper-class heroine's conventional daily round. Ralph
asks Katharine what she has been doing since they last met.

> 'Doing?' she pondered. 'Walking in and out of other people's
> houses.' (p. 341)

Virginia Woolf, similarly, pushes her plot along by having the
characters walk in and out of people's houses in order to talk and
think. They seem always to be having tea with each other, while
their emotions interact in as elaborate a pattern as that of the
mathematical equations which the heroine constructs in the privacy
of her room. Ralph Denham loves Katharine, but Katharine is
engaged to William Rodney. Mary Datchet loves Ralph, but knows
that he loves Katharine, and so refuses his offer of marriage.
Katharine realizes that her marriage with William is impossible,
and eventually (guided selflessly though reluctantly by Mary)
comes to love Ralph. At the highest point of 'muddle' in the story,
Katharine arranges for William to court Cassandra Otway, while,
in the eyes of the world, he is still engaged to Katharine. These
private affairs become public when the interfering Aunt Celia
discovers the relationship between William and Cassandra. Mrs
Hilbery steps in to seal the union of the two couples, in spite of
Mr Hilbery's half-hearted opposition. Mary has withdrawn into a

[1] Bell II, p. 69.   [2] *CE* II, p. 105.

self-abnegating, impersonal life of work. The shifts in the pattern all take place between Chapters 18 and 22, so that there is a longer first part of muddle and a shorter second part of enlightenment.

Important visits are made to the Otways at Stogdon House and to Mary's family at Disham, but in the main the action centres on five places in London: the Hilbery home in Cheyne Walk, where Katharine pours tea, helps her mother to write the life of the poet Richard Alardyce, and works secretly in her room at mathematics; Ralph's shabby, middle-class house in Highgate, full of relatives, where he barricades himself in his room to dream of Katharine; Mary Datchet's flat at the top of a block of offices off the Strand, and the suffragette office in Russell Square, where her increasingly self-reliant life takes place; and William Rodney's comfortable eighteenth-century rooms in King's Bench Walk, the rooms 'of a person who cherishes a great many personal tastes, guarding them from the rough blasts of the public with scrupulous attention' (p. 65).

'Tahsome' though the form of *Night and Day* may be, it is appropriate that the story of Katharine's escape from nineteenth-century traditions should be described in the kind of novel which was in its turn to be escaped from. Ten years later, in *A Room of One's Own* and in 'Women and Fiction',[1] Virginia Woolf was to write brilliantly about the enormous and special problems facing the woman writer who has so many inhibiting traditions to resist in order to write at all, let alone to write well and with her own voice. But in *Night and Day* the discussion is already taking place in disguised form, so that a retrospective analogy may be drawn between Katharine's emancipation as a woman and Virginia Woolf's development as a writer. In order to be truthful and free and to work at her 'art' in daylight, as 'mistress in her own kingdom' (p. 445), Katharine has to reject the phantom voices of traditional authority which decree that 'Insanity is not a fit subject for fiction' (p. 323), that women are only 'half alive' without marriage (p. 59), that a wife must be 'ambitious for her husband' (p. 140) and that 'a woman who wants to have her own way' should not get married (p. 196). Katharine's tentative resistance to these voices is described in an extremely important passage.

[1] *CE* II, pp. 141–8.

Like all people brought up in a tradition, Katharine was able, within ten minutes or so, to reduce any moral difficulty to its traditional shape and solve it by the traditional answers. The book of wisdom lay open, if not upon her mother's knee, upon the knees of many uncles and aunts. She had only to consult them, and they would at once turn to the right page and read out an answer exactly suited to one in her position [. . .] But in her case the questions became phantoms directly she tried seriously to find an answer, which proved that the traditional answer would be of no use to her individually. Yet it had served so many people, she thought, glancing at the rows of houses on either side of her, where families, whose incomes must be between a thousand and fifteen-hundred a year lived, and kept, perhaps, three servants, and draped their windows with curtains which were always thick and generally dirty, and must, she thought, since you could only see a looking-glass gleaming above a sideboard on which a dish of apples was set, keep the room inside very dark. [. . .]

The only truth which she could discover was the truth of what she herself felt – a frail beam when compared with the broad illumination shed by the eyes of all the people who are in agreement to see together; but having rejected the visionary voices, she had no choice but to make this her guide through the dark masses which confronted her. (pp. 290–1)

Katharine's predicament is vividly rendered through images. The book upon the knees of older relatives suggests security as much as repression (anticipating the vision in *The Waves* of 'the old nurse who turns the pages of the picture-book').[1] Not to read that book is to go out into the unknown, away from the stability of childhood. But the alternative to the unknown is those dark, stuffy, nineteenth-century rooms, which Virginia Woolf uses again and again as images for the attitudes they contain.[2] The symbol for Katharine's own search for truth, the 'frail beam', grows in strength, like the search itself, until it dominates the latter part of the novel.

[1] *The Waves*, p. 247.
[2] See, for example, 'Lappin and Lappinova' (written in 1919), *A Haunted House and Other Short Stories*, p. 83; *Orlando*, Ch. 5; *The Years*, pp. 10–40; *Flush*, Ch. 2 and 3.

It is not easy for Katharine to find her own way, partly because she is fond of what she must reject. Certainly she resents having to spend her mornings surrounded by manuscripts and letters and old photographs, trying to organize her mother's scatty, eloquent recollections into a 'Life' of Richard Alardyce, and her afternoons showing visitors the 'shrine' of her grandfather, the poet. But, though she longs to climb out of this 'deep pool of past time' (p. 104), it is attractive: living on in her mother, the past seems richer and more serene than her own time, and Richard Alardyce a more romantic figure than any she can find in the present:

> Sometimes she felt [. . .] that the past had completely displaced the present, which, when one resumed life after a morning among the dead, proved to be of an utterly thin and inferior composition. (p. 39)

The present consists of Aunt Celia fulminating over the immorality of Cousin Cyril's living with a woman not his wife, and William Rodney demanding constant sympathetic subservience. Katharine's feelings for William in no way measure up to her secret ideal of romantic emotion, and she therefore assumes that her 'imaginary world', 'a place where feelings were liberated from the constraint which the real world puts upon them', cannot be linked with the actual. She turns from her dreams, with 'resignation and a kind of stoical acceptance of facts' (p. 131), to marry William as a means to independence. At least, as a married woman, she will be able to work at maths and not at the life of her grandfather. Her marriage 'seemed no more than an archway through which it was necessary to pass in order to have her desire' (pp. 200–1). Since William has conventional ideas about marriage and women ('Don't ask them for their reasons. Just ask them for their feelings' (p. 190)), their conflict is inevitable. Though he is not presented as a sexually potent character, his desire to put Katharine in a doll's house creates a fierce sexual hostility between them, anticipating the more powerfully imagined relationships between Mr and Mrs Ramsay and Isa and Giles Oliver:

> William's exacting demands and his jealousy had pulled her down into some horrible swamp of her nature where the primeval struggle between man and woman still rages. (p. 344)

– an observation which is made, appropriately, at the zoo. William (whose intellectual refinement and egotistical chauvinism are not quite happily fused, making him an unsatisfactory combination of St John Hirst and the first Richard Dalloway) has an aesthetic appreciation of Katharine which is balked by her inability to act up to his concept of womanly behaviour. He is not likely to realize that she represents 'the manly side [. . .] of the feminine nature' (p. 317), since the possibility of deviation from standard sexual roles is foreign to his way of thought, but he can tell that the 'womanly' Cassandra, who soothes his pride, makes him feel happier.

Katharine is offered a very different kind of consolation by Ralph Denham: the possibility of freedom and equality, without pretence. Katharine's androgynous qualities will be able to express themselves; space, privacy and rational understanding will be the enlightened alternatives to the 'horrible swamp' of jealousy and possessiveness. Though the word 'androgynous' is not used, the relationship is a serious early version of the light-fantastic androgynous marriage in *Orlando* and of the sexless relationship between Sara and Nicholas in *The Years*.[1] Ralph and Katharine's love, however, is not sexless. Though Virginia Woolf apologized to Lytton Strachey for the lack of 'tupping' in the novel,[2] it is clear that the lovers are sexually attracted: Mr Hilbery, though never jealous of William, feels that Ralph Denham is a rival:[3]

> She might have married Rodney without causing him a twinge. This man she loved [. . .] Had he loved her to see her swept away by this torrent, to have her taken from him by this uncontrollable force? [. . .] [He] strode out of the room, leaving in the minds of the women a sense, half of awe, half

[1] The type of relationship is based partly on Virginia Woolf's own marriage and partly (see p. 7 above) on her sister Vanessa's life with Duncan Grant at Wissett Farm in 1916. See Bell II, pp. 31–2, 42.

[2] *Virginia Woolf and Lytton Strachey: Letters*, ed. Leonard Woolf and James Strachey (London, Hogarth Press, 1956), Virginia Woolf to Lytton Strachey, 28 October 1919, p. 84.

[3] The reader is put in mind here of Leslie Stephen, whose character is used as material both for Mr Hilbery – a jealous father and a reader of Scott – and for the eccentric Mr Ambrose in *The Voyage Out*, in anticipation of Mr Ramsay (see p. 38 above).

of amusement, at the extravagant, inconsiderate, uncivilized male, outraged somehow and gone bellowing to his lair [. . .] (p. 464)

Her father's outrage suggests too that Ralph is to enfranchise Katharine from the world of her childhood. He is a spokesman for modernism, who will enable her to move into the twentieth century, partly by virtue of his coming from another class and working for his living. He opens the doors for Katharine to the outside world of human activity from which she has been sheltered in Cheyne Walk by privilege and tradition. The challenge he embodies to her family history is summed up in a companion piece to the passage on tradition quoted above.

> At any moment she might hear another summons of greater interest to her than the whole of the nineteenth century. [. . .]
> The alcove on the stairs, in which the telephone was placed [. . .] was a pocket for superfluous possessions, such as exist in most houses which harbour the wreckage of three generations. Prints of great-uncles, famed for their prowess in the East, hung above Chinese teapots [. . .] [which] stood upon bookcases containing the complete works of William Cowper and Sir Walter Scott. [. . .] Whose voice was now going to combine with them, or to strike a discord? [. . .]
> She dropped the machine, and looked fixedly at the print of the great-uncle who had not ceased to gaze, with an air of amiable authority, into a world which, as yet, beheld no symptoms of the Indian Mutiny. And yet, gently swinging against the wall, within the black tube, was a voice which recked nothing of Uncle James, or of China teapots, or of red velvet curtains. (pp. 287–8)

Katharine's emancipation from the nineteenth century in all its forms – her parents, the house, William's idea of marriage, the family tea-kettle (p. 460)[1] – is the result of her emotion for Ralph, and its reward is their marriage. Though she has to undergo a private and difficult struggle in order to understand her feelings, the struggle takes her towards a mutual experience. By contrast,

[1] The image is used again in *The Years*, pp. 10–11.

Mary Datchet's struggle takes her towards isolation. Though Katharine is the heroine, Mary is the more heroic character, the first of several single women – Lily Briscoe, Miss La Trobe, the 'Marys' of *A Room of One's Own* – whose life is their work. She has removed herself from her version of Cheyne Walk – a quiet country rectory in the medieval village of Disham – six months before the start of the novel, and, by means of a private income, is able to devote herself to the cause of women's suffrage.[1] When she has to suppress her love for Ralph, she marshals her generous affections in the service of the world's troubles, and determines on a life which is 'not happiness', but which involves her in 'the vast desires and sufferings of the mass of mankind' (p. 243). In practical terms she may not achieve much. The work of Mary's suffrage office is not idealized, and her colleagues, Mrs Seal and Mr Clacton, are treated satirically. The society which she joins towards the end of the novel is vaguely described. It seems as though the value of her work lies more in its ennobling effect on the personality than in its political effects. Even at the moment of Mary's apotheosis, when Ralph and Katharine look up at the light burning in her window and see it as 'a sign of triumph shining there for ever', the figure whom Ralph associates with Mary's 'plans' is the absurd one of Sally Seal (p. 469). But Mary's stature in the novel is not undermined by the reservations felt for her work. She is a source of strength – as is comically indicated by the continuous visits she is paid by the other characters. Though she is wrenching herself away from personal involvements she is necessary to less self-reliant people, particularly to Katharine, whose developing relationship with her is the most interesting and the most convincing in the novel.

Mary, Ralph and Katharine find, in different ways, that it is possible to forge links between 'the life of solitude and the life of society' (p. 315), and that the dark, inner states of the personality can have some active relation to the external, daylit world, and need not always be suppressed or kept separate. That the characters can

---

[1] Virginia Woolf had experience of such work. In 1910 she was employed in addressing envelopes for the suffrage movement (Bell I, p. 161) and from 1916 to 1920 she was an active member of the Richmond Branch of the Woman's Co-operative Guild (Bell II, p. 35).

achieve this assimilation makes *Night and Day* the most optimistic of the novels; but at the same time the difficulty of their attempt gives it a 'melancholy' tone:

> Yet if one is to deal with people on a large scale, and say what one thinks, how can one avoid melancholy? I don't admit to being hopeless though: only the spectacle is a profoundly strange one; and as the current answers don't do, one has to grope for a new one, and the process of discarding the old, when one is by no means certain what to put in their place, is a sad one.[1]

The comment might be a description of narrative innovations as much as of subject matter: it directs us to the relationship between Virginia Woolf's attempt to find the right 'modern' way of mastering and communicating reality, and Ralph and Katharine's similar struggle to translate the truer, secret areas of the mind into communicable terms.

At the heart of the comic vacillations between different partnerships is the emphasis on the difficulty of knowing others and on the extreme obscurity and remoteness of the self. Underlying the comic cross-purposes and misunderstandings is the isolation of social beings. Katharine, in a conversation with her cousin Henry, sums up the despondency produced by attempts to communicate.

> She knew that any intercourse between people is extremely partial; from the whole mass of her feelings, only one or two could be selected for Henry's inspection, and therefore she sighed. (p. 184)

Conversations are repeatedly being carried on against the ironically different activity of the inward mind – a condition of existence to which Virginia Woolf will give increasing attention in the novels. There seems no possibility of reconciling the external and the internal, when a proposal of marriage (for instance) can spring from such incommunicable depths as these:

> He had been building one of those piles of thought, as ramshackle and fantastic as a Chinese pagoda, half from words

[1] *AWD*, 27 March 1919, p. 10.

let fall by gentlemen in gaiters, half from the litter in his own mind, about duck shooting and legal history, about the Roman occupation of Lincoln and the relations of country gentlemen with their wives, when, from all this disconnected rambling, there suddenly formed itself in his mind the idea that he would ask Mary to marry him. (p. 211)

'Oh, dear me! The mystery of life; the inaccuracy of thought!' Virginia Woolf exclaims in 'The Mark on the Wall', written in 1917, where she enters into the kind of mental process which is here being descriptively paraphrased. Since the arbitrary process of connection in Ralph's mind cannot be understood by anyone else, it seems unlikely that the attempt to know others will result in anything but confusion and dismay, the aimless, hopeful crying out of names: 'Jacob! Jacob!' 'Mrs Ramsay! Mrs Ramsay!' But for all this we cannot help 'arrows of sensation striking strangely through the envelope of personality, which shelters us so conveniently from our fellows' (p. 252). In spite of its impossibility, the task of communication is attractive, because participation is life; absolute isolation is death. The antithesis is powerfully expressed by Mary's dilemma over whether to tell Katharine that Ralph loves her. In terms of the plot, it means that Mary will lose Ralph for ever. But the problem is not explored in those terms:

> After all, she considered, why should she speak? Because it is right, her instinct told her; right to expose oneself without reservation to other human beings. [. . .] But if she did keep something of her own? Immediately she figured an immured life, continuing for an immense period, the same feelings living for ever, neither dwindling nor changing within the ring of a thick stone wall. (p. 255)

It is an image of hell. The barren sterility of isolation which Mary imagines here is one of several horrific visions which haunt the three principal characters. All three are aware of an aspect of the world without joy or hope, a 'heart of darkness'[1] which is an appal-

---

[1] Conrad is called to mind, particularly in the words of Marlow in *Lord Jim*: 'He appealed . . . to the side turned perpetually to the light of day, and to that side of us which, like the other hemisphere of the moon, exists stealthily in

ling kind of reality. Ralph, hearing of Katharine's engagement,
gives way to it, to the accompaniment of the appropriate passage
from *Measure for Measure*:

> To be imprison'd in the viewless winds,
> And blown with restless violence round about
> The pendant world . . .

> All things had turned to ghosts; the whole mass of the world
> was insubstantial vapour, surrounding the solitary spark in his
> mind [which] burnt no more [. . .] He saw the truth. He saw
> the dun-coloured race of waters and the blank shore. (pp. 143,
> 146)

Katharine, isolated by William's love for Cassandra, before her
union with Ralph, undergoes a similar experience:

> The dream nature of our life had never been more apparent
> to her, never had life been more certainly an affair of four
> walls, whose objects existed only within the range of lights
> and fires, beyond which lay nothing, or nothing more than
> darkness. She seemed physically to have stepped beyond the
> region where the light of illusion still makes it desirable to
> possess, to love, to struggle. (p. 327)

It is difficult for Ralph and Katharine to establish a relationship in
the face of this dark, nihilistic vision, since, in Katharine particularly,
there is a part that embraces the vision in preference to the muddle
of personal relationships. The inward effect of her bondage to
social tradition is that she has come to resent the demands made on
her inner life by other people; she dislikes having to be involved in
'all that part of life which is conspicuously without order' (p. 308).
Looking out of her window, she yearns, not for participation, but for
space, darkness, silence, 'the nothingness of night' (p. 97). So that
when the hero and heroine approach each other, they are engaged

---

perpetual darkness, with only a fearful ashy light falling at times on the
edge' (Ch. 8). 'For a moment I had a view of the world that seemed to wear a
vast and dismal aspect of disorder' (Ch. 33). Allen McLaurin compares the
passage about Ralph on p. 146 to the introduction of Heyst in Ch. 1 of
Victory (*The Echoes Enslaved* (Cambridge University Press, 1973), pp. 36–7).

not only in a mutual defiance of their vision of a world entirely dark, but also against Katharine's wariness of daylight communication. Their desire, and their task, is to fill both 'night' and 'day' with meaning by linking the two, jumping 'this astonishing precipice on the one side of which the soul was active and in broad daylight, on the other side of which it was contemplative and dark as night' (p. 315). They attempt to actualize their daydreams. Both have existed, in the earlier part of the novel, in a dream world which seems to have no possible meeting place with reality. Ralph is obsessed by a mythical 'Katharine', but even before her advent he had been prone to 'strange voyages' of the mind, and has had to divide his life 'rigidly' into 'hours of work and those of dreams' (p. 117). Katharine, similarly, has been used to wandering in a dream world with an ideal lover: 'They rode through forests together, they galloped by the rim of the sea' (p. 98). As we have seen, in agreeing to marry William, she is resigned to suppressing the reality of her dreams for the task of living, like the cave dwellers in Plato's *Republic*, in a prison of appearances (p. 131). The only person she knows who does not have to make any distinction between dreams and life is her mother, who, when asked about her past, can reply: 'It was life, it was death. The great sea was round us. It was the voyage for ever and ever' (p. 449). This is the language of Katharine's dreams, and she gazes admiringly at her mother, 'that ancient voyager'. Even when Ralph and Katharine begin to link their real lives with their daydreams, they find it hard to achieve Mrs Hilbery's serene harmonizing of the two; instead they are continually in difficulties, because their dreams threaten to dominate their understanding of each other. These moments they call their 'lapses'.

'Reality – reality' [. . .] 'I cease to be real to you [. . .] We come together for a moment and we part.' (pp. 438–9)

The romantic language used for their dream lives is uninteresting: the jungles and seashores and mountains (which will recur more subtly in Rhoda's and Isa's monologues) do not have the vigour and sharpness of their real surroundings. Where the language does become interesting is in the increasingly impressionistic images of air, light, fire and gloom, which are used for the vision of truth to which the lovers aspire. Towards the end of the book, as the vision is realized, the dialogue between Ralph and Katharine loses its previously naturalistic tone, and becomes anticipatory of the lyrical speech in *Between the Acts*. The relationship is increasingly described in terms of light. Ralph sits on the Embankment thinking of Katharine and an old tramp approaches him and asks for money.

> When the elderly man [. . .] mumbled on, an odd image came to his mind of a lighthouse besieged by the flying bodies of lost birds, who were dashed senseless, by the gale, against the glass. He had a strange sensation that he was both lighthouse and bird. (p. 365)

Later he thinks of the light from the Hilberys' house as a lighthouse beam irradiating the 'trackless waste'. It is interesting to find that Virginia Woolf is already using the image – in a book which has no excuse for a lighthouse – for its flexibility. It suggests ideas of hope and of desolation, of loneliness and of sanctuary. And it provides the alternative to the hard, bright electric light of 'society', the light Mrs Hilbery rejects when she says: 'Shall we give a little party in complete darkness? There'd have to be bright rooms for the bores . . .' (p. 18). Towards the end of the book Ralph tries to write Katharine a letter expressing his belief that relationships are the only means to the kind of impersonal state which she desires. It is as near as the novel comes to defining its vision of true reality, which for most of the time remains as unspecific as the alternatives it rejects are clear-cut.

> Human beings [. . .] make it possible for each to have access to another world independent of personal affairs, a world of law, of philosophy, or more strangely a world such as he had had a glimpse of the other evening when together they seemed to be sharing something, creating something, an ideal – a vision flung out in advance of our actual circumstances. (p. 452)

The letter turns itself into a drawing, the only expression he can find for his idea: a 'little dot' with 'flames round it' (p. 457).

> It represented by its circumference of smudges surrounding a central blot all that encircling glow which for him surrounded,

inexplicably, so many of the objects of life, softening their sharp outline, so that he could see certain streets, books, and situations wearing a halo almost perceptible to the physical eye. (p. 458)

Katharine, to whom Ralph appears as 'fire burning through smoke' understands the symbol: 'She said simply [...] "Yes, the world looks something like that to me too."' Very soon after, Virginia Woolf was to write a non-fictional description of true reality in the same terms, in the passage in 'Modern Fiction' which says that life is not a 'series of gig-lamps symmetrically arranged' but 'a luminous halo'.[1] Again, the relationship between the discovery of a truer life in *Night and Day* and Virginia Woolf's search for a 'truer' form of narrative realism is clear. Because the vision is exploratory and owes nothing to received ideas, it has no ready-made concrete form, and cannot be firmly expressed – 'reality, was it, figures, love, truth?' (p. 466) – except in such images as a dot with flames round it or a luminous halo. The obscure and melancholy tone of the last chapter of *Night and Day* results from the great difficulty which the lovers find in expressing their 'vision of an orderly world'.

> She felt him trying to piece together in a laborious and ele-
> mentary fashion fragments of belief, unsoldered and separate,
> lacking the unity of phrases fashioned by the old believers.
> Together they groped in this difficult region, where the un-
> finished, the unfulfilled, the unwritten, the unreturned, came
> together in their ghostly way and wore the semblance of the
> complete and the satisfactory. (p. 470)

But the truth is hard to retain. It appears in 'moments, fragments, a second of vision, and then the flying waters, the winds dissipating and dissolving' (p. 470). The struggle to sustain the moment of vision against the forces of chaos, to send the lighthouse beam across the trackless waste, will be found in the later novels. In its pre-occupation with this struggle, *Night and Day*, in spite of its traditional and comic form, is integral to the whole of Virginia Woolf's work.

---

[1] *CE* II, p. 106.

3

Jacob's Room

1922

Virginia Woolf discovered a form for *Jacob's Room* before she knew what the subject of the novel would be. The discovery sprang from the commentaries on modern fiction and the short experiments in narrative which she had been making since 1917. Quite suddenly, in 1920, she realized how they would lead to her next book. The relevant passage in the diary is a major landmark, prefacing a novel so different in appearance from *The Voyage Out* and *Night and Day* that its similarities of themes and perspectives, and its considerable debt to traditional ingredients such as epigrams, mock-heroic diction and comic dialogue, may easily be overlooked.

... having this afternoon arrived at some idea of a new form for a new novel. Suppose one thing should open out of another – as in *An Unwritten Novel* – only not for 10 pages but 200 or so – doesn't that give the looseness and lightness I want; doesn't that get closer and yet keep form and speed, and enclose everything, everything? My doubt is how far it will enclose the human heart – Am I sufficiently mistress of my dialogue to net it there? For I figure that the approach will be entirely different this time: no scaffolding; scarcely a brick to be seen; all crepuscular, but the heart, the passion, humour, everything as bright as fire in the mist. Then I'll find room for so much – a gaiety – an inconsequence – a light spirited stepping at my sweet will. Whether I'm sufficiently mistress of things – that's the doubt; but conceive[?] *Mark on the Wall*, K.G. and *Unwritten Novel* taking hands and dancing in unity. What the unity shall be I have yet to discover; the theme is a blank to me . . .[1]

It is the techniques of the short stories that are uppermost in her mind, but these arise from and express their subject matter. The 'Unwritten' search for Minnie Marsh's hidden character, the impressionistic perspective of the snail in 'Kew Gardens', the mind that seeks an impersonal peace in lieu of facts and generalizations in 'The Mark on the Wall' are attempts to fuse the experience and the presentation of true reality. And, when she envisages that 'one thing should open out of another' in *Jacob's Room* and that all will be 'crepuscular', she points to its version of life – intangible characters and mixed perceptions – as much as to its narrative 'approach'. The form of *Jacob's Room is* the subject: an alternative to the false reality of the biography of fact. The momentary 'shower of innumerable atoms' [2] of the short sketches is now sustained to the extent of a whole life: a biography of fragments.

The ingredients of traditional biography are there. When the book begins on 'the third of September', Jacob is a small boy on holiday in Cornwall, with his widowed mother, Betty Flanders, and his two younger brothers Archer and John. Cornwall becomes Scarborough, their home, where Jacob grows up, learns Latin from Mr Floyd (who proposes to his mother), and collects butterflies. When he is nineteen he goes to Cambridge, where he makes friends with Richard Bonamy and Timothy Durrant. He goes by boat, one long vacation, to Timothy's home (again in Cornwall) where he meets Timothy's sister Clara. Coming down from Cambridge, aged twenty-two, he lives in elegant eighteenth-century rooms in Lamb's Conduit Street, has affairs, goes to parties, works in an unspecified office, rides to hounds, pays visits to his mother's old friends one day and to prostitutes the next, writes essays, goes to the opera, and reaches the age of twenty-five. He goes abroad, to France, Italy and Greece, where he falls in love with an older

[1] *AWD*, 26 January 1920, p. 23.
[2] 'Modern Fiction' (1919), *CE* II, p. 106.

married woman. When he returns, the war is beginning, in which he is killed.

There is very little drama in Jacob's life except his death, and that is kept as quiet as possible. The biographer is looking for interest other than action, and the attention is not on facts. Jacob's age, place of residence and acquaintances are slid into the texture of a description or a meditation. The 'fact' that his home town is Scarborough is merged on the first page with Betty Flanders's letter, her tears, and her view. Captain Barfoot's conversation with Mrs Flanders about the advisability of 'sending a boy to one of the universities' leads brusquely to: 'Jacob Flanders, therefore, went up to Cambridge in October, 1906' (p. 27), while the fact of his going still seems an idea taking root in his mother's mind. Though every chapter shows Jacob's life, there is no impartial account of it. Instead he is evoked by numerous points of view which add up to a portrait strongly anticipating that of Percival in *The Waves*:[1] a fine upstanding English youth, blue-eyed (p. 28), beautiful (p. 71), distinguished-looking (p. 67), silent and awkward in company unless fired with enthusiasm, expressing himself in inarticulate 'public school' language in which the word 'rot' frequently appears, physically healthy and sensual (p. 87), attractive, to all kinds of women, liking sincerity (p. 136), slow-thinking (p. 142), and interested in politics (p. 131) as well as in literature. Florinda and Fanny Elmer both compare him to Greek statues (as Mary Datchet does Ralph). Sandra Wentworth-Williams thinks he is like a small boy. Clara, the most sensitive of the women who love him, calls him 'unworldly' (p. 67). All the onlookers, however, are more or less baffled. Though evidently a simple type, he is also aloof and mysterious. Bonamy (anticipating Neville's love for Percival) is

---

[1] Both *Jacob's Room* and *The Waves* are elegies for Virginia's brother Thoby Stephen, who died of typhoid fever, after a holiday in Greece, in November 1906. Thoby's intellectual and personal influence on Virginia was a strong one (and it was, of course, his Cambridge friends who formed the nucleus of the Bloomsbury Group). But, though Virginia was very fond of her brother, she was not very close to him. Both novels reflect not only her sense of loss ('after twenty years it still seemed to her that her own continuing life was no more than an excursion without him') but also her feeling that Thoby had been a mystery to her. (Bell I, p. 112.)

drawn to Jacob and at the same time in awe of him. He finds him 'barbaric, obscure' (p. 156) – also romantic, gloomy, enthusiastic, incoherent, and liable to 'get into the doldrums' and look 'like a Margate fisherman out of a job, or a British admiral' (p. 137). But Bonamy's view – like Betty Flanders's, or Mrs Durrant's, or Lucinda's, or Sandra's – is incomplete. The method of portrayal bears comparison to the modelling of Greek statues, on which Jacob himself remarks: 'The side of the figure which is turned away from view is left in the rough' (p. 141).

This shadowy but consistent vision of life and character requires its own tone of voice. *Jacob's Room* uses a fluid, complex sentence which has been conceived in the short sketches and which, though much developed in the later novels, is always to be the hallmark of Virginia Woolf's style. Its 'looseness and lightness' is well illustrated by the account of Betty's letter to Jacob, which is first quoted and then paraphrased:

'And Mrs Jarvis tells me – ' Mrs Flanders liked Mrs Jarvis, always said of her that she was too good for such a quiet place, and, though she never listened to her discontent and told her at the end of it (looking up, sucking her thread, or taking off her spectacles) that a little peat wrapped round the iris roots keeps them from the frost, and Parrot's great white sale is Tuesday next, 'do remember,' – Mrs Flanders knew precisely how Mrs Jarvis felt; and how interesting her letters were, about Mrs Jarvis, could one read them year in, year out – the unpublished works of women, written by the fireside in pale profusion, dried by the flame, for the blotting-paper's worn to holes and the nib cleft and clotted. Then Captain Barfoot. Him she called 'the Captain', spoke of frankly, yet never without reserve. The Captain was inquiring for her about Garfit's acre; advised chickens; could promise profit; or had the sciatica; or Mrs Barfoot had been indoors for weeks; or the Captain says things look bad, politics that is, for as Jacob knew, the Captain would sometimes talk, as the evening waned, about Ireland or India; and then Mrs Flanders would fall musing about Morty, her brother, lost all these years – had the natives got him, was his ship sunk – would the

Admiralty tell her? – the Captain knocking his pipe out, as Jacob knew, rising to go, stiffly stretching to pick up Mrs Flanders's wool which had rolled beneath the chair. Talk of the chicken farm came back and back, the woman, even at fifty, sketching on the cloudy future flocks of Leghorns, Cochin Chinas, Orpingtons; like Jacob in the blur of her outline; but powerful as he was; fresh and vigorous, running about the house, scolding Rebecca. (p. 86)

Mrs Flanders's mind and letters are runny and hazy, as we know from earlier in the novel; but so is the style of the narrator. What are the ingredients of this characteristic 'blur of outline'?

Two of the sentences in the passage, the first and the fourth, are enormous. The first has a simple main clause (Mrs Flanders liked Mrs Jarvis, and knew how she felt), with two dependent passages, one describing a typical conversation between Mrs Flanders and Mrs Jarvis ('and though she never listened [. . .] told her [. . .]'), the other making a generalization which hangs from a semicolon at the end of the main clause. Betty's letter is turned into 'the unpublished works of women' by the non-fictional tone of comment in 'could one read them' and then, quite simply, by a dash which jumps us through the connection between the particular and the general. But the generalization is not allowed quite to hang loose. The past-participle phrases describing womens' letters lead, by way of the loosely linking 'for', back into a present tense ('for the blotting-paper's worn') which could indicate a return to the particular: it might be Betty's blotting-paper. The other very long sentence derives a more firmly structured air from its string of past-tense, elliptical clauses linked by semicolons. As the account of Captain Barfoot's and Mrs Flanders's evening continues, the tenses shift us from a particular to a typical evening ('was saying [. . .] would talk') and then, by way of present participles, ('the Captain knocking his pipe out') to a fusion of the two. The point of view of this sentence, as well as the point in time, fluctuates. At first the clauses seem to depend on an invisible 'Mrs Flanders wrote that'. But, when we reach the first 'for as Jacob knew', Mrs Flanders's writing voice is replaced by Jacob's recollections. A new sentence might have been started, with a new set of dependent clauses depending on 'Jacob knew that'. But this would destroy the ambiguity essential to the whole passage, which allows us to take in all at once the sense of several, habitual scenes in Mrs Flanders's life; the particular incidents which she has put in her letter; the tone in which it is written; and the memories it might evoke, if read. The sad quality of the whole arises from the fact that the letter is in fact lying unread on the hall table. The ambiguity allowed by the syntax matches the haziness of some of the images. 'A little peat wrapped around the iris roots' is linked incongruously with 'Parrot's great white sale', mixing ideas of dark earth and billowing sheets; and the image of the flocks of chickens sketched on 'the cloudy future' almost suggests the beating of wings in the air. The odd juxtaposition of these images gives the passage a faint blur of lyricism.

The long, rambling sentences which allow for so many possibilities are characteristic of *Jacob's Room*; but there is more to tone of voice than sentence length. Much of the effect of the passage is made by its interpolation of direct or free indirect speech into the main narrative structure, creating a flexible interchange of voices which was to be most brilliantly used in *To the Lighthouse* and *Between the Acts*. Another noticeable feature, strongly anticipating *The Waves*, is the rhythm, provided by the semicolon connectives, by the lists of details such as the chickens' names, by the alliterative pairings ('pale profusion', 'cleft and clotted'), the repeated ellipses, the participles, and the inversions. A larger rhythm, made out of the constant repetition of these techniques, energizes the whole book.

The most striking syntactical feature of the passage is perhaps its change of tense, from the past to the present or from the past imperfect to the past perfect. Such shifts are found throughout the novel. The historical past in which Jacob spoke or acted is mixed with the present-tense commentary of the narrator. Often the past is made, by a startling switch of tense, to loom into the present:

> Rose Shaw [. . .] said that life was wicked because a man called Jimmy refused to marry a woman called (if memory serves) Helen Aitken.
>   Both were beautiful. Both were inanimate. [. . .] And now Jimmy feeds crows in Flanders and Helen visits hospitals. Oh,

life is damnable, life is wicked, as Rose Shaw said. (pp. 91–2)

As for Cruttendon and Jinny, he thought them the most remarkable people he had ever met – being of course unable to foresee how it fell out in the course of time that Cruttendon took to painting orchards; had therefore to live in Kent; and must, one would think, see through apple blossom by this time, since his wife, for whose sake he did it, eloped with a novelist; but no; Cruttendon still paints orchards, savagely, in solitude. (pp. 123–4)

A sense of Jacob's doom is created by the fairytale formula:[1] we feel a double sense of sadness at the outcome of early promise and at the continuation of life without Jacob.

The switching of tenses is frequently preceded by the use of the pronoun 'one', which allows the narrator to hover over the characters without being too assertive. The ladylike tentativeness of this 'compromise pronoun'[2] has been criticized,[3] while, on the other hand, the narrator of *Jacob's Room* has been attacked for being over-intrusive.[4] But the essential quality of the novel is, surely, the fluid relationship between biographer and subject: it is a novel about writing about Jacob. Hence the great importance of 'one', which is often used to distinguish the narrator's thoughts from those of her characters:

One must do the best one can with her report. Anyhow, this was Jacob Flanders, aged nineteen. It is no use trying to sum

[1] Compare, for example, the ending of the story which Mrs Ramsay will read to James: 'And there they are still living to this day.' ('The Fisherman and his wife', *Grimm's Fairy Tales*, translated Margaret Hunt and James Stern (London, Routledge, 1938), p. 112.)

[2] David Daiches, *Virginia Woolf* (London, Nicholson and Watson, Editions Poetry, 1945), p. 65.

[3] *The Language of Fiction* (London, Routledge and Kegan Paul, 1966), p. 86.

[4] See Joan Bennett, *Virginia Woolf: Her Art as a Novelist* (Cambridge University Press, 1945; 2nd ed. 1964), p. 77; R. L. Chambers, *The Novels of Virginia Woolf* (Edinburgh and London, Oliver and Boyd, 1947), p. 42; and Nancy Bazin, *Virginia Woolf and the Androgynous Vision* (New Brunswick, NJ, Rutgers University Press, 1973), p. 98.

people up. One must follow hints, not exactly what is said, nor yet entirely what is done. (p. 28)

In short, the observer is choked with observations. [. . .] But the difficulty remains – one has to choose. For though I have no wish to be Queen of England – or only for a moment – I would willingly sit beside her. (p. 65)

In the second excerpt, the change to the first person pronoun lays the emphasis squarely on the narrator and her problems of selection. But such comments on life and art are not always so clearly dissociated from the fiction. Often they seem to belong partly to the characters:

But the thought saddened him. It's not catastrophes, murders, deaths, diseases, that age and kill us; it's the way people look and laugh, and run up the steps of omnibuses. (p. 78)

The observation hovers between Jacob and the narrator, as on the frequent occasions when an apparently impersonal generalization is concluded by 'thought Jacob' or 'such were Bonamy's views', or when, on the other hand, the thoughts of the characters are uncertainly rendered:

But whether this is the right interpretation of Jacob's gloom [. . .] it is impossible to say; for he never spoke a word (p. 46)

Jacob, no doubt, thought something in this fashion. (p. 130)

These constant fluctuations between the biographer and her subject make us as interested in her struggle to discover and communicate character as we are with character itself. Jacob, like Minnie Marsh, is the narrator's field of experiment. Sometimes, abandoning all reserve, as at the end of 'An Unwritten Novel', she tells us point blank about the difficulties of her task. The reader is thus as much engaged with her character as with Jacob's; it is a similar position to that of the reader of *Lord Jim*, where the subtle consciousness of Marlow clouds, while it explores, a personality which may in itself be quite simple. If the reader is moved by Jacob or by Jim, it is largely because the narrators of their stories are moved, both by their heroes and by the very process of discovering character:

> It is when we try to grapple with another man's intimate need that we perceive how incomprehensible, wavering, and misty are the beings that share with us the sight of the stars and the warmth of the sun. It is as if loneliness were a hard and absolute condition of existence; the envelope of flesh and blood on which our eyes are fixed melts before the outstretched hand, and there remains only the capricious, unconsolable, and elusive spirit that no eye can follow, no hand can grasp.[1]

> In any case life is but a procession of shadows, and God knows why it is that we embrace them so eagerly, and see them depart with such anguish, being shadows. And why, if this and much more than this is true, why are we yet surprised [. . .] by a sudden vision that the young man in the chair is of all things in the world the most real, the most solid, the best known to us – why indeed? For the moment after we know nothing about him.
>
> Such is the manner of our seeing. Such the condition of our love. (p. 68)

It is apparent that the technique of *Jacob's Room* is necessary to the expression of Virginia Woolf's beliefs in the shadowiness of character and the elusiveness of relationships. 'The people are ghosts,' Leonard Woolf commented acutely,[2] remarking not only on the sad air that Jacob and his acquaintances have of being already dead ('and now Jimmy feeds crows in Flanders') but on the 'crepuscular' nature of their fictional existence. Virginia Woolf is reapplying the impersonal vision of the descriptive sketches to the personal.

> But after life [. . .] As for saying which are trees, and which are men and women, or whether there are such things, that one won't be in a condition to do for fifty years or so. There

---

[1] Joseph Conrad, *Lord Jim* (1900), Ch. 16.

[2] *AWD*, 26 July 1922, p. 47.

will be nothing but spaces of light and dark, intersected by
thick stalks, and rather higher up perhaps, rose shaped blots
of an indistinct colour . . .[1]

Yellow and black, pink and snow white, shapes of all these
colours, men, women and children were spotted for a second
upon the horizon, and then [. . .] they wavered and sought
shade [. . .] dissolving like drops of water in the yellow and
green atmosphere, staining it faintly with red and blue.[2]

In both these examples, the idea of personality is transposed into
impressions of indistinct colours and dissolving shapes. Jacob is
similarly merged, at each stage of his life, with objects and surroundings. His feelings are frequently suggested through colours or
scenes, or environments such as Cambridge and Greece, in passages
of lyrical descriptive prose in which we are apparently, but not
effectually, removed from the contemplation of Jacob. The merging
of personality into impersonality is not confined to the hero. Clara
Durrant, for example, is first seen as a figure from 'Kew Gardens':

Opposite him were hazy, semi-transparent shapes of yellow
and blue. [. . .] Nothing settled or stayed unbroken. [. . .]
    'Oh, Clara, Clara!' exclaimed Mrs Durrant, and Timothy
Durrant adding 'Clara, Clara,' Jacob named the shape in
yellow gauze Timothy's sister, Clara. (p. 54)

The calling of a name evokes nothing more certain than a shape
and a colour. Picking grapes on a ladder, Clara is 'semi-transparent,
pale [. . .] the lights swimming over her in coloured islands' (p. 59).
We hear, not her voice, but her diary; when she sleeps we see, not
her, but 'dishevelled roses and a pair of long white gloves' (p. 73);
we associate her with the paper flowers which open in water (p. 80)
and with 'a white satin shoe' (p. 114). Thus, though facts about
Clara's life (which is very like Katharine Hilbery's) are glimpsed –
her social milieu, her relationship with her mother and her love for

---

[1] 'The Mark on the Wall', *A Haunted House and Other Short Stories* (1944)
p. 45.
[2] 'Kew Gardens', ibid. p. 41.

Jacob – the reality lies in images rather than facts. Jacob too is suggested by the crab struggling to escape from the bucket of water, by the butterflies he hunts in the woods, by the tree falling with a sound as of shots,[1] by the sheep's jaw he preserves as a child and the ram's skull carved over his doorway. These objects spread him into the world of solid objects. We do not think of Jacob as a crab or a butterfly. But their struggles and deaths in a hostile universe suggest him.

Though aiming at a shadowy effect, the figures of speech are far from hazy in themselves, but frequently sharp, ironic and grotesque:

> the monster shark[. . .] being only a flabby yellow receptacle, like an empty Gladstone bag in a trunk. (p. 15)

> St Paul's Cathedral, like the volute on the top of a snail shell (p. 61)

> the noise of the voices served like a clapper in little Mrs Withers's mind, scaring into the air flocks of small birds (p. 104)

> For however long these gossips sit, and however they stuff out their victims' characters till they are swollen and tender as the livers of geese exposed to a hot fire, they never come to a decision. (p. 147)

In these dry, vivid decorations, there are noticeable transpositions between the human and the inhuman. The monster becomes a bag, the cathedral a snail-shell. Voices are a clapper to scare the birds of thought; reputations are roasted geese livers.[2] These small things encapsulate the method of the whole whereby Jacob is fused with shapes, colours, rooms, streets, cities and countries. In miniature it is possible to see that the effect of haziness (which has already been seen to arise largely from the syntactical qualities of the writing) is created from extremely precise elements. And, on a larger scale, Jacob's merging with the impersonal world often takes the form of sharp, acerbic accounts of the environments to which he is currently

---

[1] The same image is used in 'Reading' (1921), *CE* II, p. 25.

[2] The anthropomorphism in these images anticipates the interludes in *The Waves*.

adapting. Cambridge and its three archetypal professors, the British Museum Reading Room, Greece and its tourists are pinned down with a comic dispatch which is solid, and not at all hazy or blurred. The same is true of very many of the characters who surround Jacob. Overall they are meant to produce an indistinct impression, and do so, by the sense of breathless confusion which arises from having so many idiosyncratic characters in the room at once. Virginia Woolf was aware of the baffling effect this could produce; she criticized Compton Mackenzie for it:

> So, at an evening party, someone might whisper in your ear, 'That lady is Mère Gontran, and she keeps owls in a shed, and when her collie barks she thinks it is the voice of her dead husband.' One looks at Mère Gontran with an access of interest, and before the interest has died down someone else is introduced, who has some different peculiarity or even little trick of the hand such as plaiting four necklaces in a rope until the string breaks and the green shells fall on the floor [. . .] Meanwhile, what has become of Mère Gontran?[1]

The ingredients of that blurred experience are extremely definite, and, similarly, Jacob's acquaintances, taken separately, are very precisely satirized, from the Countess of Rocksbier – 'fed upon champagne and spices for at least two centuries' (p. 94) – to Miss Jinny Carslake – 'pale, freckled, morbid' (p. 121). There is always a conflict in the novel between the wealth of detail, and a sense that life cannot be pinned down by detail; between precision and strangeness; between comedy and pathos. The tension is central to the description of Jacob's room.

> Jacob's room had a round table and two low chairs. There were yellow flags in a jar on the mantlepiece; a photograph of his mother; cards from societies with little raised crescents, coats of arms, and initials; notes and pipes; on the table lay paper ruled with a red margin – an essay, no doubt – 'Does History consist of the Biographies of Great Men?' There

---

[1] Review of 'Sylvia and Michael' (20 March 1919), in *Contemporary Writers* (London, Hogarth Press, 1965) p. 86.

were books enough; very few French books; but then anyone
who's worth anything reads just what he likes, as the mood
takes him, with extravagant enthusiasm. Lives of the Duke of
Wellington, for example; Spinoza; the works of Dickens;
the *Faery Queen;* a Greek dictionary with the petals of poppies
pressed to silk between the pages; all the Elizabethans. His
slippers were incredibly shabby, like boats burned to the water's
rim. Then there were photographs from the Greeks, and a
mezzotint from Sir Joshua – all very English. The works of
Jane Austen, too, in deference, perhaps, to someone else's
standard [...] Listless is the air in an empty room, just swelling
the curtain; the flowers in the jar shift. One fibre in the wicker
armchair creaks, though no one sits there. (p. 36)

The elements of the passage are mostly matter-of-fact, creating by
implication a satire on the young Cambridge man's intellectual life,
with its absurd mixture of literary influences, and its obeisance to
Elizabethan and Greek culture. But the details are not entirely
straightforward; a strange air of sadness is conveyed even before the
elegiac lyricism of the last two sentences. Their shift in diction –
summed up in the difference between the colloquial 'all very English'
and the inverted 'listless is the air' – is augured by the images of the
slippers 'like boats burned to the water's rim' and of the poppies
'pressed to silk between the pages'. The first is more unexpected
than the second, but both evoke the same idea of death and oblivion,
vaguely associated with classical legend – the Greek fleet and the
god Morpheus. Jacob seems to become part of a mythical world, and
the implication contributes to the sense of bereavement arising from
his absence. At the end of the book, Jacob's room, again empty, is
described with phrases taken from this passage and from the first
account of his London rooms with the ram's skull over the door
(p. 67). Such repetition implies that Jacob's death is foreshadowed,
even predetermined. While he moves towards it, the death is always
there. Archer's sad call for his brother on the beach anticipates
Bonamy's last calling of Jacob's name. Everything that will happen
to Jacob is always a part of him; similarly, the experiences that
have formed him – 'the moors and Byron; the sea and the lighthouse; the sheep's jaw with the yellow teeth in it' (p. 33) – remain

a part of him. He moves through a life which moves with him. The rhythmic repetition of phrases and images thus creates a combination of motion and stillness, reflected in our feeling, through the novel, that Jacob is always present and yet always disappearing: he remains elusive.

The emptiness of Jacob's room has led to the novel's being criticized. Jacob 'is absent'.[1] He 'escapes us'.[2] We have the luminous halo, but nothing inside it. The justice of such views is mitigated by the positive sense we have of Jacob, if not as an individual, then as a figure of a recognizable class, at a particular time, doomed to a particular tragic fate. While Virginia Woolf repudiated the didactic and 'materialistic' approach of, say, H. G. Wells, and while in her own criticism she might say 'we do not like war in fiction',[3] in *Jacob's Room* she is morally committed to a fierce attack on the barren realities which include war. Like the narrator's meanderings in 'The Mark on the Wall', the stylistic innovations of *Jacob's Room* constitute an attack on an abhorrent system of life. Jacob's enemy, like Katharine's, is both the burdensome past and the harshly lit realities of the present, which rob him of Clara and send him to war. And, as in *Night and Day*, Jacob's struggle against these forces is analogous to the novelist's struggle against the conventions of realism.

'Does History consist of the Biographies of Great Men?' The essay question can be applied to the novel: can we understand the history of the period from the biography of Jacob? And doesn't the history of *this* period most appropriately consist of an entirely new form of biography? The questions set up the analogy between *Jacob's Room* and Jacob. The novel attempts an experiment in fictional biography, in its pursuit of a true 'modern' reality. Jacob, similarly, is for ever writing, or (like Virginia Woolf) criticizing the writing of others, in order to establish a true vision of life. His essays, indeed, are something of a joke. In adolescence he is found carefully correcting Morris's statements about moths. Coming

[1] Dorothy Brewster, *Virginia Woolf* (London, Allen and Unwin, 1963), p. 103.
[2] Ralph Freedman, *The Lyrical Novel* (Princeton University Press, 1963), p. 125.
[3] Review of 'Before Midnight' (1 March 1917), in *Contemporary Writers*, p. 54.

down from Cambridge, he writes an attack on the Leeds Professor's expurgated edition of Wycherley:

> Aristophanes and Shakespeare were cited. Modern life was repudiated [. . .] Leeds as a seat of learning was laughed to scorn. (p. 66)

Embarking on his affair with Florinda (by giving her the poems of Shelley), he copies out his essay 'upon the Ethics of Indecency' (p. 74). His stand for youthful independence is continued in the British Museum:

> Youth, youth – something savage – something pedantic. For example, there is Mr Masefield, there is Mr Bennett. Stuff them into the flame of Marlowe and burn them to cinders. Let not a shred remain. Don't palter with the second rate. Detest your own age. Build a better one. And to set that on foot read incredibly dull essays upon Marlowe to your friends. (p. 101)

On his way to Greece, he plans an 'essay upon civilization' with 'some pretty sharp hits at Mr Asquith' (p. 128). While he is there his musings take shape in 'a note upon the importance of history – upon democracy' (p. 142). But the note may well lead to nothing; 'it had better be burnt.'

In all these references to Jacob's literary efforts the tone is humorous, emphasizing Jacob's extreme youth. But the effect is of gallantry rather than silliness. Jacob's literary opinions are (like literary opinions in *The Voyage Out*) reflective of his spiritual condition. His missionary zeal on behalf of Shakespeare, the Greeks and the eighteenth-century robustness of Fielding, his exalting of Marlowe over Masefield, are indicative of his personal resistance to the civilization he inhabits. His natural imaginative affiliations are constantly being threatened by organized conventions of education and society. Jacob is naturally 'Greek': he looks like a Greek statue, he is quite happy lying alone on the top of Mount Olympus, and at Cambridge he and Timmy Durrant are convinced that they 'are the only people in the world who know what the Greeks meant' (p. 72). But such youthful arrogance is not allowed. The governesses and professors, Mr Plumer and his like, have taken over the

'Greek myth' (p. 130): they are the 'sole purveyors of this cake' (p. 37). Education, tradition and authority attempt to deprive Jacob of his inner conviction of reality. The opposition is not just between different writers or different ways of thinking about Greece. It is, more broadly, between the spontaneous impulses of childhood and the graceless imposition of authority and convention, which will always attempt to overshadow natural joy and freedom. It is clear from the passage that centrally describes this conflict that the impulses of childhood are at one with nature. The argument is Romantic: Jacob is like the protagonist of *The Prelude*:

> It must come as a shock about the age of twenty – the world of the elderly – thrown up in such black outline upon what we are; upon the reality; the moors and Byron; the sea and the lighthouse; the sheep's jaw with the yellow teeth in it; upon the obstinate irrepressible conviction which makes youth so intolerably disagreeable – 'I am what I am, and intend to be it,' for which there will be no form in the world unless Jacob makes one for himself. The Plumers will try to prevent him from making it. Wells and Shaw and the serious sixpenny weeklies will sit on its head. Every time he lunches out on Sunday – at dinner parties and tea parties – there will be this same shock – horror – discomfort – then pleasure, for he draws into him at every step as he walks by the river such steady certainty, such reassurance from all sides, the trees bowing, the grey spires soft in the blue, voices blowing and seeming suspended in the air, the springy air of May, the elastic air with its particles – chestnut bloom, pollen, whatever it is that gives the May air its potency, blurring the trees, gumming the buds, daubing the green. (p. 33)

The child of nature cannot commune for ever with the chestnut bloom; he must also be a social being. Night and day are again in contrast. Jacob's 'crepuscular' quality is set against the world of rapid, bright, sharp character sketches. Though the more complex and sympathetic figures like Betty and Mrs Durrant and Bonamy are given a blurred outline which arouses interest in their hidden selves, most of the figures 'at dinner parties and tea parties' are merely names. The novel is attempting to pluck out the heart of only one mystery. Is it then a limitation in Virginia Woolf's ideas that Jacob is so infinitely ambiguous, while everyone else is so dismissively defined? By analogy, all the characters should be as elusive as Jacob. But the distinction between him and the others, though disturbing, is necessary if there is to be any treatment at all of the external, social superficialities which are alien to Jacob's secret springs of character. And, although the caricaturing of minor figures is in direct contrast to the patient pursuit of Jacob, a consistent idea of character results. Jacob's name is all that we finally know him by, and this is no knowledge at all. How much less, then, do we know those that surround him! Over 160 characters are introduced into this short book, of whom many have names which are ludicrously similar. It is not possible to distinguish carefully between Norman (p. 27), Budgeon (p. 61), Sturgeon (p.6 1), Masham (p. 47), Bonham (p. 79), Stretton (p. 82), Gresham (p. 84) and Sherborn (p. 136); between Gage (p. 126), Graves (p. 105) and Gravé (p. 143); between a Miss Edwards (p. 82), a Milly Edwards (p. 113) and a Cissy Edwards (p. 153); between two gardeners called Barnet (p. 21) and Barnes (p. 159); between Mallet (p. 80), Springett (p. 104), Lidgett (p. 62) and Barrett (p. 163); between Pearce (pp. 10, 11), Perry (p. 116) and Parry (p. 159); between Mr Curnow (p. 8) and the boy Curnow (p. 52); and between Helen Aitken (p. 91) and Helen Askew (p. 105). No wonder that Jacob, introduced to an American called Pilcher (p. 84), remembers him as Pilchard (p. 130). Evidently there is more to this than mere paucity of invention. The motives are partly the same as those which inspire Dickens in *Bleak House* to call his politicians Boodle, Coodle, Doodle, and so on: their names don't matter, so long as they sound ridiculously interchangeable. But Virginia Woolf is also interested in putting an emphasis on the names, so that we end by feeling a sense of irritation at the pointlessness of their number and their similarity. They become symptoms of the futility of public life:

'Are you going away for Christmas?' said Mr Calthorp.
'If my brother gets his leave,' said Miss Edwards.
'What regiment is he in?' said Mr Calthorp.
'The Twentieth Hussars,' said Miss Edwards.

'Perhaps he knows my brother?' said Mr Calthorp.
'I am afraid I did not catch your name,' said Miss Edwards.
'Calthorp,' said Mr Calthorp. (p. 82)

The social comedy is the brightly lit side of the forces which are increasingly felt to oppress Jacob. Silly names and the sixpenny weeklies are at the surface of a mechanical system of classification and rigidity whose rhythm is the tick of the clock and the boom of the guns, a system which is the enemy to nature, childhood, integrity and imagination. The threat of the war is only introduced at the very end, but it is the culmination of what Jacob, and Jacob's biographer, have been resisting. At the darkest and most bitterly ironic point of the novel, warfare, as the extreme form of the mechanical 'reality' of modern life, confronts the imagination.

> The battleships ray out over the North Sea, keeping their stations accurately apart. At a given signal all the guns are trained on a target which (the master gunner counts the seconds, watch in hand – at the sixth he looks up) flames into splinters. With equal nonchalance a dozen young men in the prime of life descend with composed faces into the depths of the sea; and there impassively (though with perfect mastery of machinery) suffocate uncomplainingly together. Like blocks of tin soldiers the army covers the cornfield [. . .] and falls flat, save that [. . .] one or two pieces still agitate up and down like fragments of broken match-stick.
> These actions [. . .] are the strokes which oar the world forward, they say. And they are dealt by men as smoothly sculptured as the impassive policeman at Ludgate Circus. [. . .] When his right arm rises, all the force in his veins flows straight from shoulder to finger-tips; not an ounce is diverted into sudden impulses, sentimental regrets, wire-drawn distinctions. The buses punctually stop.
> It is thus that we live, they say, driven by an unseizable force. They say that the novelists never catch it; that it goes hurtling through their nets and leaves them torn to ribbons. (pp. 147–8)

The 'unseizable force' is master of an existence (unfairly but effectively summed up by domestic life in Surbiton) which is graceless, automatic, secularized, and where dreams are regulated by alarm clocks and work sirens. Its victims wake to 'all the jolly trappings of the day' and go off like insects in 'the conduct of daily life' (p. 155). This 'reality' is the enemy of the individual and of the novelist. But its mechanical bondage is contrasted with another possibility, a more impersonal and timeless existence, found at midnight on the moors above Scarborough:

> The moonlight destroyed nothing. The moor accepted every-thing. Tom Gage cries aloud so long as his tombstone endures. The Roman skeletons are in safe keeping. Betty Flanders' darning needles are safe too and her garnet brooch. And sometimes at midday, in the sunshine, the moor seems to hoard these little treasures, like a nurse. But at midnight [...] it would be foolish to vex the moor with questions—what? and why?
> The church clock, however, strikes twelve. (p. 127)

The true reality, lying beyond the limits imposed by clocks and policemen and administrators planning world war, may itself be alarming, a dark formless world of wind and air. But it is also comforting, in that it sustains life rather than destroying it, by merging individuals into the stream of nature – as Seabrook Flanders is merged with the earth:

> At first, part of herself; now one of a company, he had merged in the grass, the sloping hillside, the thousand white stones [...] Seabrook was now all that. (pp. 13–14)

This anticipates the only possible consolation for Jacob's death. Like his father, he leaves behind a name, objects, letters, bits and pieces, a pair of old shoes. These are, as always, useless as identifiers of personality. What may possibly remain, distilled into various memories and into the earth itself, is the imaginative life which Jacob was trying to sustain in the face of 'the unseizable force'. There is a very faint suggestion of this consolatory, and again Wordsworthian, idea, at the moment when 'all the leaves seemed to raise themselves' (p. 167) before Bonamy calls out for Jacob. But it has been implicit in the tension throughout between spirit and world, and it is present in the title itself: 'Jacob's Room' suggests the 'room' of the universe into which he is merged; and it is also the book itself.

4

Mrs Dalloway

1925

JACOB's biographer was hampered by an inhibition which
Clarissa Dalloway also feels:

> She would not say of anyone in the world now that they
> were this or were that. (p. 10)

In *Jacob's Room*, the first novel to concentrate on the impossibility
of pinning down the identity, there is, to some extent, a failure
where Virginia Woolf expected it: 'My doubt is how far it will
enclose the human heart.' *Jacob's Room* cannot begin to be a novel
about the personality in action, engaged in relationships or recollection, because the emphasis is all on how it can be *known*. The
only relationship of any real vitality in the novel is onesided – it is
that between the biographer and her subject. But the struggle for
knowledge, an end in itself in *Jacob's Room*, provides the groundwork for the consideration, in *Mrs Dalloway*, of personalities at
work. While we retain our sense of the inscrutability of the self, we
are now taken from the narrator's efforts at penetration of those to
the characters. We move inside 'the human heart'.

The background to this achievement was, as for *Jacob's Room*, a
series of short stories, the first of which, 'Mrs Dalloway in Bond
Street',[1] soon 'ushers in a host of others'.[2] On 14 October 1922

[1] 'Mrs Dalloway in Bond Street', an experimental version of the first chapter
of *Mrs Dalloway*, was published in 1923.

[2] *AWD*, 16 August 1922, p. 48. Stella McNichol has collected the stories

she recorded that 'Mrs Dalloway has branched into a book', but it was some time before she could find the necessary balance between 'design and substance':

> Am I writing *The Hours* [its working title] from deep emotion? [. . .] Have I the power of conveying the true reality? Or do I write essays about myself? [. . .] This is going to be the devil of a struggle. The design is so queer and so masterful, I'm always having to wrench my substance to fit it.[1]

Her ability to master the difficulties seems to have come upon her quite suddenly, as when she realized how to write *Jacob's Room*:

> My discovery: how I dig out beautiful caves behind my characters: I think that gives exactly what I want; humanity, humour, depth. The idea is that the caves shall connect and each comes to daylight at the present moment.[2]

The discovery of the 'tunnelling process'[3] enabled her to forge ahead, and the book was written in a year, gaining as it developed, a 'more analytical and human [. . .] less lyrical'[4] quality. These phrases suggest how different its concentration on the personality made it from *Jacob's Room*; but she wanted it to retain at the same time the haziness of the earlier novel, so that in spite of its carefully controlled design she would 'keep the quality of a sketch in a finished and composed work.'[5] The terms, of course, are taken from painting, an analogy which was more extensively used in a correspondence she had with the painter Jacques Raverat towards the end of the writing of *Mrs Dalloway*. They discussed fictional form. The problem about writing, Raverat said, is that it is 'essentially

---

written about Mrs Dalloway's party before, during and after the writing of the novel itself. Though the collection (*Mrs Dalloway's Party* (London, Hogarth Press, 1973)) contains stories available elsewhere, it draws attention to the way in which the idea of a party allowed Virginia Woolf to experiment with a narrative technique which could encompass changing patterns within a fixed social situation.

[1] *AWD*, 19 June 1923, pp. 57–8.   [2] *AWD*, 30 August 1923, p. 60.
[3] *AWD*, 15 October 1923, p. 61.   [4] *AWD*, 26 May 1924, p. 62.
[5] *AWD*, 7 September 1924, p. 66.

linear'; it is almost impossible, in a sequential narrative, to express
the way one's mind responds to an idea, a word or an experience,
where, like a pebble being thrown into a pond, 'splashes in the
outer air' are accompanied 'under the surface' by 'waves that
follow one another into dark and forgotten corners'. Virginia
Woolf replied that it is 'precisely the task of the writer to go
beyond the "formal railway line of sentence" and to show how
people "feel or think or dream [. . .] all over the place" '.[1] The
concept of tunnelling into 'caves' behind characters enfranchised her
from the unwanted linear structure in which an omniscient narrator
moves from points A to B. She arrived instead at a form which
could 'use up everything I've ever thought',[2] giving the impression
of simultaneous connections between the inner and the outer
world, the past and the present, speech and silence: a form patterned
like waves in a pond rather than a railway line. Many of the ingredients of the form had been tried out in *Jacob's Room:* the pronoun
'one' allowing a fluid transference of recurrent images from one
character to another, the connective 'for' making a leap in thought
seem like a progression, the use of 'nothing but present particles'[3] to
evoke the simultaneity of thought and action, are recognizable
techniques. But they are now more unobtrusively used for a style
which is really very different from that of *Jacob's Room* in its
fusion of streams of thought into a homogeneous third-person, past-
tense narrative.

The maturing of techniques since *Jacob's Room* accompanied the
maturing of characters. But, although *Mrs Dalloway* was the first of
the novels to concentrate on middle age, its social milieu, in part,
returned Virginia Woolf (as the reappearance of characters from
The Voyage Out suggests) to experiences of her adolescence. The
Dalloways in *The Voyage Out* are considerably different from the
later Dalloways. Richard is a sententious, prosing chauvinist who
considers England to be demeaned by her bohemians and suffra-
gettes. Clarissa, worshipping her husband, and sharing all his
grandiloquent beliefs ('Think of the light burning over the House,
Dick!')[4] is presented as a creature of frills, charms and affectations.
The satire in the later book is more complex and less obvious. But

[1] Bell II, pp. 106-7.   [2] *AWD*, 15 October 1923, p. 61.
[3] *AWD*, 7 September 1924, p. 66.   [4] *The Voyage Out*, p. 47.

the social arena of the Dalloways, in both novels, reflects Virginia
Woof's fascinated dislike of the world of society hostesses, eminent
politicians, distinguished doctors and lawyers, and grand old
dowager ladies, in which powerful men talk a great deal of nonsense and the woman's place is decorative, entertaining and subservient. As the marriageable Miss Stephen, she had been miserably
dragged round this world by her half-brother George Duckworth[1] and
later by a family friend, Kitty Maxse, the original of Clarissa.[2]
Virginia Stephen found Kitty brittle and superficial and felt that
her qualities might have over-influenced the portrayal of Clarissa:
was she not 'too stiff, too glittering and tinsely [*sic*]?'[3]

> I remember the night [. . .] when I decided to give it up,
> because I found Clarissa in some way tinselly. Then I invented
> her memories. But I think some distaste for her persisted. Yet,
> again, that was true to my feeling for Kitty, and one must
> dislike people in art without its mattering, unless indeed it is
> true that certain characters detract from the importance of
> what happens to them.[4]

Other adolescent feelings were recalled in the book; like Clarissa,
Virginia Woolf was tunnelling back into her past when she described Sally Seton, who was based on her cousin, Madge Symonds.
When she was fifteen she was in love with Madge, who was,
Quentin Bell says, 'very much a girl of the nineties'. He describes
how 'Virginia . . . gripping the handle of the water-jug in the top
room at Hyde Park Gate . . . exclaimed to herself: "Madge is here;
at this moment she is actually under this roof." '[5] But present
acquaintances were also used. Lydia Lopokova, the dancer (and
future wife of Maynard Keynes), was 'observed' 'as a type of
Rezia',[6] and Lady Bruton was probably based on Virginia Woolf's
knowledge of the forthright Lady Colefax.[7] Her hostility to high
society was not all drawn from memory:

> I want to bring in the despicableness of people like Ott
> [Ottoline Morrell]. I want to give the slipperiness of the

---

[1] Bell I, pp. 76 ff.   [2] Bell I, pp. 80–1.
[3] *AWD*, 15 October 1923, p. 61.   [4] *AWD*, 18 June 1925, p. 79.
[5] Bell I, pp. 60–1.   [6] Bell I, p. 90.
[7] Bell II, p. 95.

soul. I have been too tolerant often. The truth is people scarcely care for each other.[1]

Clarissa's world is, then, familiar to Virginia Woolf, as Septimus's is not. But her personal experience was used in the characterization of Septimus at a more profound level than that of social identity: 'I adumbrate here a study of insanity and suicide; the world seen by the sane and the insane side by side.'[2] For the first time since the account of Rachel Vinrace's fever, she was drawing on her own intermittent states of madness, which had led, in 1915 and in 1913, to suicide attempts. In *The Voyage Out*, *Mrs Dalloway* and the characterization of Rhoda in *The Waves*, we are given vivid accounts of these mental states, which were evidently painful studies for her to make: 'Of course the mad part tries me so much, makes my mind squirt so badly that I can hardly face spending the next weeks at it.'[3] In September 1923, while writing about Septimus, she had a 'mental tremor'[4] fleetingly reminiscent of her periods of insanity: she was evoking them too intensely.

That the madness of Septimus was close to her own experience is clear from the accounts given by Leonard Woolf and Quentin Bell. Both make only tentative diagnoses. Quentin Bell follows Woolf in saying that 'her symptoms were of a manic depressive character',[5] usually contenting himself with formulations such as 'all that summer she was mad',[6] or with a jocular reference to Virginia Woolf at her worst as a 'raving lunatic'.[7] Leonard Woolf also refers to his wife's illness as 'manic depressive insanity',[8] though 'the doctors called it neurasthenia ... a name which covered a multitude of sins, symptoms, and miseries'.[9] His painfully clinical accounts of these symptoms – the progression from exhaustion and insomnia to states of excitement, violence and delusions alternating with comatose melancholia, depression, guilt and disgust at food – have points of resemblance to Septimus's. Virginia Woolf's

[1] *AWD*, 4 June 1923, p. 55.   [2] *AWD*, 14 October 1922, p. 52.
[3] *AWD*, 19 June 1923, p. 57.   [4] Bell II, pp. 100–1.
[5] Bell II, p. 20.   [6] Bell I, p. 90.
[7] Bell II, p. 23.
[8] Leonard Woolf, *Beginning Again: An Autobiography of the Years 1911–1918* (London, Hogarth Press, 1964), p. 161.
[9] Ibid. pp. 76–7.

hostility to her doctors, particularly to Sir George Savage (the model for Sir William Bradshaw), whom Leonard himself distrusted, is one such parallel. Both Leonard Woolf and Quentin Bell remark on the thin dividing line between her normal psychology and her insanity.[1] Woolf comments on the rational quality of her delusions: the most fearful aspect of her disease was that, during its course, she was 'terribly sane in three-quarters of her mind'.[2] Though such information adds nothing to a literary estimation of *Mrs Dalloway*, it is inevitably of interest to know how much the 'mad part' owes to her recollections of being mad herself – listening to the birds singing in Greek and imagining that King Edward VII lurked in the azaleas using the foulest possible language.[3]

That Virginia Woolf should be combining, as materials for *Mrs Dalloway*, her social acquaintances and her madness, suggests how carefully the different areas of the book have to be welded together.

> In this book I have almost too many ideas. I want to give life and death, sanity and insanity; I want to criticize the social system, and to show it at work, at its most intense.[4]

This is written while the book is still being called 'The Hours'. The change of title (uncharacteristic in that it rejects the abstract concept in favour of the individual name) points to the way in which she was having to manipulate the centres of interest. She decides that the emphasis is to fall on Clarissa in the title; but in the careful structure of the novel she tries to prevent any one of the book's 'many ideas' from dominating the others. This is immediately apparent if one summarizes the 'story' of *Mrs Dalloway*.

At 10 a.m. on a warm, breezy Wednesday early in June 1923, Clarissa Dalloway, aged fifty-two, the wife of a Conservative MP, goes to Bond Street to buy some flowers for a party she is giving that evening at her house in Dean's Yard. She meets an old friend, Hugh Whitbread, on the way through Green Park. While she is buying the flowers, a VIP's car – the Queen's? the Prime Minister's? – goes past; it also passes a young couple, Septimus and Lucrezia

[1] Ibid. p. 79 and Bell I, p. 112.   [2] Woolf, op. cit. p. 164.
[3] Bell I, p. 90.   [4] *AWD*, 19 June 1923, p. 57.

Warren Smith, he an estate agent's clerk and shell-shocked veteran
of the war, she an Italian girl who used to make hats in Milan.
Septimus's madness has necessitated the calling in of doctors, first
Dr Holmes, the GP, and now Sir William Bradshaw, the famous
nerve specialist, with whom they have an appointment at 12.00.
The Smiths walk up to Regent's Park, Clarissa walks home; both
see an aeroplane advertising 'Toffo' in the sky. When Clarissa gets
home she finds a message to say that her husband is going out to
lunch with Lady Bruton. She is disturbed at not having been
invited. She starts to mend her dress for the party and is interrupted
by an unexpected visit from Peter Walsh, the man she used to love
in her youth, at her family house at Bourton, and from whom she
parted, with great pain, after she met Richard Dalloway. They
have seen each other occasionally in the last thirty years. Peter went
to India, married, was widowed, and is now in love with Daisy, a
young married woman with two children. His conversation with
Clarissa, in which he bursts into tears as he tells her this, is interrupted by the entrance of Clarissa's seventeen-year-old daughter
Elizabeth. Peter leaves Dean's Yard and walks up to Regent's
Park, pursuing an attractive girl for part of his way. At a quarter
to twelve he glimpses the Warren Smiths in the Park, who leave
at 12.00 for their appointment with Sir William. The interview
lasts precisely three-quarters of an hour and results in Sir William's
arranging for Septimus (whom he can see to be a very serious case)
to go into one of his homes.

At half past one Richard Dalloway and Hugh Whitbread meet
for lunch at Lady Bruton's, where they help her to write a letter
to *The Times*. Richard, hearing that Peter is in London, thinks of
his own love for Clarissa and decides to go and see her after lunch.
He buys her some flowers and goes home at three, to find her
annoyed, because she has had to invite an unwanted guest to her
party, and because Elizabeth is closeted in her room with her odious
history teacher, Miss Kilman. After Richard has gone Elizabeth
and Miss Kilman – whom Clarissa feels to be her enemy – leave
for tea.

Elizabeth, though full of respect for Miss Kilman, is made uneasy by her emotional, possessive, greedy manner. She leaves her in
the Army and Navy Stores and catches a bus up the Strand, while

Doris Kilman, in despair, goes to pray in Westminster Abbey. At about five, when Elizabeth is going home from her bus ride, Septimus, lying in his room, experiences a momentary freedom from insanity, much to Rezia's relief. But this is interrupted by the intrusion of Dr Holmes, and Septimus, hearing the sounds of pursuit, jumps out of the window. The clock strikes six.

Peter Walsh, going back to his hotel, is passed by the ambulance carrying Septimus's body. He goes in to change, finds a note from Clarissa, has dinner, and, as evening falls, goes out again to walk to her party. At the party, Sally Seton, an old friend of Peter and Clarissa, of whom both have been thinking during the day, arrives uninvited. The Prime Minister, Lady Bruton, Hugh Whitbread, Ellie Henderson (Clarissa's unwanted guest) – all characters who have in some way been important during the day – are there. The Bradshaws come and Clarissa learns through them of Septimus's death, with which she feels a strong connection. Peter Walsh, who has spent much of the day criticizing Clarissa, is forced yet again into a moment of intense emotion for her – 'for there she was'.

Two things are apparent from this résumé of the plot. The first is that all the activity is carefully held together by a specific use of time and place. The second is that the meat of the book does not lie in the sequence of events: they are its bare bones. It would be difficult to discover from the summary how the book could be about the relationship of the past to the present, or how there could be any possible link between Clarissa and Septimus. This is because a plot summary, apart from mentioning the time at which things happen, leaves out the narrative texture, in which images, descriptive passages, leitmotifs and internal thought processes create the 'substance' of the book.

For Clarissa does not, of course, simply walk through Green Park and up Bond Street and back again during the first thirty pages of the novel. She also perceives, thinks, remembers and generalizes, and in doing so she suffuses her present experience with the feelings and experiences of thirty years ago. What she remembers becomes a part of what she sees now, and these in turn contribute to what she thinks; her attitude to 'life: London: this moment in June'. No sooner have we read the first sentence of the novel, which looks deceptively like the start of a conventional 'story', than we are plunged ('What a plunge!' (p. 5)) into Clarissa's past. The delight of plunging into the London morning reminds her of similar feelings experienced as a girl at Bourton, and makes her think of Peter Walsh, which brings into her mind the fact that he is soon due to return from India. (Already we are made aware that the past is not in contrast with the present, but involved with it. Clarissa feels the same now as she did at Bourton; Peter, we shall find, is still making remarks about vegetables and playing with his pocket knife, which, like Hugh Whitbread's silver fountain pen and Rezia's delicate hats, is a symbol of his personality.) As she thinks how odd it is that only a few things about Peter stick in her mind – 'his eyes, his pocket-knife, his smile, his grumpiness' – she is watched, while she waits to cross the road, by a neighbour, Scrope Purvis, who thinks how charming she is, and compares her to a bird, a 'jay, blue green, light, vivacious' (p. 6), and notices how white she has grown since her illness. Already we hold in balance an external view of her – ageing, pale, elegant, charming – with the emotional life of which we are learning.

With this exception, we remain inside Clarissa's mind all the way to the flower shop. Her love of life, her admiration of fortitude, her pleasure in what she sees; the mixture of fondness and satire in her thoughts of Hugh; her memory of how she quarrelled with Peter about Hugh; their arguments, their parting; her ignorance, her intuitiveness, her feeling that in spite of death she might survive in 'the ebb and flow of things' (p. 11) . . . so it continues, and, by the time she has reached the flower shop and Miss Pym, the flower lady, has noticed how much older she looks this year, we can recognize and analyse the method, and already have a sense of Clarissa's existence taking place on several levels.

The external level, at which Scrope Purvis and Miss Pym can approach her, is the social level: Clarissa as the society hostess, the ageing MP's wife. We are warned against judging people at such a level by the nature of the book – Peter Walsh assuming the Warren Smiths to be an ordinary young couple quarrelling emphasizes the danger of saying 'of anyone in the world [. . .] that they were this or were that'. Yet, though the external level may be a mockery of the inner self, it is, at the same time, a part of the self. All the judgements made about Clarissa, whether satirical or sympathetic, have a certain kind of truth in them. Scrope Purvis and Miss Pym hardly know her. But both bring to our notice the fact that she has been ill and looks older, thereby giving her love of life and vitality an air of pathos. At the same time, Scrope Purvis and Miss Pym both praise her; the former for her charm and elegant uprightness, the latter for her kindness.

Lady Bruton cannot see the sense in 'cutting people up, as Clarissa Dalloway did' (p. 115). Richard reflects that 'she wanted support' (p. 129); Elizabeth notices that 'her mother liked old women because they were Duchesses' (p. 145). At the party there are numerous 'external' views of Clarissa. Ellie Henderson guesses that Clarissa 'had not meant to ask her this year' (p. 187), Sir Harry, the Academician, likes her 'in spite of her damnable, difficult, upper-class refinement, which made it impossible to ask Clarissa Dalloway to sit on his knee' (p. 194). Jim Hutton, the young intellectual, thinks her 'a prig. But how charming to look at!' (p. 195).

There is, then, a recognizable external self, with characteristics which are appreciated or criticized in different ways by different people; up to a point, it is possible to say of someone that 'they were this or were that'. By this method of showing us external views of Clarissa, Virginia Woolf lets us 'see' her without making any impersonal comment. Hence she emphasizes the 'streaked, involved, inextricably confused'[1] nature of existence, since any one person's view of anyone else is determined and qualified by their own limitations.

Clarissa, too, thinks of herself as a 'character' and sums herself up rather as other people do. She looks in the mirror and sees herself, 'pointed; dart-like; definite' (p. 42). She knows that this face is the result of drawing the parts together, and that the parts are infinitely different and incompatible. But it is this 'definite' self, seen also by others, which has permanent, distinct characteristics; it is this self which 'could not think, write, even play the piano [. . .] muddled Armenians and Turks' (p. 135), which admires old dowagers like Lady Bexborough, and which stiffens with pride when the Queen may be going past. It is this public, definite self,

[1] 'The Russian Point of View' (CE I, p. 242), published in The Common Reader (London, Hogarth Press, 1925); the date is unknown.

this 'being Mrs Richard Dalloway', which stands at the top of the stairs being the perfect hostess, and wanting 'that people should look pleased as she came in' (p. 12).

Below this lies her deeper self, made up partly of her feelings about experience – her love for Sally Seton and for Peter Walsh – and partly of her present emotions – for Elizabeth, Richard, Miss Kilman, her party, life itself. In this self there is a continual interplay between her sense of reaching out to others and withdrawing from them; between her sense of failure, loss and coldness, and her involvement with the vivid, energetic pulse of life. The party is the central image for the outgoing self:

> But to go deeper. [. . .] what did it mean to her, this thing she called life? Oh, it was very queer. Here was So-and-so in South Kensington; someone up in Bayswater; and somebody else, say, in Mayfair. And she felt quite continuously a sense of their existence; and she felt what a waste; and she felt what a pity; and she felt if only they could be brought together; so she did it. And it was an offering; to combine; to create; but to whom? (p. 135).

In contrast with her desire to bring people together, the image of the old lady moving from room to room in the house opposite sums up Clarissa's fierce resistance to emotional possession, 'love and religion', which attempt to force the soul and own people. Clarissa respects 'the privacy of the soul' (p. 140), which is signified for her by the idea that 'here was one room; there another' (p. 141). On the one hand, the party – the drawing together and harmonizing of people – expresses Clarissa's love of participation, as she felt it in her emotions for Sally and Peter. She still retains such strong, passionate feelings in moments of sympathy, sometimes for another woman, when she may have the 'illumination; a match burning in a crocus' (p. 36), an emotional experience which is described as a sexual orgasm. She still has a strong passion of hatred for Miss Kilman, who is trying to steal Elizabeth from her, and in hating whom there is an energy and a life; 'It was enemies one wanted, not friends' (p, 193). But in contrast with such involvement is her withdrawal. Clarissa going indoors like 'a nun who has left the world' (p. 33), going upstairs to her narrow bed like 'a child exploring a tower' (p. 35), virginal, failing Richard sexually, unable to abandon herself, feeling her slice of life dwindling away because Lady Bruton has not asked her to lunch, is possessed of a cold, ageing world, in contrast with the warm passionate experiences of her youth, to which Peter's visit recalls her. The contrast is expressed in a strange and brilliant image, unexpectedly but arrestingly appropriate:

> It was all over for her. The sheet was stretched and the bed narrow. She had gone up into the tower alone and left them blackberrying in the sun. (pp. 52–3)

There is a deeper and more remote level of existence in Clarissa which has nothing to do with failure or success and is not susceptible of satire. At this level, furthest removed from her 'external', social self, Clarissa feels the possibility (one already found in *Jacob's Room*) of going beyond the exigencies of time and place to participate in the ebb and flow of existence. This elusive, intangible self awaits death as a release, a way into communication with the general life of things:

> [. . .]or did it not become consoling to believe that death ended absolutely? but that somehow in the streets of London, on the ebb and flow of things, here, there, she survived, Peter survived, lived in each other, she being part, she was positive, of the trees at home [. . .] part of people she had never met; being laid out like a mist between the people she knew best [. . .] but it spread ever so far, her life, herself. (pp. 11–12)

On this plane she experiences a sense of identity with Septimus, feeling that his death redeems the hollowness, the 'corruption, lies, chatter' (p. 204) of her life. The connection cannot be known at any more external level, being, in fact, in sharp contrast to the world of the party in which it takes place.

The method by which layer upon layer of Clarissa's character is revealed holds good for all the other figures in the novel. Peter Walsh, for example, is, on a public level, jobless, in love, aged fifty-three, and just back from India. Deeper down, he dwells on his past and present feeling for Clarissa; and, beyond that, he is dimly aware of some kind of universal, shared life-force, suggested by the old woman singing outside Regent's Park tube. On that plane, he becomes the 'solitary traveller' of his dreams. Rezia is summed up at an external level by comfortable, endearing images: she makes a noise like 'a kettle on a hob' or 'a contented tap left running' (p. 159); she tries to keep out Holmes 'like a little hen, with her wings spread' (p. 164). But this simple, sympathetic character is in possession of one of the most fluid and ambiguous trains of thought in the novel. There is no such thing as simplicity of character: all minds work, deep down, in the immensely complex manner used to describe the aftermath of Rezia's words in Regent's Park 'You should see the Milan gardens.' The words, spoken to no one, fade like 'the sparks of a rocket' into the darkness. In the darkness, invisible houses give out 'trouble and suspense' until the relief of daylight. Rezia's loneliness is like the darkness seen by the Romans in their first visit to the country. Then, in the middle of her thoughts, 'as if a shelf were shot forth and she stood on it', she remembers that she is Septimus's wife; but then, like a shelf falling, she thinks for a moment that he has gone away to kill himself (p. 28). This cumbersome, elongated, disconnected image portrays the leaps and bounds of the mind, as well as incorporating the plot—the Romans landing in England being a reminder that Rezia has come from Italy. In some characters the penetration into their underworld may be so brief as to have the quality of a vignette; in this way, for a page or so, we drift into Lady Bruton's childhood, or slip into an experience of Maisie Johnson's which will 'jangle again among her memories' fifty years hence (p. 30), or share, briefly, the daydreams of Clarissa's maid Lucy as she sets out the silverware, and anticipates her mistress's triumph at the party: 'Of all, her mistress was loveliest – mistress of silver, of linen, of china' (p. 43). The language makes Clarissa seem slightly ridiculous, and is characteristic of a mock-heroic diction used to impress on us the worthlessness of her social existence. Thus, Lucy, 'taking Mrs Dalloway's parasol, handled it like a sacred weapon which a goddess, having acquitted herself honourably in the field of battle, sheds, and places it in the umbrella stand' (p. 34). Thus, Clarissa's objects of veneration – Royalty, the Empire, the Government – are made to look silly, as in the description of the VIP's car, for which Clarissa, thinking 'It is probably the Queen', wears 'a look of extreme dignity' (p. 20):

> [. . .] greatness was passing, hidden, down Bond Street, removed only by a hand's-breadth from ordinary people who might now, for the first time and last, be within speaking distance of the majesty of England, of the enduring symbol of the state [. . .] (p. 19)

Similarly satirical tones are used of Hugh Whitbread, whom Clarissa likes:

> He had been afloat on the cream of English society for fifty-five years. He had known Prime Ministers. His affections were understood to be deep. (p. 114)

Clarissa's feeling of rejection at having been excluded from Lady Bruton's lunch party is put in proportion when the lunch party itself is described:

> With a wave of the hand, the traffic ceases, and there rises instead this profound illusion [. . .] about the food – how it is not paid for; and then that the table spreads itself voluntarily with glass and silver, little mats, saucers of red fruit; [. . .] and with the coffee (not paid for) rise jocund visions before musing eyes [. . .] (pp. 115–16)

Lady Bruton herself, one of several grand old dowagers whom Clarissa admires and respects, is, like Hugh, an object of explicit satire:

> Debarred by her sex, and some truancy, too, of the logical faculty (she found it impossible to write a letter to the *Times*), she had the thought of Empire always at hand, and had acquired from her association with that armoured goddess her ramrod bearing, her robustness of demeanour [. . .] (p. 199)

Clarissa is indicted with her society. Peter Walsh has no patience with her in her role as a 'perfect hostess':

> Here she's been sitting all the time I've been in India; mending her dress; playing about; going to parties [. . .] (p. 46)

He attacks her assimilation of Richard Dalloway's standards:

> The public-spirited, British Empire, tariff-reform, governing-class spirit [. . .] With twice his wits, she had to see things through his eyes [. . .] (p. 86)

He attacks her worldliness, her coldness, her 'timid; hard; arrogant; prudish' manner (p. 66), her conventionality, her party air, 'effusive, insincere' (p. 185). Though our view of the characters is entirely opposed, Peter Walsh's attacks on Clarissa's social self have something in common with Doris Kilman's. Miss Kilman attacks Clarissa from hatred and jealousy, not, like Peter, from love and admiration; but the grounds of the attack – Clarissa's useless, luxurious existence, her 'delicate body, her air of freshness and fashion' (p. 138) – are similar. Their criticisms are borne out by the trivial elements in Clarissa's inner thoughts; it is not only from the outside that she is satirized. When Clarissa considers with admiration 'Mrs Foxcroft at the Embassy last night eating her heart out because that nice boy was killed and now the old Manor House must go to a cousin' (p. 7), or when she includes in her vision of 'life: London: this moment in June', 'the mothers of Pimlico' giving 'suck to their young' (p. 9); when she muses over the artistry of her dressmaker, now retired in Ealing, and says of her dresses that 'You could wear them at Hatfield; at Buckingham Palace. She had worn them at Hatfield; at Buckingham Palace' (p. 44); when she considers that by loving her roses she is helping 'the Albanians, or was it the Armenians?' (p. 133) (whose concerns she leaves to Richard): at these points we are invited to direct against her the kind of hostility felt by Doris Kilman, or, at least, the kind of satire expressed by Peter Walsh.

At the party the various methods of satire used throughout the book cohere; Clarissa's feeling of identity with Septimus is set as sharply as possible against the 'corruption, lies, chatter' of her life. The party emphasizes the ironic dichotomy between youthful aspirations and middle-aged resignation, most startlingly in the actual appearance of Sally Seton: no wild young thing (as we have continually imagined her) but a complacent Mancunian housewife. Sally and Peter compare past hopes with present achievements: ' "Have you written?" she asked him [. . .] "Not a word!" '

(p. 207). Lady Bruton observes that Richard has lost his chance of the Cabinet (p. 198). Those who are failures are thriving on a system of which Septimus Smith has been the victim. Hugh Whitbread eating cake with Duchesses, the Prime Minister ('You might have stood him behind a counter and bought biscuits' (p. 190)), Lady Bradshaw 'a sea lion at the edge of its tank, barking for invitations' (p. 201) – all are ridiculous,[1] even when, like Sir Harry or Professor Brierly, they are harmless. They are seen mostly through the eyes of Peter Walsh who has throughout been the most ruthless critic of Clarissa's society. But his criticisms are not the only means of undercutting Clarissa's 'triumph': the way the party starts in the servants' quarters, and moves up the stairs, sets it in its full triviality against the world of the 'lower classes' which Virginia Woolf (though never very realistically) likes to use as a contrast to the world of the 'gentry'. And Ellie Henderson, neglected and overawed, whom Clarissa despises, is, more endearingly than Doris Kilman, a critic of the society in that she is excluded by it.

Thus Clarissa's 'offering', her 'triumph', her attempt to 'kindle and illuminate' (p. 7), on which the book converges, is seen as hollow, trivial and corrupt, providing satisfaction for the least satisfactory part of her character. It is not at this level, but at the deepest one, that her real triumph takes place, in her response to the death of Septimus, of which she hears from the Bradshaws.

Sir William Bradshaw is the most repulsive character in the book. His presentation is even stronger than that which turns Miss Kilman, through emphasis on her ugliness, her mackintosh, her greed and her lust for possession, into nothing more than a great hand opening and closing on the table. For Sir William, the mock-heroic language is used at full strength.

> Proportion, divine proportion, Sir William's goddess, was acquired by Sir William walking hospitals, catching salmon, begetting one son in Harley Street by Lady Bradshaw, who caught salmon herself and took photographs scarcely to be

[1] The ridiculous, as often in Virginia Woolf's work, is associated with food (cf. Doris Kilman's éclairs), of which she had an extreme horror during her periods of madness (see Bell II, p. 15).

distinguished from the work of professionals. Worshipping proportion, Sir William not only prospered himself but made England prosper, secluded her lunatics, forbade childbirth, penalized despair, made it impossible for the unfit to propagate their views until they, too, shared his sense of proportion [. . .] (p. 110)

Sir William 'forces the soul'; and he is the representative of a way of life, supported by Clarissa's Prime Minister, in which individuals are made to tow the line, or are put away. Septimus sees Sir William (and Dr Holmes) as human nature, 'the repulsive brute, with the blood-red nostrils' (p. 102) which wants to attack and pin him down. Clarissa recognizes that Sir William would 'force the soul', and responds as Septimus does to the goddesses of Proportion and Conversion. As an alternative to the lust for domination which Sir William calls Proportion and Miss Kilman calls 'love and religion', Clarissa recognizes an underlying unity of all things which can coexist with the privacy and integrity of the individual. In this she is against Sir William, against the social world of which she is a part, and on the side of Septimus.

Virginia Woolf's main concern about *Mrs Dalloway* was that 'the reviewers will say that it is disjointed because of the mad scenes not connecting with the Dalloway scenes'.[1] Certainly the plot does not connect Clarissa and Septimus, apart from the arbitrary link provided by Sir William, and the situational resemblance of their both having witnessed the death of someone close to them. But the connection between them at an experiential level is intimate and vital, and in it consists the novel's most remarkable achievement. The similarity in the way they respond to life leads the reader to feel that madness is an intensification or distortion of the method of perception that Virginia Woolf feels to be normal. Their response to experience is always given in physical terms, often remarkably similar ones:

> It rasped her, though, to have stirring about in her this brutal monster! to hear twigs cracking and feel hooves planted down in the depths of that leaf-encumbered forest, the soul;

[1] *AWD*, 13 December 1924, p. 69.

never to be content quite, or quite secure, for at any moment the brute would be stirring, this hatred, which, especially since her illness, had power to make her feel scraped, hurt in her spine [. . .] (p. 15)

Septimus heard her say 'Kay Arr' close to his ear, deeply, softly, like a mellow organ, but with a roughness in her voice like a grasshopper's, which rasped his spine deliciously and sent running up into his brain waves of sound which, concussing, broke. (p. 25)

[. . .] this gradual drawing together of everything to one centre before his eyes, as if some horror had come almost to the surface and was about to burst into flames, terrified him. The world wavered and quivered and threatened to burst into flames. (p. 18)

Why, after all, did she do these things? Why seek pinnacles and stand drenched in fire? Might it consume her anyhow! Burn her to cinders! Better anything, better brandish one's torch and hurl it to earth than taper and dwindle away [. . .] (p. 185)

In these two pairs of quotations, both Septimus and Clarissa translate their emotions into physical metaphors, which are indistinguishable from the emotion itself. The climax to this method of perception is Clarissa's response to Septimus's death: 'her body went through it' (p. 203).

The difference between Clarissa and Septimus – between sanity and madness – is that Clarissa does not lose her awareness of the outside world as something external to herself even while she responds to it at a physical level. The physical response does not, in her case, become so overwhelming that it subsumes the reality which induced it. She hears Big Ben, and her thoughts about it are translated into a physical response: she 'feels' the sound as leaden circles dissolving, or as a bar of gold flat on the sea, or as a finger falling into 'the midst of ordinary things' (p. 141). But Clarissa does not, hearing the sound, appropriate and respond to its qualities without understanding what the sound means, nor does she think Big Ben is speaking to her. She retains her awareness of reality while she responds to it. Septimus, by contrast, is not always able to distinguish between his personal response and the indifferent, universal nature of external reality. He struggles to do so: in Regent's Park he keeps trying to remind himself that the 'shocks of sound' which assault him come from 'a motor horn down the street' or 'an old man playing a penny whistle' (p. 76), and he is capable of sane, indeed satirical comments on reality: 'The upkeep of that motor car alone must cost him quite a lot,' he says of Sir William (p. 109). But, in his madness, he feels that if the birds sing they must be speaking to him; if the aeroplane writes in the sky it must be signalling to him. The distinction between self and external reality is as blurred, in his mind, as the distinction between different forms of physical response: sight, sound, touch. In an attempt to sort this out as it happens to him, Septimus, the victim of Science and Proportion, tries to be 'scientific'; but the universe he inhabits, in which the usual categories are merged beyond recognition, defies analysis:

> [. . .] leaves were alive; trees were alive. And the leaves being connected by millions of fibres with his own body, there on the seat, fanned it up and down; when the branch stretched he, too, made that statement. The sparrows fluttering, rising, and falling in jagged fountains were part of the pattern; the white and blue, barred with black branches. Sounds made harmonies with premeditation; the spaces between them were as significant as the sounds. (p. 26)

This impressionist picture is very like the picture Virginia Woolf creates in a sketch such as 'Kew Gardens'. Septimus's perceptions are those of a normal sensibility taken to its illogical conclusion.

Clarissa and Septimus are linked by a mutual leitmotif, the quotation from *Cymbeline* ('Fear no more the heat o' the sun'), which Clarissa reads in Hatchard's shop window in the morning, and which comes into Septimus's mind as he lies in his room:

> [. . .] his hand lay there on the back of the sofa, as he had seen his hand lie [. . .] on the top of the waves, while far away on shore he heard dogs barking and barking far away. Fear no more, says the heart in the body; fear no more. (p. 154)

His experience is like a re-enactment of Clarissa's while she is sewing her dress. For both it is a moment of tranquillity, an escape from the body, and possibly an anticipation of death. The quotation from *Cymbeline* is appropriate, not only to their mutual sense of death as a triumphant escape, but also to their situations. The lines are spoken over one who only appears to be dead, by those who don't know themselves to be her brothers. So, Clarissa is unaware of her kinship with Septimus; so, neither of them can be thoroughly known and understood by those who look at and speak to them. The lament is spoken for Imogen, an outcast from her society, and an innocent victim of cruelty and lies: and isolation from society is experienced both by Septimus and Clarissa. 'Fear no more the heat o' the sun' casts an air of serenity over the encounter with death to which the whole book leads up. For the major connection between Clarissa and Septimus is, of course, that his death enables her to encounter hers.

Septimus thinks of himself as a scapegoat for society, as a 'drowned sailor, on the shore of the world' (p. 103), who has died and come back, a risen God from the dead, in order to communicate the true meaning of life. When he asks himself 'to whom' he should speak (as Clarissa asks herself 'to whom' the offering of a party should be made), the reply comes (rather as in Clarissa's case) – 'the Prime Minister'. This suggests that Septimus's sense of the true meaning of life is no more compatible with the superficial social fabric epitomized by the Prime Minister than is Clarissa's inner self. His message is given, indeed, not to the world at large, but to Clarissa. Like

> . . . Lazarus, come back from the dead,
>   Come back to tell you all, I shall tell you all[1]

he speaks to Clarissa after his death, showing her that 'Death was defiance. Death was an attempt to communicate [. . .] There was an embrace in death' (p. 204). At this impressive climax, where the 'too many ideas' cohere, the book's strongly moral nature, as well as its structural unity, can be thoroughly perceived.

[1] T. S. Eliot, 'The Love Song of J. Alfred Prufrock', *Prufrock and Other Observations* (1917).

Clarissa and Septimus connect at an intense moment of consciousness which is ironically contrasted with the moments measured out by the striking clock. Their communication defies 'real' time, since it is made after, and in spite of, the hour of Septimus's death, and takes place outside the room where the 'strained time-ridden faces'[1] of the partygoers bears evidence to the domination of 'clock time'. Within the party, the effort to vanquish 'clock time' fails: the youthful idyll of life at Bourton, which has been painfully and pleasurably recollected throughout the novel, is time lost, not time regained.[2] Though its protagonists are all reassembled at the party, they are ageing, unsuccessful, disillusioned; the victims of real time.

The party is the climax to the tension between the two kinds of time in the novel. The strictly limited 'clock time', covering just over twelve hours, and impressed on the reader (as we saw in the plot summary) at regular intervals, is combined with a continuous flowing of various consciousnesses (reflected by the fluid sentence structures) in which past, present and future are merged.[3] 'Consciousness time' is frequently associated with the image of a vista. During her conversation with Peter, Clarissa has an image of herself as

a child throwing bread to the ducks, between her parents, and at the same time a grown woman coming to her parents who stood

[1] T. S. Eliot, 'Burnt Norton', V (1936), *Four Quartets.*

[2] The last scene of *Mrs Dalloway*, Virginia Woolf's most Proustian novel, invites comparison with Marcel's last party in *Time Regained* (1927).

[3] It has often been noticed that Virginia Woolf's concept of inner time set against clock time is very like Henri Bergson's theory of *la durée*, which was in fashion at the time. Bergson's *durée*, or durational flux, is the inner reality of the personality flowing through time. 'Our moods and sensations are queer blendings of such elements as memories impinging upon and conditioning our present sensory impressions of confused sounds, smells and sights, all forming themselves into highly fluid states of consciousness ever merging into one another.' (Shiv Kumar, *Bergson and the Stream of Consciousness Novel* (London and Glasgow, Blackie, 1962), p. 22.) Kumar is illuminating on the parallels between Bergson's philosophy and Virginia Woolf's perceptions, but makes it clear that the resemblances were coincidental: it seems very unlikely that she had read him. The 'Bergsonian' flavour of *Mrs Dalloway* was more probably filtered through her reading of Proust.

by the lake, holding her life in her arms which, as she neared them, grew larger and larger in her arms, until it became a whole life, a complete life, which she put down by them and said, 'This is what I have made of it! This!' (p. 48)

Clarissa's approach to her parents down a vista of time is rather like the vision of the 'solitary traveller', who may or may not be Peter Walsh. As he falls asleep in the park, the figure of the nurse knitting at the end of the bench becomes transformed into a giant female figure seen at the end of a forest ride by the traveller, which leads him on, 'taking away from him the sense of the earth, the wish to return, and giving him for substitute a general peace' (p. 64). Our feeling that this is meant as Peter Walsh's dream comes from the fact that elsewhere he uses two images related to this passage – the nurse waving at the window, and Clarissa like a 'lolloping mermaid' with her Prime Minister. But the image is purposely generalized into a universal idea of death as peace. Looking down the vista of time, the traveller sees his own end in sight. It is an alarming, but at the same time a consolatory vision.

The figure seen at the end of a vista is used again to show the characters struggling to approach each other through the barriers of generation, separation and death. Septimus sees Evans coming towards him through the trees. Richard watches Elizabeth through a press of people at the party and, for a moment, does not recognize her. At the end, Clarissa is framed in the doorway and Peter apprehends her reality in a moment which transcends time; 'for there she was.'

The most complex example of the 'vista' used as an image for 'consciousness time' is the passage in which Peter, taking off his boots in the hotel, considers whether or not he should marry Daisy. At one point in present time in his hotel room, he remembers one point in past time when Daisy ran to meet him, crying that she would give him everything. At the same moment he imagines a hypothetical future time when he might 'go to Oxford and poke about in the Bodleian':

Vainly the dark, adorably pretty girl ran to the end of the terrace; vainly waved her hand; vainly cried she didn't care a straw what people said. There he was, the man she thought the world of [. . .] padding about a room in a hotel in Bloomsbury, shaving, washing, continuing, as he took up cans, put down razors, to poke about in the Bodleian, and get at the truth about one or two little matters that interested him. (p. 174)

The actual past moment, the actual present moment and the hypothetical future moment are here merged in one.

The clocks in *Mrs Dalloway* recall people from such inner fluidity to the burden of real time and place, and in this sense the leaden circles are the enemy, the spokesmen of Proportion, like Sir William:

Shredding and slicing, dividing and subdividing, the clocks of Harley Street nibbled at the June day, counselled submission, upheld authority, and pointed out in chorus the supreme advantages of a sense of proportion [. . .] (p. 113)

Against them is set an infinity which goes beyond all limits, even that of the personal consciousness, as in the song of the old woman outside Regent's Park tube:

Through all ages – when the pavement was grass, when it was swamp, through the age of tusk and mammoth, through the age of silent sunrise – the battered woman – for she wore a skirt [. . .] stood singing of love – love which has lasted a million years [. . .] love which prevails, and millions of years ago her lover, who had been dead these centuries, had walked, she crooned, with her in May [. . .] and when at last she laid her hoary and immensely aged head on the earth, now become a mere cinder of ice [. . .] then the pageant of the universe would be over. (pp. 90–1)[1]

This impersonal infinity is felt, too, in the music Elizabeth hears in Fleet Street:

[. . .] this voice, pouring endlessly, year in, year out, would take whatever it might be; this vow; this van; this life;

---

[1] This passage strongly anticipates *Between the Acts*, in its fusion of prehistory with the idea of a universal 'pageant'.

> this procession; would wrap them all about and carry them on,
> as in the rough stream of a glacier the ice holds a splinter of
> bone, a blue petal, some oak trees, and rolls them on. (p. 153)

As in *Jacob's Room*, that natural infinity is in contrast with the
time by which history is measured and wars are made, leaving a
world (in which manners and customs, as Peter notes, are greatly
changed) where the people who pick up life as it was, who open
bazaars and go shopping and give parties and write letters to *The
Times*, are ironically contrasted with the victims of the war, the
poor, the shell-shocked, and the dead:

> Really it was a miracle thinking of the war, and thousands of
> poor chaps, with all their lives before them, shovelled together,
> already half forgotten; it was a miracle. Here he was walking
> across London to say to Clarissa in so many words that he loved
> her. (pp. 127–8)

But it is an over-simplification to say that 'consciousness time' is
always in conflict with 'clock time'. The leaden circles dissolving
in the air may be reminders of death, but they are also, for Clarissa,
the pulse of life itself. Big Ben and St Margaret's often usher in the
moments of intense feeling, those still points of concentration like a
'falling drop', in which all life seems to be contained. The notes
strike like warnings but, as they dissolve, they seem to sum up and
become part of the activity of life. Big Ben's first stroke in the book
is followed by Clarissa's response: 'Heaven only knows why one
loves it so' (p. 6) – 'it', as so often, being life itself. Later, the
different sounds of the clocks suggest the different sides to her life:

> [. . .] but here the other clock, the clock which always struck
> two minutes after Big Ben, came shuffling in with its lap full
> of odds and ends, which it dumped down as if Big Ben were all
> very well with his majesty laying down the law [. . .] but she
> must remember all sorts of little things besides – Mrs Marsham,
> Ellie Henderson, glasses for ices [. . .] (p. 141)

Peter Walsh thinks of the bell of St Margaret's ('like a hostess')
as being Clarissa herself; the sound suggests to him both her life
('as if this bell had come into the room years ago') and her death
('Clarissa falling where she stood, in her drawing-room') (p. 56).

The bells, which are fluid symbols of life and death, and which act at the same time as structural connections, are the precursors of a similarly used motif, the lighthouse, in Virginia Woolf's next, and greatest, novel.

5

To the Lighthouse

1927

So that is marriage, Lily thought, a man and a woman looking at a girl throwing a ball [. . .] And suddenly the meaning which, for no reason at all [. . .] descends on people, making them symbolical, making them representative, came upon them, and made them in the dusk standing, looking, the symbols of marriage, husband and wife. Then, after an instant, the symbolical outline which transcended the real figures sank down again, and they became [. . .] Mr and Mrs Ramsay watching the children throwing catches. (p. 84)

The passage draws together, as in the curve of the ball, the three centres of this tripartite novel: the Ramsays' family life; the 'symbolical outline', which transcends the 'real figures'; and Lily's attempt to master both symbol and reality.

Prue and Jasper, throwing catches, are watched by their parents on a September evening before dinner. It is a family party in a shabby house on the Isle of Skye; there are eight children and some guests – Charles Tansley, a young philosopher; Augustus Carmichael, an old college friend of Mr Ramsay's; William Bankes, a widowed botanist; Lily Briscoe, who paints; and Minta Doyle and Paul Rayley, who are falling in love. One of the younger children, James, has just gone to bed, disappointed because the weather (as his father and Charles Tansley have unkindly assured him) will not be good enough to make the long-promised journey to the lighthouse the next day. Two of the older children are still at the beach with Paul and Minta. Mrs Ramsay, upset by the conversation about the lighthouse, is worried in case they will be late: the cook has made a *bœuf en daube* which cannot be kept waiting.

These are 'real figures', and this is the stuff of a more than usually uneventful family saga. Charles Tansley, ill at ease in the rather snobbish family who don't like his ties, might find a place in Arnold Bennett's *Clayhanger*. James's disappointment could form a part of Hugh Walpole's *Jeremy*. But the scene in which Mr and Mrs Ramsay watch the children throwing catches suggests that the novel reaches beyond its realistic materials. The people are also shapes, and the shapes convey larger meanings than can be contained in the lives of individuals. The point of view from which the scene is described hovers between the personal and the general.

Nevertheless, *To the Lighthouse* is at an important level a dramatic, realistic, ironic story of a family life which was, to a great extent, Virginia Stephen's. 'Writing the *Lighthouse* laid them in my mind'[1] she says of her preoccupation with her parents; and Vanessa Bell, best qualified to judge, comments:

> In the first part of the book you have given a portrait of mother which is more like her than anything I could have conceived of as possible. You have made me feel the extraordinary beauty of her character ... It was like meeting her again with oneself grown up and on equal terms ... You have given father too I think as clearly, but perhaps ... that isn't quite so difficult. There is more to catch hold of.[2]

Vanessa herself is part of *To the Lighthouse*, as one of the Stephen children whose lives with their widowed father inspired James's and Cam's relationship with Mr Ramsay in the last part of the novel, and as Lily Briscoe, whose struggle with her art is as much Vanessa's as Virginia Woolf's own: 'God! how you'll laugh at the painting bits in the Lighthouse!' Virginia wrote to her.[3]

The marriage of Leslie Stephen and Julia Duckworth seemed to Virginia Woolf to present an archetypal pattern of sexual antitheses. Her portrayal of the Ramsays makes these contrasts so obvious, and

---

[1] *AWD*, 28 November 1928, p. 138.
[2] Bell II, p. 128.   [3] Bell II, p. 127.

is so characteristic of her treatment of the differences between male and female sensibilities, that the grandeur and subtlety of the relationship seems all the more extraordinary. Mrs Ramsay is beautiful, queenly, shortsighted, philanthropic and inventive. Her intimacy with her children nourishes her natural tendency towards fantasy and exaggeration. Like Mrs Hilbery she is associated with poetry, Mr Ramsay (like Mr Hilbery) with prose. Mr Ramsay does not see what is close to him – the flowers, or his own children's beauty. Instead, with 'an eye like an eagle's' (p. 81), he seeks for truth. He is awkward and ungainly in company. He is a stickler for facts, and cannot bear exaggeration or imprecision. Their conflict over the weather is a paradigm of the sexual battle: Mrs Ramsay becomes a fountain of fecundity and Mr Ramsay a 'beak of brass'. The woman's emotional act of giving sympathy paradoxically fertilizes the man, but more in the manner of a mother feeding her child than a lover:

> He wanted [. . .] to be taken within the circle of life, warmed and soothed, to have his senses restored to him, his barren-ness made fertile, and all the rooms of the house made full of life – the drawing-room; behind the drawing-room the kitchen; above the kitchen the bedrooms; and beyond them the nurseries; they must be furnished; they must be filled with life. (p. 44)

But this is not a simple dialectic. Mrs Ramsay is as dependent on Mr Ramsay for comfort and protection. She rests on the hard certainties of the masculine world 'as a child' (p. 122). It is she who is the more pessimistic and who relies on him to turn her thoughts away from doubt and gloom. And, in spite of their contrasted characteristics, they are engaged on the same field of battle, in which they evince similar characteristics of courage and endurance. Mr Ramsay struggles to overcome his sense of failure and transience, Mrs Ramsay brandishes her sword (p. 70) – an image shared by them both – against the 'little strip of time' which threatens her. She attempts to build something that will endure, from social and domestic materials.

Both are trying to come to terms with the fact of death; but there is a difference in the way their attempts are treated. Mr Ramsay is very largely a comic character. His bawling 'Best and brightest, come away!' at Miss Giddings (p. 82), like a character out of Lewis Carroll, his fury at Augustus Carmichael's asking for another plate of soup, his delight when Lily praises his boots, his pose of desolation on the boat, all emphasize the ludicrous side of Leslie Stephen which is summed up by the story

> that he was heard one night slowly ascending the stairs, groaning at each step and loudly exclaiming: 'Why won't my whiskers grow? Why won't my whiskers grow?'[1]

The language associated with Mr Ramsay's thoughts frequently takes on the extravagant mock-heroic tone which was used in *Mrs Dalloway* as an instrument of satire:

> his own children [. . .] sprung from his loins, should be aware from childhood that life is difficult; facts uncompromising; and the passage to that fabled land where our brightest hopes are extinguished, our frail barks founder in darkness (here Mr Ramsay would straighten his back and narrow his little blue eyes upon the horizon), one that needs, above all, courage, truth, and the power to endure. (p. 6)

The metaphor of a dangerous expedition also colours the passage in which he is trying to 'reach R'. Though it is a satirical image imposed from the outside in order to make Mr Ramsay's heroic struggle seem absurd, it is also part of his train of thought; again the mental image is turned into a physical action:

> when the search party comes they will find him dead at his post, the fine figure of a soldier. Mr Ramsay squared his shoulders and stood very upright by the urn. (p. 42)

Mr Ramsay thus participates in the imagery which is used to satirize him. The same is true of the description of his mental processes as the struggle to 'reach R', in part an ironical shorthand used by the narrator, but also Mr Ramsay's own method of summing up the extent of his achievement as a philosopher. The subtlety with which the figures of speech hover between the inside and the outside of Mr Ramsay's mind makes it difficult for us to find him

[1] Bell I, p. 74.

altogether comic. At the same time, it is evident that Virginia Woolf did mean Mr Ramsay to be ludicrous, from the way in which she has extrapolated him from Leslie Stephen. Her father was an excellent mountaineer, identified by Thomas Hardy with the Shreckhorn which Stephen (as 'gaunt and difficult' as the mountain) was the first to climb.[1] He was also a great walker until late on in life, leading the arduous 'Sunday tramps' for fifteen years. But Mr Ramsay's idea of himself as the leader of an expedition is an unreal self-dramatization, and his desire to 'be off for a day's walk' 'with nothing but a biscuit in his pocket' (p. 79) is felt by Mrs Ramsay to be negligible, mere nostalgia for his youth. The real expedition he leads to the lighthouse is not a strenuous adventure; his children feel the falsity of his identifying on the boat with the brave, simple fishermen. Virginia Woolf has transformed Leslie Stephen's genuine attributes of physical daring and stamina into facets of Mr Ramsay's emotional self-indulgence.

There is no comparable ridicule of Mrs Ramsay's courage and endurance. Nevertheless, an equivalent satirical tone is associated with her which suggests that, like Clarissa, she is not inviolate from criticism. The tone is grandiose, affected, and full of second-rate literary clichés:

> There was something in this of the essence of beauty which called out the manliness in their girlish hearts [. . .] (p. 9)

> Had she not in her veins the blood of that very noble, if slightly mythical, Italian house, whose daughters [. . .] had lisped so charmingly, had stormed so wildly, and all her wit and her bearing and her temper came from them [. . .] (pp. 11–12)

> Like some queen who, finding her people gathered in the hall, looks down upon them, and descends among them, and acknowledges their tributes silently, and accepts their devotion and their prostration before her [. . .] she went down [. . .] (p. 95)

An association is made between Mrs Ramsay and the kind of sentimental Victorianism which is to be parodied in *Orlando*. And Mrs Ramsay is at one point explicitly identified with Queen

[1] F. W. Maitland, *Life and Letters of Leslie Stephen* (London, Duckworth, 1906), p. 276.

Victoria (p. 17). But there is a rather different ironic tinge to her imaginary words to Lily at the dinner table:

> 'I am drowning, my dear, in seas of fire. Unless you apply some balm to the anguish of this hour and say something nice to that young man there, life will run upon the rocks [. . .] My nerves are taut as fiddle strings.' (p. 106)

Sounding here more like Gwendolen Fairfax than Queen Victoria, she is now being satirized not for her Victorianism but for the littleness of her society feelings, as Clarissa is satirized by Peter Walsh. In both women the compulsion to be loved (whether as wife, mother, hostess or friend) is presented as a weakness. And Mrs Ramsay has other limitations. She is afraid, like the speaker in Hardy's poem, to

> look into my glass
> And view my wasted skin

She is uninformed (like Mrs Wilcox in *Howards End*), leaving factual knowledge and differences of opinion to the men. She believes fervently and defensively in the essential value for women of marriage and child-bearing. She is deeply inhibited in her emotional life and, at the same time, interfering and even malicious in her dealings with the lives of others.

The evidence about the Ramsays is constantly reshuffled through the attitudes of different onlookers. Mr Carmichael shows up Mrs Ramsay's desire to be liked by not liking her; Mr Bankes exposes Mr Ramsay's egotistical concern with his works and fame by his own disinterestedness; Lily is amazed at Mrs Ramsay's misjudgements of people and at her universal recommendation of marriage. The children resent, as well as admire, both their parents; beneath the main current of the book there is another story, to be fully expressed in *The Years*, of the second generation's attempt to escape their nineteenth-century background. And the future that the Ramsays set in motion is also a means of judging them. In the last part of the novel Mrs Ramsay is dead, and so are the two children of brightest promise: Andrew, whom Mr Ramsay had said 'would be a better man than he had been' (p. 80), and Prue, whom Mrs

Ramsay intended to be 'happier than other people's daughters' (p. 126). The Rayleys' marriage, which she arranged, has not been a success; and Lily and William Bankes have not married as she hoped they would. At a realistic level it appears that the Ramsays' marriage was an incompatible union between unsatisfactory characters whose plans for others were all unfulfilled.

If one is thus to deny the value of the 'real life' of the Ramsays, the only satisfactory conclusion in the book is an aesthetic one. But to say that their relationship is only triumphant when resolved by Lily as part of her picture is to be false to the complex and powerful balance of the novel, which has two moments of climax, not just one. There is a resolution of conflict between Mr and Mrs Ramsay at the end of Part I which is weighed against Mr Ramsay's arrival at the lighthouse and Lily's completion of her picture in Part III.

And what then? For she felt that he was still looking at her, but that his look had changed. He wanted something – wanted the thing she always found it so difficult to give him; wanted her to tell him that she loved him. And that, no, she could not do [. . .] A heartless woman he called her; she never told him that she loved him. But it was not so – it was not so. It was only that she never could say what she felt [. . .] Getting up she stood at the window with the reddish-brown stocking in her hands, partly to turn away from him, partly because she did not mind looking now, with him watching, at the Lighthouse. For she knew that he had turned his head as she turned; he was watching her. She knew that he was thinking, You are more beautiful than ever. And she felt herself very beautiful [. . .] Then, knowing that he was watching her, instead of saying anything she turned, holding her stocking, and looked at him. And as she looked at him she began to smile, for though she had not said a word, he knew, of course he knew, that she loved him. He could not deny it. And smiling she looked out of the window and said (thinking to herself, Nothing on earth can equal this happiness) –

'Yes, you were right. It's going to be wet tomorrow.' She had not said it, but he knew it. And she looked at him smiling. For she had triumphed again. (pp. 141–2)

The moment is controlled, and described, by Mrs Ramsay; it is the victory of her beauty and intuition over his desire for speech and hard facts. In a sense she is subjugating him to her will; her smile is one of mastery. But her triumph is also achieved by a relinquishing of the will: she admits his monopoly of the truth, and allows that it will be wet the next day. The scene, by its lyrical fluidity (an intensification of the manner of the whole novel) gives the impression that both minds are simultaneously revealed to each other in silence, even though the narrative is really centred in Mrs Ramsay's consciousness. Thus, although she dominates the moment, it creates a moving sense of unification. A reconcilement of considerable grandeur has taken place between temperaments of extreme emotional disparity.

The force of this scene, however, does not arise entirely from our interest in the realistic personal relationship between Mr and Mrs Ramsay. We come to it after the long first part of the novel has established, in a brilliant variety of ways, an elastic interplay between the real and the metaphysical, so that Mr and Mrs Ramsay's marriage by now seems to be a reconcilement between abstract qualities which gives it a more than merely personal importance. The most obvious of the techniques used to achieve this effect is the manipulation of participles, by now a familiar device for expressing the simultaneity of different levels of experience, whose limitation is that it requires an equally refined sensibility of all its characters: 'We do not always think of eternity while serving potatoes; sometimes we just think of serving potatoes. Virginia Woolf's characters never do.'[1] Furthermore, they are often ironically aware of the dichotomy between their thoughts and their actions: 'Raising her eyebrows at the discrepancy – that was what she was thinking, this what she was doing – ladling out soup [. . .]' (p. 96). The point of this constant emphasis on the disparity between thought and action is not that it should be psychologically convincing. Perhaps not everyone thinks like this; but everyone in this novel must, because the characters are being used in the service of an abstract argument about the difficulty of infusing

[1] David Lodge, *Language of Fiction: Essays in Criticism and Verbal Analysis of the English Novel* (London, Routledge and Kegan Paul, 1966), p. 86.

shapes with sense. The recognizable shapes of daily life are frequently at odds with the sense which underlies them. This is evident in some of the dialogue, which, like the ladling of soup, is often irrelevant to the flow of consciousness behind it, as in the climatic scene between Mr and Mrs Ramsay:

> 'They're engaged [. . .] Paul and Minta.'
> 'So I guessed.'
>
> [PAUSE]
>
> 'How nice it would be to marry a man with a wash-leather bag for his watch.'
>
> [PAUSE]
>
> 'You won't finish that stocking tonight.'
> 'No [. . .] I shan't finish it.'
>
> [PAUSE]
>
> 'Yes, you were right. It's going to be wet tomorrow.' (pp. 140–2)

Like James's memory of his mother saying 'We shall need a big dish tonight. Where is it – the blue dish?', which illustrates his belief that 'she alone spoke the truth' (p. 212), the commonplace words are ironically remote from their emotional significance. But the novel does not insist on a simple opposition between the actual and the intangible. Very often, the spoken words sum up, rather than deflect the underlying meanings, as when the Swiss girl says 'The mountains are so beautiful' (p. 33) or Mr Ramsay says 'Damn you' to Mrs Ramsay (p. 38) or 'Well done' to James (p. 234). And colloquial phrases may take on a resonance beyond the control of the speaker. Mrs Ramsay, giving William Bankes a second helping of *bœuf en daube* at the moment of realizing that her dinner party has become a thing of 'coherence' and 'stability', says 'Yes, there is plenty for everybody' (p. 121). The trite remark is suggestive of her bountifulness and creativity. Lily speaks of Mr Ramsay's landing at the lighthouse in an oddly uncolloquial sentence: 'It is finished,' she says (p. 236), and then completes her picture. There is an irresistible suggestion of Christ's last words on the cross, not for any precise analogy but for the idea of sacrifice which they express. The first section of 'Time Passes' eerily combines the sense of an ordinary conversation with prophetic notes: 'It's almost too dark to see,' says Andrew (p. 143), involuntarily anticipating his own death.

Andrew's remark seems to hover between the spoken and the implied, as though it is hanging in the air. This effect contributes to the narrative method of the whole book, in which very many phrases and images seem only partly to be attached to the characters,[1] so that their mental processes are fused with an impersonal voice, which takes over in 'Time Passes'. Such ambiguity in the creation of real characters applies, very often, to their spoken words, in that we are frequently unsure as to whether they are really spoken. Mr Bankes, one presumes, does not say 'Nature has but little clay like that of which she moulded you' on the telephone to Mrs Ramsay. He says he will catch the 10.30 at Euston (pp. 34–5). Mrs Ramsay is far from saying 'Nothing on earth can equal this happiness' to Mr Ramsay. Mr Ramsay does not actually step from the boat shouting 'There is no God' (p. 236). Indeed, most of the characters are extremely inhibited. Mr Ramsay makes everyone very uncomfortable by *saying* 'You find us much changed' (p. 168) or by bursting out with the lines from Cowper's 'The Castaway'. Lily's great cry for Mrs Ramsay, which reaches the level of the spoken word, is immediately an embarrassment to her: 'Heaven be praised, no-one had heard her cry that ignominious cry' (p. 205). But the inhibition is not merely one of character; it reveals the immense difficulty of connecting the life of the mind and the world of external signs in any way that is at all meaningful: a difficulty that is central to Lily's attempt to paint. Because the appropriate utterances or signs are usually so much simpler than the complex of meanings they contain – 'It is finished', or a line down the middle of the canvas – it is always necessary to understand that 'Nothing was simply one thing' (p. 211).

The infusion of the commonplace with an enriching significance extends from words to things. Everyday matters of fact take on, largely through reiteration, the sort of resonance we have already seen apportioned to trite phrases. Thus the bill for the greenhouse

---

[1] There is a brilliant analysis of this aspect of the novel by Erich Auerbach in the last chapter of *Mimesis* (New York, Anchor Books, 1957).

roof becomes, in Mrs Ramsay's mind, a synecdoche for the whole corpus of material worries which have prevented Mr Ramsay, husband and father of eight children, from being also a first-class philosopher. The banging of doors, similarly, echoes throughout the book. Open doors and broken locks annoy Mrs Ramsay as she sits contemplating the shabbiness of the house; during the long, destructive onslaught of nature, the abandonment of the house by human agencies is accompanied by the ghostly banging of doors, and its undignified resurrection at the hands of Mrs McNab and Mrs Bast is, in part, a mending of doors:

> Attended with the creaking of hinges and the screeching of bolts, the slamming and banging of damp swollen woodwork, some rusty laborious birth seemed to be taking place [. . .] At last [. . .] keys were turned all over the house; the front door was banged; it was finished. (pp. 159, 161)

Though the house may have triumphed over death, its inhabitants, returning, have yet to work out their salvation. Without Mrs Ramsay, Lily feels it is 'a house full of unrelated passions' (p. 168), suggested by 'doors slamming and voices calling' (p. 166) and questions which 'opened doors in one's mind that went banging and swinging to and fro' (p. 166). The image has come to stand for loss of control, and is used again by Lily in her memories of Mr and Mrs Ramsay's quarrels:

> He would whizz his plate through the window. Then all through the house there would be a sense of doors slamming and blinds fluttering as if a gusty wind were blowing and people scudded about trying in a hasty way to fasten hatches and make things shipshape. (p. 226)

The major image here is of course that of the sea voyage, and the overlap between the real and the metaphorical is most obvious in the multiple significances which are drawn from the novel's island setting. In this *To the Lighthouse* resembles *The Voyage Out*; their titles could be run together, and suggest how close in both novels is the interrelationship between the external environment and the inner meanings. In *Mrs Dalloway, The Waves* and *Between the Acts*, though there is great use of water imagery, the characters' lives are landlocked. But in *To the Lighthouse* 'the sea is all about us':[1] it dominates the actual and imaginative lives of the characters. An illustration of this is provided by the story Mrs Ramsay reads to James. In the fairy tale, the fisherman who has caught and released a magic flounder is urged by his bullying wife to ask the flounder for more and more exorbitant requests on her behalf: she must be king, emperor, pope, and at last God. Each request is granted to the accompaniment of a stormier sea, and at the final blasphemy the flounder sends them back to their original pigsty. The story can be read as a grotesque parody of Mrs Ramsay's protective, energizing relationship with her husband, suggesting that she is responsible for his constant need of reassurance: 'perhaps it was her fault that it was necessary' (p. 124), and even that it is only her death which enables him to make his voyage: 'There was no helping Mr Ramsay on the journey he was going' (p. 175). Or, its increasingly terrifying descriptions of the state of the sea might be used as analogies to Mrs Ramsay's periodic dread of the sound of the waves, which make her think 'of the destruction of the island and its engulfment in the sea' (pp. 19–20). Or the throwing back of the magic flounder might suggest the fish with a piece cut out of it, thrown into the sea on the voyage to the lighthouse like a sacrificial offering. Or the wife's blasphemy might carry a faint resemblance to Mr Ramsay's imagined words of triumph, 'There is no God.' These are fluid possibilities: the fairy tale is by no means meant to serve as a definite analogy to the novel. But they become possibilities by virtue of the consistent association between the sea and the lives of the characters.

Mrs Ramsay telling a fairy story to James, sitting at the window like a picture of a Madonna and Child (which Lily 'without irreverence' may turn into a purple triangle), presides over a mythical world. Her powers seem to be those of a pagan goddess or a fairytale witch. But she has to work magic within the confines of the fierce, scientific world of real facts ruled by her husband, by Charles Tansley and by William Bankes: the masculine world of which Andrew would have been, and James will be, the inheritor. *To the Lighthouse*

[1] T. S. Eliot, 'The Dry Salvages' (1941), *Four Quartets*.

continually hovers on the edge of becoming a fairy tale, or, more ambitiously, a mythical or even Christian allegory, whose subject – a frequent subject of myth – is the conquest of death.

Mrs Ramsay's mythical qualities seem to arise partly from her close involvement with the imaginative life of her children: the idea of the circus fills her with glee (p. 14); as a child might, she hears in the waves a drum roll or a lullaby (p. 19); the end of the fairy story is told as though in her own words (p. 71); she fantasizes about the rooks, calling them Joseph and Mary, for her own pleasure as well as for the children (p. 93); and her lullaby to Cam is a fairy story (p. 132) transforming reality into a mythical paradise which lingers in Cam's mind for life (p. 232).

While her imaginings thus transform the real world into a story for children, she is seen by others as a superhuman figure with goddess-like creative powers. Dry, precise Mr Tansley finds himself singing a lyric paean to her beauty (p. 17); Mr Bankes is moved to similarly exalted language: 'The Graces assembling seemed to have joined hands in meadows of asphodel to compose that face' (p. 35). To Lily she is an 'august shape' (p. 60) in whose heart 'were stood, like the treasures in the tombs of kings, tablets bearing sacred inscriptions' (p. 59). In the mythic universe which Mrs Ramsay inhabits and Lily tries to recreate, all objects and characters may be transformed, as in a sea-change 'in that underworld of waters [. . .] where in the green light a change came over one's entire mind [. . .]' (pp. 207–8). Prue, at the point of death, seems to Lily to become Proserpina, letting 'her flowers fall from her basket' (p. 228). Augustus Carmichael, who druidically intones the mysterious poem at the end of the dinner, 'holding his table napkin so that it looked like a long white robe' (p. 128), turns at the end into 'an old pagan God, shaggy, with weeds in his hair and the trident (it was only a French novel) in his hands' (p. 236). Drugged and remote, evidently a man of vision, he becomes an acolyte at the ceremonies of creation engendered by Mrs Ramsay and Lily.

His trident concludes the association made throughout between mythic powers of creation and the powers of the sea, whose potential for enfranchising the solid universe from its apparently fixed boundaries is sinister as well as creative. Not surprisingly, the imagination tends towards monsters when thinking of the marine underworld, and its mythical inhabitants, the sirens, are emblems of danger for hardy seamen such as Mr Ramsay:

> Steer, hither steer your winged pines,
> All beaten Mariners!
> Here lie Love's undiscovered mines,
> A prey to passengers –
> Perfumes far sweeter than the best
> Which make the Phoenix' urn and nest.
> Fear not your ships
> Nor any to oppose you save our lips;
> But come on shore,
> Where no joy dies till Love hath gotten more.

So reads Mrs Ramsay, from an undistinguished seventeenth-century poem by William Browne of Tavistock, which identifies her with the insidious, beguiling elements of femininity. But Mr Ramsay, who is to be a triumphant, not a beaten mariner (and who is mainly associated with land imagery), resists the siren:

> The whole of life did not consist in going to bed with a woman, he thought, returning to Scott and Balzac, to the English novel and the French novel. (p. 139)

Few others can resist her power, particularly at the dinner party, where she appears as a pagan deity presiding over a sacrificial rite in which Paul and Minta are the victims, 'led [. . .] Lily felt, to the altar' (p. 117). As Mrs Ramsay put 'a spell on them all' (p. 116), the bowl of fruit becomes for her 'a trophy fetched from the bottom of the sea' (p. 112), and the dish of *bœuf en daube* the celebration of 'a festival' (p. 115), creating a sense of eternity. As the meal draws to a close the voices of people talking at the table 'came to her very strangely, as if they were voices at a service in a cathedral [. . .] some Roman Catholic cathedral' (p. 127). Earlier betrayed by her love of rhythm and need for security into murmuring 'we are in the hands of the Lord' (p. 74) – which she does not really believe – she now, more actively, creates her own service, her own church full of worshippers, which she knows will outlast her. Lily, recreating her in 'The Lighthouse', 'felt as if a door had opened, and one went in and stood gazing silently about in a high cathedral-like place' (p. 195). The mythical and religious associations allow a superhuman aspect to Mrs Ramsay's power of creating harmony and radiance, like a stroke of light laid over a chaotic waste of waters. Her ability to reconcile 'scraps and fragments' (p. 104), culminating in the dinner scene, justifies the association with mythical deities: Mrs Ramsay is herself a creator.

The spiritualization of character hovers between the real and the abstract areas of the novel. Mr Carmichael's trident is also a French novel; but, at the other extreme, the mythical apparatus provides for an almost entirely impersonal presentation in 'Time Passes'. Through death and absence, character is merged with nature, and becomes the stuff of folklore and legend in the myth-creating minds of Mrs McNab and Mrs Bast. The section shows an advance on the attempt in *Mrs Dalloway* to turn the characters into super-human beings. The solitary traveller of Peter Walsh's dream, who is and is not Peter, encountering the figure of a woman who is and is not Clarissa, anticipates the 'sleeper' of 'Times Passes', the walker on the beach who tries to find some meaning in appearances, and whose search for hope is thwarted by the 'brute confusion' of the universe (p. 154). Peter's dream stands out oddly in *Mrs Dalloway*. In *To the Lighthouse* the hovering vantage point of the 'sleeper' is more firmly integrated into the impersonal fabric of 'Time Passes'. His quest for truth, set first against the pseudo-biblical rhetoric which describes the decay of the house ('Let the wind blow; let the poppy seed itself and the carnation mate with the cabbage' (p. 157)) and then against the 'wantoning memories' of Mrs McNab, ensures that though the Ramsays' house is almost entirely given over to 'the fertility, the insensibility of nature' (p. 157) there is, nevertheless, a constant reminder of human consciousness. The walker on the beach is not Lily, but he anticipates and recalls Lily's attempt to find some 'vision' affirmed in 'the sea and sky' (p. 152).

The empty house in 'Time Passes' is full of empty shapes.

> What people had shed and left – a pair of shoes, a shooting cap, some faded skirts and coats in wardrobes – those alone kept

the human shape and in the emptiness indicated how once they were filled and animated [. . .]

So loveliness reigned and stillness, and together made the shape of loveliness itself, a form from which life had parted. (p.147)

Shapes imply space, an emptiness at the centre. The abstract relationship between shapes and space is vital to the novel.[1] Lily's painting (unfinished in 'The Window', begun again and finished in 'The Lighthouse') creates, and then has to solve, this relationship.

And so lightly and swiftly pausing, striking, she scored her canvas with brown running nervous lines which had no sooner settled there than they enclosed (she felt it looming out at her) a space. [. . .] What could be more formidable than that space? (pp. 179–80)

Filling a space entails a sense of perspective. As the morning wears on, two parallel perspectives are achieved (the structure of the narrative making the double achievement seem simultaneous). As Mr Ramsay's boat nears the lighthouse and to those on board the land becomes 'very small: shaped something like a leaf stood on end' (p. 214), Mr Ramsay drops his melodramatic pose of suffering and James and Cam are momentarily reconciled to him. The approach to the stark actuality of the lighthouse, like the approach to death, enables the complex land entanglements to be put in proportion. Meanwhile on shore Lily too discovers that 'so much depends [. . .] upon distance' (p. 217). As the boat draws away she is more able to understand Mr Ramsay; as she tunnels through her picture into the past she finds that the time and space dividing her from Mrs Ramsay make it possible to find her again.

Lily's visionary translation of life into shapes is the culmination of a similar process carried on throughout the book, which constantly reiterates a tension between simple and complex shapes. The importance of the lighthouse in the first part, 'The Window', lies

---

[1] It extends to her description of the writing of *To the Lighthouse*: 'I [. . .] got down to my depths and made shapes square up.' (*AWD*, 7 November 1928, p. 136.)

not in itself, but in the stroke of light it throws in a circular sweep across space, seen through the frame of the window. To some extent this light is identified with Mrs Ramsay's creation of harmony and rhythm, and she herself appropriates it, as Clarissa does the bells of London, finding it expressive of certain qualities in herself and of certain moments in her experience (comparable to Clarissa's in their translation of sexual into emotional exaltation (p. 76)). Only in the third part is the lighthouse seen in its concrete shape, not as a beam of light but as a tower: Mr Ramsay's lighthouse.[1] James makes the comparison:

> The Lighthouse was then a silvery, misty-looking tower with a yellow eye that opened suddenly and softly in the evening. Now –
> James looked at the Lighthouse. He could see the white-washed rocks; the tower, stark and straight; he could see that it was barred with black and white [. . .] So that was the Lighthouse, was it?
> No, the other was also the Lighthouse. For nothing was simply one thing. (p. 211)

Though different, the two personae of the lighthouse, tower and beam, are simple. All the simple shapes of the book – the dome shape which Lily associates with Mrs Ramsay and Nancy with Minta, the triangular shadow cast by Mrs Ramsay, the wedge shape of her dark and secret self, the line drawn down the middle of Lily's picture – give a sense of fulfilment and evoke the obscure, unapparent levels on which the personality works. In contrast with such simple shapes are found repeated references to twists, knots, nets, meshes and weaves: the shape of the active life of relationships in which people speak, judge, worry, laugh at each other,

---

[1] An important letter to Roger Fry warns us against forcing the lighthouse to 'mean' any one thing:

> I meant nothing by *The Lighthouse*. One has to have a central line down the middle of the book to hold the design together. I saw that all sorts of feelings would accrue to this, but I refused to think them out, and trusted that people would make it the deposit for their own emotions [. . .] I can't manage Symbolism except in this vague, generalized way. (Bell II, p. 129.)

give parties and arrange things. Mrs Ramsay at the window is continually stretched between her deep-sunk contemplative life and the external demands made on her in the scene. The indivisibility of these two areas of experience is suggested by her knitting, which, like her life of personal entanglements, she resents ('making some little twist of the reddish-brown stocking she was knitting, impatiently' (p. 7)) but can continue unconsciously while she sinks down into herself. Her inner simplicity is contrasted with the life of 'strife, divisions, difference of opinion, prejudices twisted into the very fibre of being' (p. 1), which she deplores. But she herself 'in active life' 'would be netting and separating one thing from another' (p. 123). It is the active side of her which leads Lily to ask what it was 'by which, had you found a glove in the corner of the sofa, you would have known it, from its twisted finger, hers indisputably?' (p. 57). Like a 'phantom net' (Mrs Ramsay's image for the lights of the town (p. 79)) she 'tangled' one's perceptions 'in a golden mesh' (p. 59) and rejoices to think that 'wound about in their hearts, however long they lived she would be woven' (p. 130).

The web of active relationships spun by Mrs Ramsay, and living on through 'Time Passes' in the 'ball of memories' unwound by Mrs McNab (p. 160), is set against the less delicate knots in 'The Lighthouse' that bind the family together under Mr Ramsay, like the knots tied and untied by Macalister's boy: 'A rope seemed to bind him there, and his father had knotted it and he could only escape by taking a knife and plunging it . . .' (p. 213). While James struggles in his bondage, Lily is trying to untie 'a knot in her mind' (p. 178): to complete the picture and to understand the Ramsays. The knotty problem of balancing 'this mass on the right hand with that on the left' (p. 62) is also the problem of balancing the evidence about the Ramsays' marriage in order to arrive at a completed picture and a moment of vision. Essentially this can only be a moment – 'The vision must be perpetually remade' (p. 206) – and at the moment of completion it is already past. 'I have had my vision,' Lily concludes, not 'I have it.'

What Lily arrives at is the proper balance of shapes; this is not an easy achievement and it is undertaken several times in the book. Mrs Ramsay's dinner party is shaped out of disparate entities – hostilities, reservations, her own reluctance to participate – into a coherent

whole, whose ingredients are of the most trivial (talk about vegetable skins and coffee) but whose effect is nevertheless grand and
transcendental, because it has come about by a creative effort. Like
Lily looking at her picture when it is done, Mrs Ramsay looks back
on her dinner party as something that takes on a new perspective as
soon as it is completed:

> With her foot on the threshold she waited a moment longer in
> a scene which was vanishing even as she looked, and then,
> as she moved and took Minta's arm and left the room, it changed,
> it shaped itself differently; it had become, she knew, giving one
> last look at it over her shoulder, already the past. (p. 128)

The search for 'significant form' must continue. A few moments
later she is reading the Shakespeare sonnet in which the lover
invests the beauties of April with the idea of his beloved:

> They were but sweet, but figures of delight
> Drawn after you, you pattern of all those.

The poem gives her a sense of completed form:

> There it was, suddenly entire shaped in her hands, beautiful
> and reasonable, clear and complete, the essence sucked out of
> life and held rounded here – the sonnet. (p. 139)

There are three analogous activities. In the poem, the lover gives
added meaning to shapes by the force of his emotion, just as the poet
has 'shaped' the sonnet to be 'beautiful and reasonable' through a
creative effort. Mrs Ramsay, reading, makes sense of the shapes on
the page. In miniature, the passage shows the sense of the whole
novel. Acts which give form to life – even the cutting out of illustrations from the Army and Navy Stores catalogue – are creative
and humanizing. Without creative actions there is only space, like
the space caused by death.

For Lily to say that 'Love had a thousand shapes' (p. 218) seems
vague and sentimental until it is put in the context of the idea that
Lily and Mrs Ramsay are both 'lovers' trying to create shapes of
wholeness:

> There might be lovers whose gift it was to choose out the
> elements of things and place them together and so, giving them

a wholeness not theirs in life, make of some scene, or meeting of people (all now gone and separate) one of those globed compacted things over which thought lingers, and love plays. (pp. 218–19)

The greatest achievements are proportionate to the greatest intensity of emotion. This is felt particularly of Lily's concentration, which is analogous to Mrs Ramsay's and is used in order to re-create Mrs Ramsay:

Mrs Ramsay saying 'Life stand still here'; Mrs Ramsay making of the moment something permanent (as in another sphere Lily herself tried to make of the moment something permanent) – this was of the nature of a revelation. (p.183)

Lily brings the mythical Mrs Ramsay back to life by her creative effort to fill space with meaning. Before she does it, all that she sees is 'like curves and arabesques flourishing round a centre of complete emptiness' (p. 203). She feels that if the meaning of life can be asked for with sufficient intensity

the space would fill; those empty flourishes would form into shape; if they shouted loud enough Mrs Ramsay would return. 'Mrs Ramsay!' she said aloud. 'Mrs Ramsay!' The tears ran down her face. (p. 205)

The passage derives its energy from the language of painting. Without that we might look askance at its emotional intensity. The last part of the novel is a delicate matter, which is made to work only by the very careful sustaining of an intimate relationship between Lily's yearning for Mrs Ramsay and her desire to get the painting right. The 'return' of Mrs Ramsay – though well prepared for by the legendary, mythical qualities with which she has always been invested – is only acceptable if we can barely distinguish Lily's two impulses. To this end, when Mrs Ramsay does appear, she is there very much as a model for the picture. The moment of climax is moving because it is very quiet, and even ironic: Mrs Ramsay's 'perfect goodness' to Lily included her complete disdain of the picture which now immortalizes her; this is Lily's triumph over Mrs Ramsay as well as her tribute to her.

> Mrs Ramsay – it was part of her perfect goodness to Lily – sat there quite simply, in the chair, flicked her needles to and fro, knitted her reddish-brown stockings, cast her shadow on the step. There she sat. (p. 230)

But the moment has three sides, not two. It also marks the arrival of Mr Ramsay at the lighthouse, where – as though encountering death – he momentarily assumes the heroic standards of behaviour which have previously been used to satirize him, and at last inspires nothing but admiration:

> He rose and stood in the bow of the boat, very straight and tall, for all the world, James thought, as if he were saying, 'There is no God,' and Cam thought, as if he were leaping into space, and they both rose to follow him as he sprang, lightly like a young man, holding his parcel, on to the rock. (p. 236)

Mrs Ramsay appearing, Lily completing her picture and Mr Ramsay arriving at the lighthouse are all victorious over the impersonal powers of chaos and death through their concentration on the task in hand and through the intensity of emotion which they possess or inspire.

The book's conclusion, then, is a moral one. Like *Jacob's Room*, *Mrs Dalloway* and *The Waves*, *To the Lighthouse* deals with the possibility of coming to terms with death. Lily's painting does not set up a romantic dichotomy between aesthetic consolation and mortal suffering. The artistic act involves suffering; it sums up the extreme difficulty of giving some moral coherence to the chaotic forms of reality;

> It was an exacting form of intercourse anyhow. Other worshipful objects were content with worship; men, women, God, all let one kneel prostrate; but this form, were it only the shape of a white lamp-shade looming on a wicker table, roused one to perpetual combat, challenged one to a fight in which one was bound to be worsted. (p. 180)

The artist here rejects the passive forms of worship (such as Christianity) for what she considers a more arduous responsibility. So Leslie Stephen, saying, like Mr Ramsay, 'There is no God', turned from the 'muscular Christianity' of his early years to a rationalist philosophy of responsibility and endurance, but retained the Evangelical belief in 'the supreme importance of the individual's relation to the good'.[1] In a novel which criticizes and mocks but finally finds admirable Mr Ramsay's bleak drama of endurance, the consolations offered for death are based on the real Mr Ramsay's principles. Completed forms, whether made from a social and family group, an abstract painting, or the journey to the lighthouse, create the only lasting victory over death and chaos. Such forms can only be brought into being by means of the arduous search for truth which is a necessary personal responsibility.

[1] Noel Annan, *Leslie Stephen: His Thought and Character in Relation to his Time* (London, MacGibbon and Kee, 1951), p. 123. Annan points out that this belief is retained in Bloomsbury's 'unalterable emphasis on personal salvation' (ibid. p. 126).

6

Orlando

1928

ORLANDO has a different quality from all Virginia Woolf's other novels, though it is interestingly comparable to many of them, particularly to *Jacob's Room* and *Between the Acts*. The difference in quality is suggested by its subtitle, 'A Biography': it is an attempt to represent the character of a real person. Though *To the Lighthouse* was also, in a sense, biographical, it was not written *for* the characters who are evoked in the novel. *Orlando*, by contrast, is a personal offering, dedicated to Vita Sackville-West in a spirit of love and fascination and also of irony.

In writing the book, Nigel Nicolson suggests, 'Virginia had provided Vita with a unique consolation for having been born a girl.'[1] *Orlando* is meant to console Vita not only for her sex, but also for her loss of Knole, the ancestral home of the Sackvilles, which came about because she was a woman and could not inherit.[2] Vita had passionate and bitter feelings of possession and loss for Knole, which one can see expressed in her novels *The Heir* (1922) and *The Edwardians* (1930) and in her letters to Harold: 'Oh God, I do wish that Knole hadn't got such a hold on my heart! If only I had been Dada's son, instead of his daughter!'[3] In *The Heir*

[1] Nigel Nicolson, *Portrait of a Marriage* (London, Weidenfeld and Nicolson, 1973; Futura, 1974), p. 214.

[2] See Harold Nicolson, *Diaries and Letters 1945–62* (London, Collins, 1968; Fontana, 1971), p. 102, note 46.

[3] Ibid. p. 182.

(subtitled 'A Love Story') a quiet little man from Wolverhampton suddenly finds himself in possession of a Kentish Elizabethan manor house. The story describes his increasingly possessive love for the place, which is heavily mortgaged and has to be auctioned. The hero, Chase, finds the thought of losing the house more and more unbearable, for 'The house *was* the soul; did contain and guard the soul as in a casket . . . the soul of England.'[1] At the sale he finds himself 'fighting to shield from rape the thing he loved'[2] and buys it back in a defiant gesture 'to cast off the slavery of the Wolverhamptons of this world'. The language of the story is equally emotional throughout, and accurately reflects Vita's passion for family property, and her idea of herself as part of the tradition she inherits:

> If I could take my England, and could wring
> One living moment from her simple year,
> One moment only, whether of place or time,
> . . . Then should my voice find echo in English ear;
> Then might I say, 'That which I love, I am.'[3]

'I loved it', she says of Knole in *Knole and the Sackvilles*, 'and took it for granted that Knole loved me.'[4] The phrase is suggestive of the aristocratic pride which united a distaste for the Wolverhamptons of this world with a strong local feeling for family, house and land. In *The Edwardians*, published two years after *Orlando*, Vita recreates her childhood at Knole ('Chevron'). Chevron's beauty dominates the book, and the thought of its becoming national property (as Knole did in 1941) is anathema to the hero. But in *The Edwardians* the way of life made necessary by the place is treated with some reservations. The hero's sister is a socialist and 'regards our love for Chevron as a weakness'.[5] Chevron's way of life is threatened, and the book is tinged with Vita's wistful acceptance of that fact – a quality similar to the tender nostalgia at

[1] Vita Sackville-West, *The Heir* (London, Heinemann, 1922), p. 59.

[2] Ibid. p. 116.

[3] Vita Sackville-West, *The Land* (London, Heinemann, 1926), p. 62.

[4] Vita Sackville-West, *Knole and the Sackvilles* (London, Heinemann, 1922; Ernest Benn, 1958), p. 29.

[5] Vita Sackville-West, *The Edwardians* (London, Hogarth Press, 1930), p. 246.

the end of *Orlando*. As in *Orlando*, too, genders overlap. The brother and sister of *The Edwardians* are called Sebastian and Viola, and both are in love with the same character. It is interesting that Vita, by this reference to Shakespeare's sexually ambiguous twins, should have followed the consolation for the loss of Knole provided by *Orlando*. There, Knole is Orlando's because she has been a man; in *The Edwardians*, Chevron is Vita's because she is a man as well as a woman. Vita's masculine sexuality, which she herself fictionalized in the melodramatic and romantic *Challenge* (written in 1919 but at the time unpublished), is closely related to her feelings about her family home, and this is made apparent both in her own novel about Knole and in *Orlando*.

Virginia Woolf understood and admired Vita's feelings for her house and her land, and was interested in the link between those feelings and Vita's sexuality, a link which she recognized as being central to Vita's character. By making Orlando's life span over 300 years and include a change of sex she suggests that Vita's personality was formed equally by its androgyny and by its inheritance from the past. The novel's general themes of history and sexual identity are thus at every point directed towards a description of personality. The historical periods that have created the house have also created Orlando. The book necessitates a double reading; its fantasy and pageantry are being used as the material of a love letter which tells the loved one the writer's opinion of her. As the book goes on, it becomes increasingly concerned with what Vita is like. Virginia Woolf feared that the book, which she had 'begun as a joke', lacked 'unity'.[1] There is some truth in this; the serious concentration on Orlando's personality is at odds with the very materials and techniques used to create it. The idealization of the character (which Quentin Bell remarks on, criticizing it for its nearness to 'the glamorous creations of the novelette'[2]) gives an oddly romantic air to a book which partly sets out to be an instrument of ridicule and satire.

For the subtitle is also a joke. The personal emphasis of *Orlando* is couched in parodic terms; the study of Vita's character is presented through the medium of a literary *jeu d'esprit*. The game

[1] *AWD*, 31 May 1928, p. 128.   [2] Bell II, p. 118.

takes various forms. Overall, the techniques of the historical biographer are being ridiculed, very much as in *Jacob's Room*. What
is life? the narrator asks, giving throughout the implied answer that
life is not what the biographers make of it, 'since a biography is
considered complete if it merely accounts for six or seven selves,
whereas a person may well have as many thousand' (p. 218). The
serious experiment in *Jacob's Room* of 'following hints' in order to
get at the truth of life and character is refashioned here into a less
arduous and more entertaining shape. Many of the techniques are
the same. The biographer is as much in evidence, hanging 'like the
hawk moth' 'at the mouth of the cavern of mystery',[1] periodically
standing back to generalize or comment about life and art, speaking
to the reader more often and more directly than Orlando does. In
Jacob's Room, however, the difficulty of discovering Jacob produced a sense of sadness, anticipating his death. *Orlando* provides
a comic version of the same difficulty. The ironic disparity between
the jaunty, factual attempt at biography and the shifting, ambiguous
quality of life is parodic rather than elegiac.

The elusiveness of the principal character is not the central
theme. Orlando is far closer to us than Jacob; her thoughts frequently overlap with the biographer's. They voice, indistinguish-
ably, questions asked by women and by writers: 'Which is the
greater ecstasy? The man's or the woman's?' (p. 109); 'What then,
was Life?' (p. 199); 'What has praise and fame to do with poetry?'
(p. 229). Unlike Jacob, Orlando is a self-conscious participant in
the biographer's quest for personality, and at times speaks for her:

> 'Hair, pastry, tobacco – of what odds and ends are we com-
> pounded,' she said (thinking of Queen Mary's prayer book).
> 'What a phantasmagoria the mind is and meeting-place of
> dissemblables!' (p. 124)

The biographer is wily. The quaintness of Orlando's vocabulary
and the humorous conclusion to her meditation ('she threw her
cheroot out of the window and went to bed') prevent us from taking
too seriously a platitude with which the biographer is very much
in agreement. The light tone avoids solemnity and at the same time

---

[1] *Jacob's Room*, p. 69.

allows for flexibility; at any moment we may find that it is the biographer rather than Orlando who is speculating:

> Had Orlando, worn out by the extremity of his suffering, died for a week, and then come to life again? And if so, of what nature is death and of what nature life? Having waited well over half an hour for an answer to these questions, and none coming, let us get on with the story. (p. 48)

Here the character of a pompous biographer is being assumed in order for it to be mocked. This satire on traditional biography (which owes a debt to Lytton Strachey's work in the same field) is carried out in various ways, all aimed at showing up the dichotomy between factual biography and true life. The predicament of the biographer whose subject does nothing but write (and whose reader may consequently ask for his money back) is wittily described; the absurdities of 'Acknowledgements' and 'Indexes' are mocked; and the solemn use of historical records is made fun of: 'We have done our best to piece out a meagre summary from the charred fragments that remain; but often it has been necessary to speculate, to surmise, and even to use the imagination' (p. 84). Orlando's career at this point is given to us through the diary of 'John Fenner Brigge, an English naval officer' and 'Miss Penelope Hartopp, daughter of the General of that name' (p. 90). Though the pastiche on 'source material' is meant to amuse, it also arises naturally from Virginia Woolf's tendency to create scenes and characters through different observers; Penelope Hartopp's account of events is reminiscent of Ellie Henderson's view of Clarissa's party. In all the literary jokes made in *Orlando* there is a similar sense of Virginia Woolf's pleasure and natural inclination. Brief satires on legal parlance, ridiculous accounts and examples of Victorian literature, pastiches of Sir Thomas Browne or Jane Austen, sidelong digs at D. H. Lawrence and his game-keeper (p. 190) or at Hemingway and his monosyllables (p. 182),[1] burst out energetically from within the general parodic vein. Virginia Woolf does not pursue the parodic line which Joyce takes

---

[1] Cf. 'An Essay on Criticism' (1927), *CE* II, p. 256. 'We find attached to this admirable frankness an equal bareness of style. Nobody speaks for more than a line or two ... But there is something faked ...'

in 'The Oxen of the Sun' section of *Ulysses*, where the development of the foetus is imaged in a gargantuan parody of the major styles of English literature from Anglo Saxon to the future time. But there is in *Orlando* a more moderate form of the same idea. Each historical period, which in itself illustrates or sets off a part of Orlando's character, is invoked by literary or artistic allusions which may (as in the references to Sir Thomas Browne) move towards actual stylistic parody. Usually, however, the allusions suggest rather than imitate the tone of the period.

A major element in the book's humour is the satire directed against Vita herself, and Vita's work. Clearly, we are allowed to view with irony the inconsistency in Orlando which allows him to be 'unaccountably ashamed of the number of his servants and of the splendour of his table' (p. 60) when he is with Nick Greene, and to describe 'with some pride' when she is with Rustum the gipsy 'the house where she was born, how it had 365 bedrooms and had been in the possession of her family for four or five hundred years' (p. 103). This fond satire on Vita's personal characteristics incorporates a literary debunking of *Knole and the Sackvilles*, which Vita published in 1922. 'I am reading *Knole*,' Virginia Woolf writes to Vita '. . . you have a rich dusty attic of a mind.'[1] The use she makes of Vita's book on Knole is well suggested by the illustrations which she chose, in consultation with Vita,[2] for the first edition of *Orlando*. Three of these are photographs of Vita, posed and dressed to suggest Orlando in the eighteenth, nineteenth and twentieth centuries. One is a photograph of Angelica Bell in outlandish costume, representing Sasha; and three are historical portraits of 'the Archduchess Harriet', of 'Marmaduke Bonthrop Shelmerdine' and of 'Orlando as a boy', which is the portrait of the young Edward Sackville, son of the fourth Earl of Dorset, one of the illustrations to *Knole and the Sackvilles*. The combination of photographs of Vita and historical portraits reflects Virginia Woolf's treatment of her subject. In part *Orlando* really is the history of the Sackvilles at Knole. Many of the details that Vita

---

[1] Vita Sackville-West, 'Virginia Woolf and *Orlando*', *The Listener*, Vol. 53 (27 January 1955), pp. 157–8.

[2] Harold Nicolson, *Diaries and Letters 1930–39*, ed. Nigel Nicolson (London, Collins, 1966; Fontana, 1969), pp. 29–30.

records are used in *Orlando*. These may be small matters like the names of the servants, the descriptions of the bowls of potpourri, the mention of King James's silver brushes or of the gallery 'whose floor was laid with whole oak trees sawn across' (p. 224).[1] But more important themes are also incorporated. Orlando's early tragedies call to mind not only Vita's juvenile historical novels and plays but also Charles Sackville's *Gorboduc*; Orlando's relationship with Nick Greene refers to the Sackvilles' patronage of the arts; the allusions to Shakespeare echo Vita's attempts to forge some connection between Shakespeare and Knole; Vita herself speaks in *Knole* of 'the disadvantage of fine birth to a poet'.[2] Vita's desire to 'resurrect the Sackvilles' in her guidebook, to destroy the concept of the house as a historic monument to the dead, is close in spirit to Orlando's wistful sympathy for the house at the end of the book:

> The house, with its exits and entrances, its properties of furniture and necessities . . . the house demands its population. Whose were the hands that have, by the constant light running of their fingers, polished the paint from the banisters? . . . Who were the men and women that, after a day's riding or stitching, lay awake in the deep beds, idly watching between the curtains the play of the firelight, and the little round yellow discs cast upon walls and ceiling through the perforations of the tin canisters standing on the floor, containing the rush lights?
>
> Thus the house wakes into a whispering life, and we resurrect the Sackvilles.[3]

Rows of chairs with all their velvets faded stood ranged against the wall holding their arms out for Elizabeth, for James, for Shakespeare it might be, for Cecil, who never came. The sight made her gloomy. [. . .] Chairs and beds were empty; tankards of silver and gold were locked in glass cases. The great wings of silence beat up and down the empty house. [. . .] The gallery stretched far away to a point where the light almost failed. It was as a tunnel bored deep into the past. As her

---

[1] Cf. *Knole and the Sackvilles*, p. 25.   [2] Ibid. p. 45.
[3] *Knole and the Sackvilles*, p. 40.

eyes peered down it, she could see people laughing and talking
[. . .] (pp. 224–5)

Orlando is an attempt to resurrect the Sackvilles. But it does not
treat Vita's literary monument to them as sacrosanct. The game
Virginia Woolf plays with *Knole* is that of exaggerating all its
details, taking her cue from Vita's descriptions of the house as
having the look of 'a medieval village', of containing within its
'four acres of building' seven courts, corresponding 'to the days of
the week; and in pursuance of this conceit . . . fifty-two staircases,
corresponding to the weeks in the year, and three hundred and
sixty-five rooms, corresponding to the days.'[1] Vita admits that she
has not verified this count, but the elaborate grandeur of the claim
(particularly because of the sense it gives of Knole as a House of
Time) attracts Virginia Woolf's attention, and sets the tone for
the passage in which she describes Orlando's refurnishing of Knole.
Every item in the list of Orlando's expenses is taken from the
inventories and lists of 'household stuff' given in the chapter
'Knole in the reign of Charles I'; but the numbers of Spanish
blankets, walnut-tree tables, cushions of crimson damask, are
wildy exaggerated. Vita's apology for her lists ('I fear lest the
detailing of these old papers should grow wearisome'[2]) is taken up:
'Already – it is an effect lists have upon us – we are beginning to
yawn' (p. 77).

But though the effect is satirical, it is also creative of atmosphere.
Knole is vividly, marvellously realized, partly through the parodic
treatment of Vita's book, partly through more lyrical descriptive
passages. Such changes of approach are characteristic of *Orlando*; its
interest, and also its weaknesses, arise from the attempt to use
several styles and several approaches interchangeably. Her diary
notes on the writing of *Orlando* lay stress on this attempt. It is to be
written, she says, in 'a mock style very clear and plain';[3] but then
again 'it has to be half laughing, half serious; with great splashes of
exaggeration'.[4] In the end she decides that *Orlando* is not a complete
success: it is 'too freakish and unequal, very brilliant now and

[1] Ibid. p. 19.   [2] Ibid. p. 102.
[3] *AWD*, 22 October 1927, p. 117.
[4] *AWD*, 20 December 1927, p. 120.

then'.[1] Presumably she would, in *Orlando*, feel open to the charge she herself levels against the purple patch – 'not that it is purple but that it is a patch'.[2]

The diary entries point to two of the stylistic variations in *Orlando*, that between satire and lyricism, and that between the early fantasy and later seriousness of the book. But there are further refinements. Each historical period is evoked in a fluent essayist's style, distinct from the satiric tone used for the pedantic biographer, or from the impressionistic, lyrical style which attempts to reach the heart of *Orlando*'s personality and the nature of life. Even within the 'clear and plain' historical style there are variations. The spirit of each age requires a different literary treatment.[3] Rich, clear, sharp, energetic details evoke the Elizabethan period like a Breughel painting; the vitality, passion and pageantry of the age are encapsulated in the personality of Queen Elizabeth, and in Orlando's affair with Sasha. The literary climate is suggested by a generalized paraphrase of all Elizabethan poetry: 'The moment is brief they sang; the moment is over; one long night is then to be slept by all' (p. 19). If one turns from this first chapter to the description of the eighteenth century in Chapter Four, one finds different techniques at work. The spirit of the age is preserved in the minds of its major literary figures; as a result the chapter consists largely of anecdotes and quotations, and is summed up by a silhouette portrait of Johnson, Boswell and Mrs Thrale. The nineteenth century, by contrast, is expansively caricatured; the emphasis is on grotesque parody, whether in the generalized account of the country's rising damp or its three-volume novels, or in the exchange about wedding rings between Orlando and Mrs Bartholemew ('The muffins is keepin' 'ot,' said Mrs Bartholemew mopping up her tears, 'in the liberry' (p. 165)). The pictorial images for the age are a Turner cloudscape and an object which suggests a mixture of the Albert Memorial and Crystal Palace:

> Draped about a vast cross of fretted and floriated gold were widow's weeds and bridal veils; hooked on to other excrescences

[1] *AWD*, 31 May 1928, p. 128.
[2] 'The Narrow Bridge of Art' (1927), *CE* II, p. 226.
[3] The method anticipates the pageant in *Between the Acts*.

were crystal palaces, bassinettes, military helmets, memorial
wreaths, whiskers, wedding cakes, cannon, Christmas trees,
telescopes, extinct monsters, globes, maps, elephants, and
mathematical instruments – the whole supported like a gigantic
coat of arms on the right side by a female figure clothed in
flowing white; on the left, by a portly gentleman wearing a
frock-coat and sponge-bag trousers.[1] (p. 163)

The list is impressionistic and elephantine, and far removed in tone
from the bizarre precision and archaic tone of the list that describes,
as the climax to a series of brilliant descriptive passages, the breaking
of the Great Frost:

Many perished clasping some silver pot or other treasure to
their breast; and at least a score of poor wretches were
drowned by their own cupidity [. . .] furniture, valuables,
possessions of all sorts were carried away on the icebergs.
Among other strange sights was to be seen a cat suckling its
young; a table laid sumptuously for a supper of twenty; a
couple in bed; together with an extraordinary number of
cooking utensils. (p. 44)

Cutting transversely across these linear, historical changes in style is
the fluctuation between wit and lyricism in the treatment of
Orlando. Where Virginia Woolf is concentrating on the absurdities
of the biographer who attempts to create Orlando, or on the relation
between Orlando and the spirit of the age, or on Orlando's moments
of action, the style is witty, 'clear and plain'. Where she is concentrating, as she does increasingly, on the true, inward nature of
personality, the style is lyrical and impressionistic. But a serious
tone is never allowed to dominate; the light-fantastic is com-
pulsively reintroduced. This is necessary if Virginia Woolf is to
sustain all the levels of the book at once, but it is often rather
irritating. It seems at times as though, in making Orlando at once a
creature of fantasy who lives for centuries and changes her sex, and

---

[1] This is reminiscent of Strachey's description of Victoria's possessions in
Queen Victoria (London, Chatto and Windus, 1921; Harmondsworth,
Penguin, 1971), pp. 232–3.

at the same time a complex person to be used as the spokesman (like Mary Seton in *A Room of One's Own*) for women and for women writers, Virginia Woolf has set herself an almost impossible task.

> When the sailors began chanting, 'So good-bye and adieu to you, Ladies of Spain,' the words echoed in Orlando's sad heart, and she felt that however much landing there meant comfort, meant opulence, meant consequence and state (for she would doubtless pick up some noble Prince and reign, his consort, over half Yorkshire), still, if it meant conventionality, meant slavery, meant deceit, meant denying her love, fettering her limbs, pursing her lips, and restraining her tongue, then she would turn about with the ship and set sail once more for the gipsies.
>
> Among the hurry of these thoughts, however, there now rose, like a dome of smooth, white marble, something which, whether fact or fancy, was so impressive to her fevered imagination that she settled upon it as one has seen a swarm of vibrant dragon-flies alight, with apparent satisfaction, upon the glass bell which shelters some tender vegetable. (p. 115)

The dome shape is a recurring image of comfort and fulfilment in Virginia Woolf, used here to express the contrast between Orlando's new feelings of restriction at being a woman and the consolation of writing. The process of thought is an extremely serious one – indeed it contains the argument of *A Room of One's Own*. But seriousness is kept within the realm of fantasy by the artificial rhythms and repetitions of the first paragraph and the elaborate image of the second part. The writer chooses to be winsome and entertaining rather than solemn or didactic; and thereby succeeds only in sounding whimsical and affected.

Though the book's carefully preserved lightness of tone may not always be interesting or persuasive, its serious, innermost intention – the analysis of Orlando's character – is convincingly achieved. Orlando, who is both man and woman, also stands in a dual relation to time. We partly feel that, although Orlando takes over 300 years to reach the age of thirty-six, she does not change. Her essential qualities are already formed when she is an Elizabethan boy of sixteen and continue, over the centuries, to express themselves in her poem, 'The Oak Tree':

> How very little she had changed all these years. She had been a gloomy boy, in love with death, as boys are; and then she had been amorous and florid; and then she had been sprightly and satirical; and sometimes she had tried prose and sometimes she had tried drama. Yet through all these changes she had remained, she reflected, fundamentally the same. She had the same brooding meditative temper, the same love of animals and nature, the same passion for the country and the seasons. (p. 167)

It is important that there should be a 'sameness' about Orlando. Although the character becomes more self-possessed and aware as a mature woman than as a young man, he/she is always sulky, beautiful, clumsy, impetuous, devoted to nature and solitude and 'afflicted with a love of literature' (p. 52). It is by this means that Virginia Woolf emphasizes Orlando's natural androgyny: she is the same character whether she is a man or a woman, and it is evident from the first line of the book that Orlando's man/womanly characteristics overlap. Orlando's 'sameness' enables Virginia Woolf eventually to attack the nineteenth century, the only age to which Orlando cannot adapt her bisexual personality, since it forces men and women into unnaturally rigid marital roles. Ironically, then, the major change in Orlando's life comes not when she turns from man into woman, but when she has to adapt herself to the Victorian age:

> Orlando had inclined herself naturally to the Elizabethan spirit, to the Restoration spirit, to the spirit of the eighteenth century, and had in consequence scarcely been aware of the change from one age to the other. But the spirit of the nineteenth century was antipathetic to her in the extreme, and thus it took her and broke her, and she was aware of her defeat at its hands as she had never been before. For it is probable that the human spirit has its place in time assigned to it; some are born of this age, some of that; and now that Orlando was grown a woman, a year or two past thirty indeed, the lines

of her character were fixed, and to bend them the wrong way was intolerable. (p. 172)

That Orlando should have permanent qualities, 'fixed lines', rather than a changing, developing character, is necessary too if we are to bear in mind that the fantasy of Orlando's moving through time is a lighthearted metaphor for her historical consciousness. By the end of the book we think of Orlando as an achieved and real personality, dominated by her powerful feelings of the past history of her house and family. We concentrate, finally, on her consistency, not on the changes she has 'lived' through. This is emphasized in the remarkable passage about the true self and the Captain self which draws to a conclusion our consideration of Orlando/Vita.

> She was [...] changing her selves as quickly as she drove [...] as happens when [...] the conscious self, which is the uppermost and has the power to desire, wishes to be nothing but one self. This is what some people call the true self, and it is, they say, compact of all the selves we have it in us to be; commanded and locked up by the Captain self, the Key self, which amalgamates and controls them all. (p. 219)

At a cursory reading the passage suggests that the conscious or true self is the *same* as the Captain self. But the Captain self is rather the guardian of the true self, standing in the same relationship to it as does the biographer to his subject. Virginia Woolf is the Captain self of the novel who 'amalgamates and controls' all the selves of Orlando. But Orlando too has a Captain self which searches for her true self, the combination of all her identities, with such questions as these:

> 'What, then? Who, then?' she said. Thirty-six; in a motor-car; a woman. Yes, but a million other things as well. A snob, am I? The garter in the hall? The leopards? My ancestors? Proud of them? Yes! Greedy, luxurious, vicious? Am I? (here a new self came in). Don't care a damn if I am. Truthful? I think so. Generous? Oh, but that don't count (here a new self came in). (p. 219)

The passage continues to delineate all her qualities, though the Captain self does not succeed in finding the true Orlando until she passes through the lodge gates to her house. The questionings suggest Orlando's infinite variety, but they also confirm the reader's sense that Orlando has a recognizable, consistent personality. Because Virginia Woolf wanted to write a lighthearted, not a serious biography, she chose to build Orlando's 'true self' out of a fantastic time sequence rather than out of a day-in-the-life, as with Mrs Dalloway, or out of a sequence from childhood to old age, as with Bernard, who, at the end of *The Waves*, is a Captain self calling for his true self in manner very similar to Orlando's.

The historical organization of *Orlando* is, then, a means of showing how Orlando stays the same, not how she changes. Similarly, the sex change does not alter Orlando's character, but her perceptions and her social behaviour. Her perceptions are enriched by it – 'She was man; she was woman; she knew the secrets, shared the weaknesses of each' (p. 112) – but her social behaviour is restricted. Because she understands both sides, but has to behave as a woman, she is both enlightened and frustrated. She thus becomes the ideal spokesman for the androgynous argument also being evolved at this time in *A Room of One's Own*, which, though a more public and straightforward statement than *Orlando*, uses some of the same techniques, such as the mingling of a chronological account of women through the centuries with the fantasy of Shakespeare's sister. In *A Room of One's Own*, as in *Orlando* (and as in the later and less engaging *Three Guineas*) women are encouraged to cherish and make use of their special qualities, which arise from centuries of oppression:

> 'Better it is', she thought, 'to be clothed with poverty and ignorance, which are the dark garments of the female sex; better to leave the rule and discipline of the world to others; better be quit of martial ambition, the love of power, and all the other manly desires if so one can more fully enjoy the most exalted raptures known to the human spirit, which are,' she said aloud, as her habit was when deeply moved, 'contemplation, solitude, love.' (p. 113)

Virginia Woolf says that this train of thought leads Orlando into 'the extreme folly [. . .] of being proud of her sex', but the comment is perhaps not quite true to the tone of the passage from which it arises. A comparison with *A Room of One's Own* is invited. Here she states that 'it is fatal for anyone who writes to think of their sex. It is fatal to be a man or a woman pure and simple; one must be woman-manly or man-womanly.'[1] Though the need for such impartiality is applied equally to both sexes, there is in her account of the two imaginary writers, Mary Carmichael and Mr A, a definite preference for the woman, insufficiently androgynous though she may be. Orlando is supposed to balance equally the qualities of both sexes, as is shown in this charming analysis of Vita which expresses very clearly Virginia Woolf's feelings about her:

> For it was this mixture in her of man and woman, one being uppermost and then the other, that often gave her conduct an unexpected turn. The curious of her own sex would argue, for example, if Orlando was a woman, how did she never take more than ten minutes to dress? And were not her clothes chosen at random, and sometimes worn rather shabby? And then they would say, still, she has none of the formality of a man, or a man's love of power. She is excessively tender-hearted. She could not endure to see a donkey beaten or a kitten drowned. Yet again, they noted, she detested household matters, was up at dawn and out among the fields in summer before the sun had risen. (p. 133)

But Orlando is more a critic of men than of women, and she does in fact become more womanly – 'a certain change was visible in Orlando' (p. 132) deeper than the change of clothes. Though she is described as an androgynous personality, her female characteristics seem to dominate. It would be hard to imagine an *Orlando* in which the sex change was the other way round. Only if Orlando had ended up as a man would the enthusiasm for the hermaphrodite mind be absolutely unbiased. Not until *The Waves* does the androgynous spokesman become a man. In *Orlando* the emphasis is feminist; Orlando really does fall into the folly of 'being proud of her sex'.

She is hauled back from such folly, however, by a consideration of the word 'love'. The satisfaction Orlando finds in her relationship with Shelmerdine (far greater than any she enjoyed in her ego-

[1] *A Room of One's Own* (1929), p. 102.

tistical masculine affairs) is reminiscent of Katharine and Ralph's achievement in *Night and Day* (and suggestive of Vita's adaptable *modus vivendi* with Harold Nicolson). Orlando's sense of freedom and excitement in the relationship provides her with those moments of ecstasy which result, here and elsewhere in Virginia Woolf's work, from the personality's being transcended:

> It is not articles by Nick Greene or John Donne nor eight-hour bills nor covenant nor factory acts that matter; it's something useless, sudden, violent; something that costs a life; red, purple, blue; a spurt; a splash; like those hyacinths (she was passing a fine bed of them); free from taint, dependence, soilure of humanity or care for one's kind; something rash, ridiculous, like my hyacinth, husband I mean, Bonthrop; that's what it is – a toy boat on the Serpentine, ecstasy – it's ecstasy that matters. (p. 203)

Colours, movements and natural objects are preferred to the masculine world of administration, articulacy and philanthropy. Orlando thrives on an incoherent plane (described in the terms of an abstract painting) where her love for one person is a mixed part of her intense susceptibility to immediate experience. Such ecstasy can only result from an emancipating relationship in which sexual characteristics are blended. The tone and structure of Orlando do not, however, lend themselves to a study of relationships. Shelmerdine is a flimsy and fantastic creature, only serviceable as an agent for the moments of ecstasy, or as an instrument of satire on the nineteenth-century matrimonial instinct, to which Orlando falls an unwilling victim. His return in an aeroplane at the end indiscreetly forces a renewal of the book's fantasy level, which, since the striking of the present time, has been abandoned in favour of a conclusive search for Orlando's 'true self'.

This self lies not in her relationships with other people, but in her relationship with her house and with her writing. The closest analogy between Orlando and her biographer is that both are struggling to find a way of expressing life (or truth, or reality: the terms are frequently interchangeable) in art. Orlando's attempts to write are, like her character, partly evolved from and partly at odds with the historical periods through which she lives. When an

Elizabethan, she writes tragedies like *Gorboduc*; when a seventeenth-century ambassador she reads Sir Thomas Browne and meditates upon tombstones (shrinking from 'the cardinal labour of composition which is excision' (p. 50)); in the eighteenth century she becomes a lover of the picturesque; and in the nineteenth century has to wrestle with the spirit of the age which would have her write 'in the neatest sloping Italian hand [. . .] the most insipid verse she had ever read in her life' (pp. 167–8). In the end Orlando writes Vita's poem 'The Land' – not perhaps a very startling departure from Victorianism, but the result of 'the transaction between a writer and the spirit of the age' which 'is one of infinite delicacy' (p. 188).

The difficulty of making the transaction when the writer is unsympathetic to his age is only one of the several difficulties which obstruct Orlando in her natural desire to write. Orlando is an aristocrat, by tradition a patron rather than a writer; to become the latter she must 'substitute a phantom' (literature) 'for a reality' (her house and lands) (p. 52). In substituting phantom for reality she is faced with the essential task of every writer (not least of Orlando's biographer, who is much preoccupied with it), that of translating reality into words. 'Life? Literature? One to be made into the other? But how monstrously difficult!' (p. 201).

Like all books about writers, *Orlando* reflects itself: the book, and the biographer's explanations of her difficulty in writing it, is a mirror, as well as a framework, for Orlando's poem, and her difficulty in writing it. Throughout, the biographer and Orlando both have to tackle again and yet again what it means to have to write; to have, for instance, to try to turn 'green' from a thing into an idea:

> He was describing, as all young poets are forever describing, nature, and in order to match the shade of green precisely he looked (and here he showed more audacity than most) at the thing itself, which happened to be a laurel bush growing beneath the window. After that, of course, he could write no more. Green in nature is one thing, green in literature another. Nature and letters seem to have a natural antipathy; bring them together and they tear each other to pieces. The shade of green Orlando now saw spoilt his rhyme and split his metre. (pp. 11–12)

At this early stage in Orlando's literary career he abandons the problem precipitately, and the biographer has done no more than crudely to impress on us the untransferability of greenness into poetry. In the second assault on the same problem, both Orlando and the biographer are more sophisticated. Orlando is at the stage of rejecting all elaboration, all rhetoric, all figures of speech. Let words be things themselves, not other things. But nature itself, he finds, does not invite such treatment, for all its things can be seen as other things. Looking at nature – even before one has written about it – must mean using metaphor. Again he abandons the problem:

> So then he tried saying the grass is green and the sky is blue [. . .] Looking up, he saw that, on the contrary, the sky is like the veils which a thousand Madonnas have let fall from their hair; and the grass fleets and darkens like a flight of girls fleeing the embraces of hairy satyrs from enchanted woods. 'Upon my word,' he said [. . .] 'I don't see that one's more true than another. Both are utterly false.' And he despaired of being able to solve the problem of what poetry is and what truth is, and fell into a deep dejection. (pp. 71–2)

Always, when Orlando returns to the attempt at representation, she works through images, as does her biographer. As the period changes, so too do the figures of speech. In the eighteenth century, 'green' is more formally decorated: 'She compared the flowers to enamel and the turf to Turkey rugs worn thin. Trees were withered hags, and sheep were grey boulders. Everything, in fact, was something else' (p. 101). But the problems of mimesis remain unsolved, and cannot be solved, since new ways of making 'green' be literature have endlessly to be struggled for. Lightheartedly, and in miniature, *Orlando* thus suggests the necessity for Virginia Woolf's own unceasing literary experimentation.

In the struggle, the writer has to establish and sustain integrity. Orlando must learn to ignore the flattery or abuse of such as Nick Greene, and come to the point of saying: 'Bad, good, or indifferent, I'll write, from this day forward, to please myself' (p. 73). All writers, of course, not only those who are also aristocrats or women, have to struggle for that defiant statement, which arises, or should arise, from the continuous tension between exposure and privacy in the writer's life.

> While fame impedes and constricts, obscurity wraps about a man like a mist; obscurity is dark, ample, and free; obscurity lets the mind take its way unimpeded. (p. 73)

It is an obvious enough conflict – *A Writer's Diary* bears evidence to it on almost every page – but not a simple one. Though the writer's initial, and essential, integrity, can be established by sloughing off external influences, there follows the pull towards the outside world, the desire for fame. Orlando has to reject Nick Greene after their first encounter in order to become her own literary master and judge. But she needs him again in his later incarnation (as a man of letters modelled on Sir Edmund Gosse) so that he can give her manuscript what it needs: 'It wanted to be read. It must be read. It would die in her bosom if it were not read' (p. 192). Only then, after the intercourse with public life, can the writer, justified, withdraw again into obscurity into the centre of her 'true self', which, for Orlando, is found in her relationship with her house and land:

> What has praise and fame to do with poetry? [. . .] Was not writing poetry a secret transaction, a voice answering a voice? So that all this chatter and praise and blame and meeting people who admired one and meeting people who did not admire one was as ill suited as could be to the thing itself – a voice answering a voice. What could have been more secret, she thought, more slow, and like the intercourse of lovers, than the stammering answer she had made all these years to the old crooning song of the woods, and the farms and the brown horses standing at the gate, neck to neck, and the smithy and the kitchen and the fields, so laboriously bearing wheat, turnips, grass, and the garden blowing irises and fritillaries?
> So she let her book lie unburied and dishevelled on the ground, and watched the vast view, varied like an ocean floor this evening with the sun lightening it and the shadows darkening it [. . .] (pp. 229–30)

The passage gently humanizes the 'crooning' landscape, and treats Orlando's meditation romantically – with a tender allusion to Vita's poem (' . . . the springing grass/Was dulled by the hanging cups of fritillaries' (p. 187)). It is a serious and restrained conclusion to a book which has been witty, extravagant, even flashy, in tone and manner. The biographer, at this point in full possession of Orlando's true self, creates a mood of sober sympathy for her heroine, and, giving up tricks and jests, herself discreetly disappears.

7

The Waves

1931

ORLANDO'S 'ease and dash'[1] only partially expressed Virginia Woolf's state of mind after *To the Lighthouse*. Behind the 'externality' of *Orlando* and *A Room of One's Own* another kind of novel was being evolved from a 'play-poem idea'[2] of 'some semi-mystic very profound life of a woman' in which 'time shall be utterly obliterated; future shall somehow blossom out of the past.'[3] The difficult development from that first mysterious hint of 'The Moths' in 1926 to the triumphant completion of *The Waves* in 1931 is thoroughly charted in the *Diary*,[4] enabling us to see that, although the form and the subject of the novel were very much changed, the original conception remained. The life of a woman against the background of flying moths became 'a series of dramatic soliloquies',[5] but there was a consistent abstract idea behind these changing forms:

> Now is life very solid or very shifting? I am haunted by the two contradictions. This has gone on for ever; will last for ever; goes down to the bottom of the world – this moment I

[1] *AWD*, 28 November, 1928, p. 139.

[2] *AWD*, 18 June 1927, p. 108.

[3] *AWD*, 23 November 1926, p. 102.

[4] There is a full and interesting account of the relationship between *The Waves* and *A Writer's Diary* in Joan Bennett's book, *Virginia Woolf: Her Art as a Novelist* (Cambridge University Press, 1945; 2nd ed. 1964), Ch. VII.

[5] *AWD*, 20 August 1930, p. 159.

stand on. Also it is transitory, flying, diaphanous. I shall pass like a cloud on the waves. Perhaps it may be that though we change, one flying after another, so quick, so quick, yet we are somehow successive and continuous we human beings, and show the light through.[1]

The diary entry combines allusions to moths and waves in a passage which recalls the language of 'Modern Fiction', but with a slightly different emphasis. The concepts of the 'semi-transparent envelope' and the 'shower of innumerable atoms' shaping themselves 'into the life of Monday or Tuesday' are now applied to 'human beings' rather than to 'life'. *The Waves*, more devoted to abstraction than any of the other novels, uses human beings as case histories to illustrate the nature of life. The concentration on abstract ends requires a further eradication of materialism from the novel; and the terms in which this is envisaged remind us, again, of the transition period between *Night and Day* and *Jacob's Room*:

> What I want now to do is to saturate every atom. I mean to eliminate all waste, deadness, superfluity: to give the moment whole: whatever it includes. Say that the moment is a combination of thought; sensation; the voice of the sea. Waste, deadness, come from the inclusion of things that don't belong to the moment; this appalling narrative business of the realist: getting on from lunch to dinner. It is false, unreal, merely conventional. Why admit anything to literature that is not poetry – by which I mean saturated?[2]

Again, as in the passage describing her discovery of a 'new form' for *Jacob's Room* in 1920, she expresses a desire to 'enclose everything, everything'.[3] But the desire to exclude and eliminate is as powerful, and the emphasis is now on concentration and intensity rather than on 'looseness and lightness'. The tone of the 1928 diary entry is sterner and more definite, and suggests some disaffection with the methods tried out in *Jacob's Room* and perfected in *To the Lighthouse*. It augurs a radical departure from her previous achievements

---

[1] *AWD*, 4 January 1929, p. 141.
[2] *AWD*, 28 November 1928, p. 139.
[3] *AWD*, 26 January 1920, p. 23.

which seemed to her inevitable: 'no other form of fiction suggests itself except as a repetition'.[1]

The third-person narrative which characterized the earlier novels is still found in the italicized passages in *The Waves*, the 'interludes',[2] but no longer in a fluid, malleable, chameleon style. Instead it is elaborately literary and impersonal, and carefully set apart from the bulk of the novel, a first-person narrative in which the six characters 'speak' of themselves. This would suggest that Virginia Woolf is now, for the first and last time, writing what could be called a 'stream of consciousness' novel,[3] in which the minds of the characters flow on, as from the inside, with no authorial interpolations. And *The Waves* does seem to fulfil our criteria for such a novel. Apart from the interludes, the action, dialogue, description, factual information, do not exist autonomously, but only (if at all) within the characters' minds. The need for more than one point of view is satisfied, not as in the earlier novels by the chameleon activity of the third-person narrator, but simply by presenting six streams of consciousness rather than one.

The definition, however, is inadequate. If we set a passage from *The Waves* against some excerpts from twentieth-century novels which might be, and have been, described by the term 'stream of consciousness', the effect is one of dissimilarity.

In this way, for two consecutive summers I used to sit in the heat of our Combray garden, sick with a longing inspired by the book I was then reading for a land of mountains and rivers, where I could see an endless vista of sawmills, where beneath the limpid currents fragments of wood lay mouldering in beds of watercress; and near by, rambling and clustering along low walls, purple flowers and red. And since there was always lurking in my mind the dream of a woman who would enrich me with her love, that dream in those two summers used to be

[1] *AWD*, 26 January 1930, p. 153.

[2] This is Virginia Woolf's term for them: 'The interludes are very difficult, but I think essential' (ibid.).

[3] Melvin Friedman, for instance, calls *The Waves* 'the most firmly rooted in stream of consciousness of all her books' (*Stream of Consciousness: A Study in Literary Method* (New Haven and London, Yale University Press, 1955), p. 22.

quickened with the freshness and coolness of running water; and whoever she might be, the woman whose image I called to mind, purple flowers and red would at once spring up on either side of her like complementary colours.[1]

The far east. Lovely spot it must be: the garden of the world, big lazy leaves to float about on, cactuses, flowery meads, snaky lianas they call them. Wonder is it like that. Those Cinghalese lobbing around in the sun, in *dolce far niente*. Not doing a hand's turn all day. Sleep six months out of twelve. Too hot to quarrel. Influence of the climate. Lethargy. Flowers of idleness. The air feeds most. Azotes. Hothouse in Botanic gardens. Sensitive plants. Waterlilies. Petals too tired to. Sleeping sickness in the air. Walk on roseleaves.[2]

First of all shall I have a haystack? Well idealized that might be quite good. First of all then we will consider the haystack. It stands up in a sunny field by the side of but out from a chestnut tree. So. The hay has been cut. Of course. It isnt imported hay in that stack. Well all the rest of the field, it is a very big field, it stretches away far and wide, and there on it are the swathes of white hay that have been left over. There it lies. So. There is a blue sky overhead and some white puff clouds bowling along in front of a summery wind. Not the sort you say as you crouch under the breakwater: 'I will say this about Shrimpton-on-Strand you can always get out of the wind one side of the breakwater or the other, or under the bathing machine.'

Well now into this picture empty of all human interest comes Pompey Casmilus. Here at last, she says, is the right haystack . . . So I lie back on my ivory haystack and there is nobody else in the whole wide world and so I fall asleep. No dreams. No dreams.[3]

[1] Marcel Proust, (translated Scott Moncrieff) *Swann's Way*, Vol. 1 of *Remembrance of Things Past* (London, Chatto and Windus, 1966), p. 114 (first published in 1913 as *Du côté de chez Swann*).

[2] James Joyce, *Ulysses* (Paris, Shakespeare and Co., and London, Egoist Press, 1922; Harmondsworth, Penguin, 1969), p. 73.

[3] Stevie Smith, *Novel on Yellow Paper* (London, Cape, 1936; Penguin, 1951; reissued 1972), p. 27.

'I shall edge behind them,' said Rhoda, 'as if I saw someone I know. But I know no one. I shall twitch the curtain and look at the moon. Draughts of oblivion shall quench my agitation. The door opens; the tiger leaps. The door opens; terror rushes in; terror upon terror, pursuing me. Let me visit furtively the treasures I have laid apart. Pools lie on the other side of the world reflecting marble columns. The swallow dips her wings in dark pools. But here the door opens and people come; they come towards me. Throwing faint smiles to mask their cruelty, their indifference, they seize me. The swallow dips her wings; the moon rides through blue seas alone. I must take his hand; I must answer. But what answer shall I give? I am thrust back into this clumsy, this ill-fitting body, to receive the shafts of his indifference and his scorn, I who long for marble columns and pools on the other side of the world where the swallow dips her wings.' (p. 90)

Evidently the stream of consciousness novel in the first third of the century is a hybrid genre. The methods used by these four narrators for examining an exotic alternative to reality are very different. Marcel orders his childhood sensations, with retrospective irony, into a completed picture designed like the illustration to a book. Bloom's fantasy, nourished by his accumulated perceptions and information, is immediate: the sentence structure, by avoiding the imposition of a verb tense, gives us the impression that we are hearing his mind as it works. Pompey Casmilus's present-tense narrative, which shows that her daydream is recurrent, creates the sound of a voice recounting a humorous anecdote. Rhoda's soliloquy resembles none of these. Like Marcel, she presents an elaborate, literary version of her thought process, but unlike him she is supposed to be thinking about a scene which is actually taking place. In spite of this, there is no attempt, as in Joyce, to evoke natural immediacy, no realistic representation of the jerks and twists of the mind as it is idly running along. Indeed, there is no sense of idleness or relaxation: the daydream and the public experience are pitched at the same level of intensity. There is no room for the humour available to the other three writers. The sound of the spoken voice is not simulated in order to create an ironic distance between the narrator and her own experience. Instead, a formal, rhythmic monologue subjugates the representation of personality or action to a series of physical images which are made to stand for a state of mind. The effect is that of a translation of life and consciousness into a rigid set of analogies, as though a character on stage were being represented by two actors, one carrying out a mime in slow motion while the other comments on the meaning of the actions. Coldness and intensity are strangely mixed; agony and fear are formalized, while they are being communicated, into rhythms and images. The rhythmic prose which is substituted for a naturalistic representation of speech or thoughts does not distinguish between descriptions, action, conversation, reflections or recollection. Whether Rhoda is young or old, happy or sad, excited or despondent, it does not vary.

The style is the same for all the characters. It is characteristic of Susan to express herself in simple statements ('The meat is stood in the oven; the bread rises in a soft dome' (p. 85)), but the others may do this too. And Susan is not confined to words of one syllable – 'I love, I hate' (p. 12). Describing how Bernard makes phrases, she makes one herself: 'Now you mount like an air-ball's string, higher and higher through the layers of the leaves' (p. 14). She is as liable as the others to employ the Latinisms which are supposed to be Neville's idiosyncrasy: going to school, she says: 'All here is false; all is meretricious' (p. 27). The tautology is there for the sake of the rhythm and is not in character. Parallelism is introduced throughout irrespective of who is speaking, patterned out of the repetition of certain parts of speech:

[Bernard:] They too bubbled up, they also escaped. (p. 186)
[Jinny:] The torments, the divisions of your lives. (p. 189)
[Rhoda:] After all these callings [. . .] these pluckings and searchings (p. 192)
[Neville:] I choose at random; I choose the obvious. (p. 182)
[Louis:] People go on passing; they go on passing. (p. 79)
[Susan:] Everything is now set; everything is fixed. (p. 122)

This rhythm creates a long prose-poem. Though recurrent rhythm has been an important ingredient of the earlier novels, nowhere else has it been consistent and insistent enough to suggest that the book should be read as lines of poetry rather than as lines of prose.

> How strange that people should sleep
> that people should put out the lights
>   and go upstairs.
> They have taken off their dresses,
> they have put on white night-gowns.
> There are no lights in any of these houses.
> There is a line of chimneypots against the sky;
> and a street lamp or two burning,
> as lamps burn when nobody needs them.
> The only people in the streets
> are poor people hurrying.
> There is no one coming or going in this street;
> the day is over.
> A few policemen stand at the corners.
> Yet night is beginning.[1]   (p. 86)

The effect is sustained with extraordinary ease throughout. *The Waves* is not difficult to read as poetry; its rhythm is agreeable and insidious. But it is difficult to read as a novel, in that its emphasis on rhythm overwhelms distinctions of character. Only the content enables us to distinguish between the voices. An idiosyncrasy of speech – Louis's Australian accent – can be described but not rendered, since, obviously, the formal framework of 'said Louis', 'said Bernard', is a sustained irony: real speech is not being represented.

Given a formal, undifferentiated style, distinctions can only be made on the basis of the images. This brings the novel dangerously close to a play of humours in which bits of the human personality are

---

[1] The passage oddly echoes Wallace Stevens's 'Disillusionment of Ten O'Clock', *Harmonium* (1923); collected in *The Palm at the End of the Mind*, ed. Holly Stevens (New York, Knopf, 1971), p. 11.

> The houses are haunted
> By white night-gowns.
> None are green,
> Or purple with green rings,
> Or green with yellow rings ..

parcelled out among the different characters. Bernard's twisting of little toys, Neville's call to 'one person', Rhoda's dreamland of swallows and pillars, Louis's vision of the Nile, Susan's screwed-up pocket-handkerchief and Jinny's yellow scarf seem at times like routine reminders of which 'humour' is speaking. But there is a counterweight to this limiting technique of identification in the fact that many images are shared between the characters. The first utterances of the six as children immediately suggest how fluid is the relationship between individual and common experience. To some extent distinctions are made. Louis voices an image which will be a constant symbol of his insecurity, the great chained beast stamping on the shore. The metaphor suggests a vivid imagination and is in contrast to Susan's direct physical impressions – 'I see a slab of pale yellow' – and her apprehension of concrete, ordinary objects – 'Biddy has smacked down the bucket on the kitchen flags' (p. 8). Rhoda's images evoke the pressure of hostile or indifferent elements on unprotected things – the snail flattening the grass blades, the cold water running on the mackerel, the bird left singing alone. But the 'first impressions' suggest the common experience of the six children as much as their differences. The mackerel in the bowl, the bucket on the kitchen flags and the scraping of fish scales might be noticed by the same voice. As they grow older, the voices become more distinct. But the narrative sustains their common consciousness through the general use of images like circles or waves, and through their participation in each other's private figures of speech, Neville and Susan, for instance, both thinking of Bernard as a loose, dangling thread (as he does himself), Jinny and Louis both associating Rhoda with the petals with which she herself identifies, and Bernard, finally, incorporating all their lives in himself:

> Here on my brow is the blow I got when Percival fell. Here on the nape of my neck is the kiss Jinny gave Louis. My eyes fill with Susan's tears. I see far away, quivering like a gold thread, the pillar Rhoda saw, and feel the rush of the wind of her flight where she leapt. (p. 249)

Percival, whose death Bernard here assimilates into his own experience, is the central, dominant example of an image shared by all the speakers. Images may become words, but they do not use words. Percival is silent, then absent, and then dead, so that he can be used as a catalyst for the feelings of the six narrators. None of them wants to think about Percival himself, only about Percival as a gauge by which to measure their own lives. This is so even when Percival is present:

> We are drawn into this communion by some deep, some common emotion. Shall we call it, conveniently, 'love'? Shall we say 'love of Percival' because Percival is going to India?
>   No, that is too small, too particular a name. We cannot attach the width and spread of our feelings to so small a mark. (p. 108)

After his death it is hard for them to concentrate on him. Once Percival's obsequies are done, Bernard and Jinny have to go back into the 'machine' of ordinary life (p. 135); it is an artificial effort to think of the dead, and after a time it becomes a false gesture, like covering him with lilies (p. 228). His death is generalized by Louis ('all deaths are one death' (p. 145)), forgotten by Rhoda ('I seldom think of Percival now' (p. 176)), and merged with other experiences even by Neville: 'You are you. That is what consoles me for the lack of many things [. . .] and the flight of youth and Percival's death [. . .]' (p. 155). Instead, the image of Percival's death gives birth, as it were, to an idea of youth and life: it is that which becomes memorable about Percival, as though he is resurrected in the continuing lives of his friends. This paradox is not only found in Bernard's last phrases, but, earlier, in the way that Susan and Jinny both turn the idea of going to India into an image of life and renewal:

> 'His eyes will see when mine are shut,' I think. 'I shall go mixed with them beyond my body and shall see India.' (p. 147)

> The activity is endless. And to-morrow it begins again; to-morrow we make Saturday. Some take train for France; others ship for India. [. . .] Life comes; Life goes; we make life. (p. 150)

Images are not only shared among the voices, but also overlap between the voices and the interludes. Interspersed with the expressions of personal consciousness from birth to death are the descriptions of an impersonal scene – a beach, a garden, a house – from dawn to dusk (which broadens out occasionally into more remote, exotic settings). Since the style of the two are different, the interludes being far more effusive, lyrical and alliterative, it is something of a shock to find the speakers appropriating details from a universe which is indifferent to them (Louis, for instance, comparing himself to 'a warden' carrying 'a lamp from cell to cell' (p. 173), an image which has been used for light on the hills (p. 127) in the fifth interlude). At such moments *the* world becomes *their* world, particularly at the end, when Bernard turns the scene of the interludes into his vision of truth, and confirms our supposition that the house of the interludes is the house where the children's lives began.

The overlap is made more plausible by the sustained anthropomorphism of the interludes. In the first one, every figure of speech is used to relate the processes of nature to those of human beings. Sea, air, waves and light, become a cloth, a veil, the sediment in an old wine bottle, the arm of a woman, a lamp, the blades of a fan and a bonfire. It is the same in the third, where we find a characteristically elaborate image for the rim of flotsam on the shore 'as if some light shallop had foundered and burst its sides and the sailor had swum to land and bounded up the cliff and left his frail cargo to be washed ashore' (p. 62). The birds are characterized as companionable, fearful, apprehensive, emulous, aware, quizzical and savage. The waves are turbaned warriors with assegais (an image also used by Rhoda and Louis in the fourth section (p. 120) to describe those involved in the dance of life). The cruelty of maturing life is imaged by the vicious warfare in the undergrowth between birds and sluggy matter; and in the third section all the voices use birds as images. Obviously a consistent analogy is being made between non-human growth and decay and the human lifespan. But the effect of the anthropomorphism is peculiar; the inhuman scenes seem, because of it, to be bursting with active life, and to provide (like the activity of nature in the 'Time Passes' section of *To the Lighthouse*) a threat to the individual human consciousness.

The mixture of analogy and opposition between nature and man is found particularly in the treatment of the waves themselves, where there is an unresolved ambiguity. Are the waves meant to suggest the human lives, or are they the detached, impersonal forces of fatality? The last sentence of the book, '*The waves broke on the shore*', may suggest that Bernard's encounter with death is itself a wave, another inevitable part of existence; but it also implies that his individual effort is set against an arbitrary, uncaring universe. But the irony of the last line has to do with language as well as life. Bernard, in his last soliloquy, has used the images of the interludes as his own phrases, almost as though he were the author of *The Waves*. The world described in the interludes is that of 'the house, the garden, and the waves breaking' which make up Bernard's vision of 'the world seen without a self'. At the moment of seeing the world as it really is, he realizes that his phrases are useless to him; only words of one syllable will serve. The criticism is not only of Bernard's phrase-making self, but also of the elaborately written interludes. And when Bernard stops speaking, only words of one syllable are left: '*The waves broke on the shore*.' Both narrators have had finally to resort to the simplest of terms.

The interweaving of images suggests that the book is about the relationships between the six characters, who all, not only Bernard, measure their own lives against the other five, bringing up in their 'spoons' 'another of those minute objects which we call optimistically "characters of our friends"' (p. 209). These lines of thought, netting the voices together like 'a string of six little fish that let themselves be caught while a million others leap and sizzle' (p. 220), create the narrative links in a book without much plot. Twice Susan thinks of Jinny in London and the next voice to speak is Jinny's, in London (pp. 86, 148). But, apart from two meetings in Percival's honour, the extent of their involvement in adult life is uncertain. Bernard pays visits to Jinny after Percival's death, to Susan in the country and to Neville in his room. Rhoda and Louis are lovers for a time; Jinny prepares her room 'in case Bernard comes, or Neville or Louis' (p. 167). Their relationships, however, do not seem vital or impassioned. The information that Susan has always loved Bernard, or that Rhoda and Louis are lovers, seems to have little relevance to the voices. The quality of the book is abstract, not personal.

In thus disallowing the emphasis on relationships which was an important part of *Mrs Dalloway* and *To the Lighthouse*, in favour of an emphasis on the essences of personality, Virginia Woolf deprives herself of some of her most powerful qualities. She loses the fine tension between outer and inner levels of experience which makes the party scenes of *Mrs Dalloway* and *To the Lighthouse* more interesting than the dinner scenes in *The Waves*. Denying her characters idiosyncrasies and social mannerisms, she denies herself the kind of humour which energized her treatment of Mr Ramsay. There are limited comic possibilities when the characters exist at a level where they must take themselves seriously, though Jinny provides comedy by virtue of being the most superficial 'humour' – 'Here is Percival [. . .] he has not dressed' (p. 105) – and Bernard by being the wittiest, as in his description of Percival's Indian triumphs:

> By applying the standards of the west, by using the violent language that is natural to him, the bullock-cart is righted in less than five minutes. The Oriental problem is solved. (p. 116)

Though the resistance of her chosen form to comedy may not seem very important, it is part of the lack of distinction between different levels of intensity which makes *The Waves* the most arduous of her novels. The important points of climax – the vision of unity at the dinner for Percival, the momentary fusion of separate selves at Hampton Court, Bernard's final vision of truth and his ensuing encounter with death – are movingly and strenuously lyrical, but they do not stand out vividly from the rest of the writing.

Yet, in spite of the levelling effect of the style, her natural bent for characterization will not be suppressed. The outer life presses in through vivid anecdotes. Neville watches distastefully as Bernard mops up with his handkerchief the pool of tea running over *Don Juan*. Louis leaves his table in the steamy eating house, slipping a too large tip under the plate. Jinny writes a note and powders her nose giving 'her body a flick with the whip' (p. 228). Though Bernard's wife, Susan's husband, and Jinny's and Neville's lovers hardly exist, the moments of active emotion they induce are as strongly and crudely presented as the ordinary material of conventional novels:

You left me. The descent into the Tube was like death. We were cut up, we were dissevered by all those faces and the hollow wind that seemed to roar down there over desert boulders. I sat staring in my own room. By five I knew that you were faithless. I snatched the telephone and the buzz, buzz, buzz, of its stupid voice in your empty room battered my heart down, when the door opened and there you stood. That was the most perfect of our meetings. But these meetings, these partings, finally destroy us. (p. 153; Neville)

And then that rasping, dog-fish-skin-like roughness – those black arrows of shivering sensation, when she misses the post, when she does not come. Out rush a bristle of horned suspicions, horror, horror, horror – but what is the use of painfully elaborating these consecutive sentences when what one needs is nothing consecutive but a bark, a groan? And years later to see a middle-aged woman in a restaurant taking off her cloak. (p. 215; Bernard)

But such activities, like the places described in the novel, are subsumed in the lyric rhythm of consciousness, and become images. Action and environment inevitably take on a universal quality when treated in this way, and this creates a difficulty about the novel's social assumptions.

Obviously all Virginia Woolf's novels deal – though not flatteringly or complacently – with a limited social milieu, and betray a lack of imaginative reach over the classes outside her own experience. Septimus Smith is convincingly portrayed (at least as well as Leonard Bast, Forster's comparable character in *Howards End*), but he is, after all, mad, which gives him a classless air. The charladies and women singing outside tube stations may act as potent symbols, but they are not characterized at any more convincing level than is found in 'The mothers of Pimlico gave suck to their young'[1] or 'A woman of the lower classes was wheeling a perambulator.'[2] Such awkward excursions into foreign territory do not greatly matter if the central social group of the novel is vividly presented. The close-knit upper-middle-class

----

[1] *Mrs Dalloway*, p. 9.   [2] *The Years*, p. 17.

society that dominates *Night and Day*, *Mrs Dalloway*, *To the Lighthouse* and *Between the Acts* is firmly in the tradition of the novel of social realism dealing with a particular class, from *Emma* to *The Egoist*. There can be no valid criticism of Virginia Woolf for staying within her own world, nor for turning working-class women like the singer in *Mrs Dalloway* and Mrs McNab in *To the Lighthouse* into mythical, subhuman figures. In *The Waves*, however, because of the determined rejection of realism, the class distinctions are, paradoxically, disturbing. The six characters are constantly talking about the proletariat. Rhoda fears and hates it:

> Oh, human beings, how I have hated you! [. . .] how hideous you have looked in Oxford Street, how squalid sitting opposite each other staring in the Tube! (p. 174)

Louis wishes he could 'look like the rest' (p. 79) but, if he cannot be assimilated, he is determined to impose his will on the flux and disorder of the 'average man's' life. Jinny is oblivious of any class but her own; Susan identifies the lives of country working people with the lives of animals:

> I [. . .] sit by the beds of dying women [. . .] frequenting rooms intolerable except to one born as I was and early acquainted with the farmyard and the dung-heap and the hens straying in and out, and the mother with two rooms and growing children. I have seen the windows run with heat, I have smelt the sink. (p. 163)

Neville uncompromisingly despises the world of 'horsedealers and plumbers' (p. 66), saying in Cambridge: 'Where there are buildings like these [. . .] I cannot endure that there should be shop girls' (p. 73). Bernard, supposedly in warm contrast to Neville as one who wants to absorb all the different lives he encounters, is in no doubt, however, of the cosmic difference between his perceptions and those of the 'small shopkeepers':

> What a sense of the tolerableness of life the lights in the bedrooms of small shopkeepers give us! Saturday comes, and there is just enough to pay perhaps for seats at the Pictures. Perhaps before they put out the light they go into the little

garden and look at the giant rabbit crouched in its wooden hut. That is the rabbit they will have for Sunday dinner. Then they put out the light. Then they sleep. And for thousands of people sleep is nothing but warmth and silence and one moment's sport with some fantastic dream. 'I have posted my letter,' the greengrocer thinks, 'to the Sunday newspaper. Suppose I win five hundred pounds in the football competition? And we shall kill the rabbit. Life is pleasant. Life is good. I have posted the letter. We shall kill the rabbit.' And he sleeps. (p. 201)

Bernard and his five friends thus, in their different ways, write off the possibility that another class of people could share their perceptions. The very lack of realism makes this assumption unpalatable in *The Waves* where it would not have mattered in *To the Lighthouse*. Because the six characters are abstracted to their essences from those material envelopes (which in their case may be semi-transparent but in the case of the small shopkeepers are certainly opaque), they seem to be giving a definitive account of the quality of all experience. But the underlying details of their real lives, protected and privileged, suggest how relative their experience must in fact be. Though their individual weaknesses are described, the one, overall weakness – that not one of them ever considers whether sensibilities as interesting might not be found among the masses they fear and despise – is not perceived by their creator.

The six voices are not equally important and complex. The images that identify Jinny and Susan are less suggestive than those for Rhoda or Bernard, since characters whose lives are dominated by their bodies require physical images which can be literally applied. When Louis speaks of his body going down to the depths of the world, the image stands for his sense of history. But when Jinny describes herself as dancing like a fire, unfurling like a fern, rippling like a plant in a river, the image does not reach beyond itself: it only describes the bodily actions of one who lives in the 'society of bodies' (p. 53). Her leitmotif – 'The door opens. O come, I say' (p. 89) – is a literal description of the pattern of her life. Very occasionally Jinny makes a statement about herself which reaches towards a complex idea of personality: 'I cannot follow any thought from present to past [. . .] I do not dream' (p. 35). The sentence deals, unusually for Jinny, with a state of mind rather than a physical sensation, though it is about her lack of mental subtlety. There is little room for complexity in the portrayal of an alluring society lady bravely facing up to the oncoming of old age, though some attempt is made to transform her interest in clothes, lipstick and facepowder into a moral stand against chaos:

> This is the triumphant procession; this is the army of victory
> [. . .]
> Look how they show off clothes here even under ground in perpetual radiance. They will not let the earth even lie wormy and sodden. There are gauzes and silks illumined in glass cases and underclothes trimmed with a million close stitches of fine embroidery. Crimson, green, violet, they are dyed all colours. Think how they organize, roll out, smooth, dip in dyes and drive tunnels blasting the rock. [. . .] I am a native of this world, I follow its banners. (pp. 166–7)

In the opposition Jinny makes between civilization and pre-historic savagery there is an interesting antithesis to Louis's sense of the links between all ages of the world. But her praise of artifice goes only as far as the formula of life lived for the body can take one. And there are limits too within that formula. Jinny is a sensual creature, living from one orgasm to the next. But the physical images which describe her – the thin rippling body, the narrow throat – suggest a barren nerve-racked sexuality, rather like Lucy Tantamount's in *Point Counterpoint* (1928), not a rich, warm bodily life. There is no such thing in *The Waves*. Susan, whose bodily life is slow, maternal and earthbound, is in direct contrast to Jinny, but hers is a sinister and gloomy sensuality. Her empathy with things of the earth, leading (predictably) from wild rural adolescence to silent motherhood, is obscure and alarming:

> What I give is fell. I cannot float gently, mixing with other people. I like best the stare of shepherds met in the road; the stare of gipsy women beside a cart in a ditch suckling their children as I shall suckle my children. For soon in the hot midday when the bees hum round the hollyhocks my lover will

come. He will stand under the cedar tree. To his one word I
shall answer my one word. What has formed in me I shall
give him. I shall have children; I shall have maids in aprons;
men with pitchforks [. . .] I shall be like my mother, silent in a
blue apron locking up the cupboards. (p. 84)

Susan, locking cupboard doors and netting fruit, 'glutted with
natural happiness' in a landscape heavy and rich with the perpetual
breeding and ripening of 'Those dying generations at their song',[1]
seems a bringer of death as much as of life. Her refusal of Percival
suggests this: 'She who had refused Percival lent herself to this,
to this covering over' (p. 230).

By contrast with Jinny and Susan, every physical image associated with Rhoda points away from the body, towards a description
of mental anguish:

I must push my foot stealthily lest I should fall off the edge
of the world into nothingness. (pp. 36–7)

I came to the puddle. I could not cross it. Identity failed me.[2]
(p. 54)

Like a ribbon of weed I am flung far every time the door
opens. (p. 92)

The walls of the mind become transparent. (p. 196)

Rhoda's fearful instability, like Septimus's, is defined throughout
by physical sensations. And, like Septimus, she combines a sense of
the reality of the life of 'Monday or Tuesday' with a desire to
escape it. She knows that she is 'a girl, here in this room' as well as
being a ribbon of weed. Rhoda's is an irreconcilable position: she is
stretched between an ideal vision of impersonality and serenity,
evoked by her imaginary journeys and the satisfaction she finds in
abstract shapes, and the torture of 'here and now'. Though she
makes journeys away from the real world, she cannot separate
herself entirely, nor does she really want to. Her real desire is to be

[1] W. B. Yeats, 'Sailing to Byzantium', *The Tower*, 1928.
[2] 'Life is [. . .] the oddest affair; has in it the essence of reality. I used to feel
this as a child – couldn't step across a puddle once, I remember, for thinking
how strange – what am I? etc.' (*AWD*, 30 September 1926, p. 101).

included and to give herself – but 'Oh, to whom?' – and her escapism is tempered by her reluctant allegiance to reality:

> But these pilgrimages, these moments of departure, start always in your presence, from this table, these lights, from Percival and Susan, here and now. (p. 119)

Rhoda expresses an extreme version of the tension between isolation and participation which dominates all Virginia Woolf's novels, and she is defeated by it. Her suicide is her judgement on the real world, with which she can never be reconciled. Should we be tempted, however, to draw a simplistic analogy between Rhoda's experience and that of her creator, Bernard's voice provides an important qualification of Rhoda's judgement: 'Cruel and vindictive as we are, we are not bad to that extent' (p. 216).

Louis is a more interesting and complex voice than Rhoda in that, though he too fears the world, he wishes to impose order on it rather than to flee it; he is more frightening than frightened. His sense of insecurity and isolation in childhood results in an authoritarian and highly ordered public life which is always to be at odds with his secret loneliness. Thus, more emphatically than with the other characters, the images that define his personality are drawn from his childhood. His feelings of inadequacy are for ever evoked by the fat woman at the children's party who gave him, in pity, the Union Jack from the Christmas tree. His fear of untidy passionate relationships will always be imaged by Jinny's kiss on the back of the neck. His desire to impose order and make his way in a hostile world are already present in the blow he lands on the oak door at school and in his respect for Crane the headmaster. From the first, he feels himself to be part of an endless process of historical growth, his veins going down into the past, and this leads him to work at putting a ring of commerce round the world in his public life and, in his solitary attic room, to write poetry which will 'forge [. . .] a ring of beaten steel' (p. 144). Like the flamboyant historical figures with whom he identifies, he wants to provide an element of the continuity of which he is so vividly aware:

> to mark this inch in the long, long history that began in Egypt, in the time of the Pharaohs, when women carried red pitchers to the Nile. (p. 56)

This recurrent image is a clear indication of the difference between Louis and Rhoda. Louis's imaginary pilgrimage to the Nile is not a terrified flight from the real world, but an implacable source of strength. In spite of his constant dread of death, of the great beast stamping, Louis is in the ranks: he is part of 'the eternal procession' of working life and, as such, is rather the odd one out of the six.

Neville, like St John Hirst and William Dodge, a clever, passionate, unattractive homosexual, is a character who cannot well be summed up by such recurrent physical images as are used for Louis. Though his life is organized around physical comforts and intimacies, the 'ordinary things' in which he finds his peace – 'a table, a chair, a book with a paper-knife stuck between the pages' (pp. 124–5) – are not symbols but descriptions of his life. His engrossment in personal relationships, which gives existence, for him, the flavour of a Shakespearian play, can only be communicated anecdotally and analytically. To some extent his life is summed up by the images of the headmaster's crucifix, the gardener raising his mallet, and the boys on deck squirting each other with hosepipes. From these figures we gather Neville's distaste for virile pomp and circumstance, and his yearning for a momentous, consuming personal intimacy. But the image of the naked boys is a pathetic one. Neville's refined scenes of intimacy are verbal rather than physical. Though he longs for a life of the body, like Jinny's, his is in fact a life of the mind.

In this passage, Neville's type, one well known to Virginia Woolf, is brilliantly portrayed. The physical images are introduced not as symbols of his personality, but as the material for his thoughts and relationships:

> Now this room seems to me central, something scooped out of the eternal night. Outside lines twist and intersect, but round us, wrapping us about. Here we are centred. Here we can be silent, or speak without raising our voices. Did you notice that and then that? we say. He said that, meaning . . . She hesitated, and I believe suspected. Anyhow, I heard voices, a sob on the stair late at night. It is the end of their relationship. Thus we spin round us infinitely fine filaments and construct a system. Plato and Shakespeare are included,

also quite obscure people, people of no importance whatsoever. I hate men who wear crucifixes on the left side of their waist-coats. I hate ceremonies and lamentations and the sad figure of Christ [. . .] Some spray in a hedge, though, or a sunset over a flat winter field, or again the way some old woman sits, arms akimbo, in an omnibus with a basket – those we point at for the other to look at. [. . .] And then not to talk. To follow the dark paths of the mind and enter the past, to visit books, to brush aside their branches and break off some fruit. And you take it and marvel, as I take the careless movements of your body and marvel at its ease, its power – how you fling open windows and are dexterous with your hands. For alas! my mind is a little impeded, it soon tires; I fall damp, perhaps disgusting, at the goal. (pp. 153–4)

If one lives by the body, as Susan and Jinny do, and as Neville attempts to, the body will fail one. Two alternatives are provided in *The Waves*. One can be a visionary and look for 'a reason', 'a plot' behind 'this ordinary scene' (p. 169), like Rhoda and Louis. To go in this direction is to go towards alienation, solitude and even suicide. Or one can commit oneself to an interest in 'this ordinary scene', but treating it not as the arena of immediate gratification but as the material for art. This is no safer direction, in that words, like the body, may fail one. Bernard's stories and phrases, his 'sense of what other people are like' (p. 200), frequently desert him. As a storyteller he is at the mercy of all his assumed identities, of his need for an audience, and of his chronic sense of imperfection. Growing old, he begins to wonder whether there are 'stories' at all (p. 160), and whether there is any point in his life's activity:

Why impose my arbitrary design? Why stress this and shape that and twist up little figures like the toys men sell in trays in the street? Why select this, out of all that – one detail? (p. 161)

He is assailed by the sense of making so many transitions and acting out so many different tales that 'there is nothing to lay hold of. I am made and remade continually. Different people draw different worlds from me' (p. 114). He relies on being able to call upon the real Bernard, 'you the usual partner in my enterprises' (p. 162), whom he thinks of as a 'faithful, sardonic man' (p. 68). But he goes in fear of the moment when he will call upon his real self, like Orlando in her motor car, and no one will reply.

When this happens – when the fist does not form, the fin does not rise above the waste of waters[1] – the story-making identity finds itself merged with an undifferentiated, 'omnipresent, general life' (p. 96). Passive, undesiring, inarticulate, it becomes part of 'the world seen without a self' (p. 247). It is paradoxical that Bernard, who is the most worldly, domestic and articulate of the voices, is the character who experiences this mystical abnegation of the self, 'at the still point of the turning world'.[2]

At the end of The Waves, after summing up his life and the lives of his friends, he admits the limitations of being always an observer, a raconteur, a separate identity. He recognizes that his moments of merging, of becoming one with the others, were 'a sort of death' (p. 240), and that to merge and become depersonalized is as necessary and inevitable as death. Through Bernard the six lives become one, and this suggests, as in Mrs Dalloway and To the Lighthouse, that the personality is not a discrete entity but can be subsumed into the general life flow of the universe. For all this, Bernard's mystical experience of a loss of personality is not the moral conclusion of the book. For Bernard (unlike the narrator of Four Quartets) the timeless moment without a self is not infinitely desirable. Though it gives one a vision of the truth, 'to let oneself be carried on passively is unthinkable' (p. 206). Loath though Bernard is to suffer from the compulsions of daily life, of having to

---

[1] The 'fin in a waste of waters' (pp. 162, 210, 234) is used by Bernard several times as an image for something – such as a word, a thought, a sense of one's own personality – which may disrupt the monotony of life. The disruption is welcome, though the image is a sinister one. Virginia Woolf uses it in the diary to describe both the increased intensity of vision which accompanies her 'mental tremors' (Bell II, p. 100) and her apprehension of the 'essence of reality' (AWD, 30 September 1926, p. 101) which she attempts to pin down in The Waves. 'I have netted that fin in the waste of waters' she writes on finishing the novel (AWD, 7 February 1931, p. 169).

[2] T. S. Eliot, Burnt Norton (1935), Four Quartets.

do one thing and then another because 'Tuesday follows Monday: Wednesday, Tuesday' (p. 243), he nevertheless accepts that action must take place within that ordinary, sequential life:

> What are days for?
> Days are where we live.
> They come, they wake us
> Time and time over.
> They are to be happy in.
> Where can we live but days?[1]

Bernard remembers the shape of his nose, he bangs his spoon on the table. He asserts the individual personality and the value of its struggle against the impersonal forces of flux and death. His childhood resilience to life's hostility, expressing itself intuitively in his explorings and his stories, becomes in later life a more conscious resistance:

> I jumped up. I said, 'Fight! Fight!' I repeated. It is the effort and the struggle, it is the perpetual warfare, it is the shattering and piecing together – this is the daily battle, defeat or victory, the absorbing pursuit. The trees, scattered, put on order; the thick green of the leaves thinned itself to a dancing light. I netted them under with a sudden phrase. I retrieved them from formlessness with words. (p. 232)

In old age, Bernard faces death, like Mr Ramsay, with an individual effort which is translated into the physical image of Percival on horseback – Percival being the epitome of the life of action and effort. Ironic though this image is, Percival having been conquered by death, it ends the book firmly in a word *with* a self:

> the theme effort, effort, dominates; not the waves: and personality: and defiance.[2]

---

[1] Philip Larkin, 'Days', *The Whitsun Weddings* (London, Faber, 1964).
[2] *AWD*, 22 December 1930, p. 162.

8

The Years

1937

'**T**HE years 1930 to 1939 were horrible both publicly and privately,' wrote Leonard Woolf.

If one was middle aged or old and so had known at least a 'sort of a kind' of civilization, it was appalling impotently to watch the destruction of civilization by a powerful nation completely subservient to a gang of squalid, murderous hooligans . . .

The twilight was in one's private as well as in public life . . . This erosion of life by death began for Virginia and me in the early 1930s and gathered momentum as we went downhill to war and her own death. It began on 21 January 1932 when Lytton Strachey died of cancer . . . After Lytton's death Carrington . . . shot herself.

Two years later Roger Fry died . . .[1]

Virginia Woolf spent a large part of the thirties writing *The Years*, interspersed with her work on *Flush* and *Three Guineas*. Though *Three Guineas* was a social and political statement, the other works seem remote from the period in which they were produced. 'The novels of Virginia Woolf . . . are irrelevant for the historian,'[2]

---

[1] Leonard Woolf, *Downhill All the Way: An Autobiography of The Years 1919–1939* (London, Hogarth Press, 1967), pp. 248–50.

[2] A. J. P. Taylor, *English History 1914–1945* (Oxford, Clarendon Press, 1965; Harmondsworth, Pelican, 1970), p. 389.

A. J. P. Taylor writes of the thirties; and Quentin Bell in his biography points out that

> in 1933 – the year of the publication of *Flush* – Hitler came to power and the Japanese were overrunning Manchuria; in the following year there was what looked like the first stage of a Fascist revolution in France; in 1935 the Italians invaded Abyssinia, in 1936 the Spanish Civil War began, in 1937 the Japanese took Shanghai and Pekin and in 1938 the Nazis annexed first Austria and then the Sudetenland.[1]

As in her life she was reluctant – though considerably urged – to identify with any political movement or ideology, so in her fiction she was anxious to avoid propaganda or didacticism. In the prevailing mood of the thirties such attitudes made her seem old-fashioned and ineffectual: 'Her gift was for the pursuit of shadows, ... when what was needed was the swift and lucid phrase that could reach the ears of unemployed working men or Trades Union officials.'[2] It took some time for the dangerous condition of Europe to affect her imagination – in 1934, as Bell says, she was 'more worried about her novel than about politics'.[3] And though her reactions were strong when they were aroused, they were politically naïve:

> To her ... it appeared that the horrible side of the universe, the forces of madness, which were never far from her consciousness, had got the upper hand again. This to her was something largely independent of the political mechanics of the world. The true answer to all this horror and violence lay in an improvement of one's own mental state; somehow one had to banish anger and the unreason that is bred of anger.[4]

The Years closely reflects this state of mind. It is a novel that examines the possibility of living a life of integrity and contentment under adverse conditions, drawing an analogy (as *Three Guineas* more explicitly does) between Victorian paternalism and the masculine militarism and egotism of twentieth-century public life. Once liberated from the long shadow of the first, the women and the

---

[1] Bell II, p. 186.   [2] Ibid.
[3] Bell II, p. 179.   [4] Bell II, p. 187.

men of the Pargiter family struggle to adapt to the second. Naturally this involves Virginia Woolf in a satire both on Victorian family life and on the social and political conditions of the years leading up to the First World War. These factors determine the relationship between individuals and society in the 'present day' of the mid-1930s. But though the novel is much occupied with the external conditions of upper-class English life between 1880 and the thirties, to say that it is 'irrelevant for the historian' is not entirely absurd. The emphasis falls not on the facts of political or social change and their implications for the individual, but on a more abstract and less tangible investigation of various attempts to reconcile the obscurity of the soul with the moral need for social participation. The story of the Pargiters traces a tension between the world and the spirit which requires analogies to be drawn, rather than developments perceived, between different historical periods.

The frustration for the historian also stems from the novel's characteristic liaison between method and intent. A rejection of the 'masculine' world of fact, aggression, propaganda and convention as being contributory to 'the horrible side of the universe', in favour of a peace-engendering, unegotistical, impersonal freedom, requires a framework which will not be factual or conventional. There are frequent references in the diary to her fear of being crudely didactic in *The Years*, like other 'social' novelists such as 'Hugh Walpole and Priestley':[1]

And conversation: argument. How to do that will be one of the problems. I mean intellectual argument in the form of art: I mean how to give ordinary waking Arnold Bennett life the form of art?[2]

She tells herself to 'lyricize the argument'[3] and is troubled by 'the burden of something that I won't call propaganda. I have a horror of the Aldous novel.'[4] 'One can't propagate at the same time as write fiction.'[5] *The Years* continually replaces the definite and the

[1] *AWD*, 19 December 1932, p. 190.   [2] *AWD*, 31 May 1933, p. 208.
[3] *AWD*, 23 January 1935, p. 238.   [4] *AWD*, 20 February 1935, p. 239.
[5] *AWD*, 13 April 1935, p. 245.

factual with more hazy and haphazard alternatives: this is both its narrative technique and its message. We are returned to the antithesis which was found twenty years before in 'The Mark on the Wall':

— but these generalizations are very worthless. The military sound of the word is enough. It recalls leading articles, cabinet ministers — a whole class of things indeed which, as a child, one thought the thing itself, the standard thing, the real thing, from which one could not depart save at the risk of nameless damnation. Generalizations bring back somehow Sunday in London, Sunday afternoon walks, Sunday luncheons, and also ways of speaking of the dead, clothes, and habits — like the habit of sitting all together in one room until a certain hour, although nobody liked it. There was a rule for everything. The rule for tablecloths at that particular period was that they should be made of tapestry with little yellow compartments marked upon them. [...] How shocking, and yet how wonderful it was to discover that these real things, Sunday luncheons, [. . .] and table-cloths were not entirely real [. . .] What now takes the place of those things I wonder [. . .]? Men perhaps, should you be a woman; the masculine point of view which governs our lives [. . .] which establishes Whitaker's Table of Precedency, which has become, I suppose, since the war, half a phantom to many men and women, which soon, one may hope, will be laughed into the dustbin where the phantoms go, the mahogany sideboards and the Landseer prints, Gods and Devils, Hell and so forth, leaving us all with an intoxicating sense of illegitimate freedom — if freedom exists ...[1]

As in *The Years*, an analogy is made here, through images, between Victorian family life, with its protocol and solid objects, and the post-war public world of masculine authority; and, as in *The Years*, resistance to such authority is founded on laughter. Freedom comes through burlesquing the traditional objects of veneration; but the possibility of freedom is only tentatively hazarded. In both

[1] 'The Mark on the Wall', *A Haunted House and Other Short Stories* (1944), pp. 47–8.

the early short story and the late novel, the 'quiet, spacious world' which is suggested as an alternative to the domain of 'hard, separate facts'[1] is difficult to reach. The difficulty applies to art as much as to life. 'The Mark on the Wall' characteristically links the desire for a more free and impersonal existence with the expectation of new developments in fiction. The narrator's reaction against tradition and 'generalizations' is involved with her hope that 'the novelists of the future' will leave 'the descriptions of reality more and more out of their stories.'[2] When she wrote this in 1917 Virginia Woolf was toiling through the traditional thirty-four chapter form of *Night and Day*, and at first sight it might seem as though *The Years*, far from being a further experiment in fiction, returns, in reaction to *The Waves*, to the traditional structure and naturalistic dialogue of her second novel. This view gains some support from the apparent similarity in the subject matter of the two books. But these resemblances, though interesting, are superficial. The concentration on personality, central to the earlier novels, has given way to a preoccupation with wider areas of experience. *Night and Day* deals with individuals, *The Years* with society: Virginia Woolf was anxious that no one character should 'become too dominant'.[3] Though much less obviously experimental than *The Waves*, *The Years* is not a retrogressive work. It is an attempt (one made with extreme difficulty) to transform the realistic saga of family life, as practised by Walpole in the Herries novels (published between 1930 and 1933) and by Galsworthy in the *Forsyte Saga* of the twenties, into an 'essay-novel'[4] dealing with the abstract themes of time, memory and society.

The differences in structure and approach between *The Years* and a conventional family saga (or between *The Years* and *Night and Day*) make themselves felt in a summary of the book's eleven sections. The first secton, 1880, takes Colonel Pargiter from his club and his mistress to his family home, Abercorn Terrace, on the day of his wife's death. Though the scene then moves to Oxford, where Edward Pargiter and his cousin Kitty are re-enacting the youthful experiences of Jacob Flanders and Clara Durrant, Mrs Pargiter's death dominates the whole section, which

[1] Ibid. pp. 45, 49.   [2] Ibid. p. 47.
[3] *AWD*, 25 April 1933, p. 197.   [4] *AWD*, 2 November 1932, p. 189.

ends with her funeral. Throughout the section, rain falls inter-
mittently, creating a mild dreariness which oppresses the Pargiter
children in London and adds to Kitty's restlessness in Oxford. We
recall the beginning of the 'Victorian' character in *Orlando*: 'Rain
fell frequently, but only in fitful gusts, which were no sooner over
than they began again.'[1]

The second section, 1891, is dominated by the death of Parnell and
the burning of autumn leaves. A 'specimen day'[2] of Eleanor's life
with her father at Abercorn Terrace is described. Through her we
find out where the other children have gone: Martin to India,
Morris to the lawcourts, Delia to the slums. The Colonel visits his
sister-in-law Eugenie and his brother Digby for the birthday of his
little niece Maggie. The juxtaposition of Eleanor's tiresome
bondage to her father with the wild gaiety of Maggie and Sara's
bonfire suggests a symbolic value for the burning of leaves: 'For it
was October, the birth of the year' (p. 74).

The third section, 1907, takes place on a hot midsummer night in
London. Digby, Eugenie and Maggie have gone to a ball. Sara, who
must rest because she is crippled, lies at home reading. Dance music
and the moon outside disturb her. When the others return,
Maggie talks of her evening out and their mother, romantic and hist-
rionic, dances a waltz for them in the bedroom until called away
by the querulous voice of her husband. The glamorous, music-filled
night sums up the pre-war social world. In the next section, 1908,
it has vanished. Digby and Eugenie are dead, a cruel March wind is
blowing. Martin and Rose visit Eleanor, more than ever a prisoner
to the ageing Colonel and Abercorn Terrace.

The fifth section, 1910, concludes with the death of Edward
VII, but all the imagery is of flowers and spring. The section deals
with older and younger women in their relationships to a male-
dominated society. Rose, Maggie and Sara have lunch together;
Rose and Sara go to a political meeting where they find Eleanor and
Kitty; Kitty leaves for a performance of *Siegfried*. A Foreign Office

---

[1] *Orlando*, p. 160.

[2] See *AWD*, 27 November 1935, p. 260, and Bell II, p. 190: 'Virginia again
recorded what she called "a specimen day." By this she meant not a normal
day but rather, I think, a specimen of the distractions, worries, absurdities,
that make up one's life.'

employee talks importantly of the King's illness. At dinner, Sara tells Maggie about the meeting, but they are interrupted by the drunken noise of the man next door.

1911, the sixth section, portrays Eleanor's feelings after the death of Colonel Pargiter. She goes on holiday with Morris's family, whose country life on a hot August day, with the bazaar in the garden for the church fund, and after-dinner coffee on the terrace, strongly anticipates *Between the Acts*. Morris's children, North and Peggy, are in their turn secretly conspiring against the restrictions of family life. The next section, 1913, set in January snow, describes the pensioning-out of the family retainer, Crosby. Like Elizabeth Barrett returning to Wimpole Street in *Flush*, Eleanor notices for the first time how 'dark' and 'low' Crosby's basement is (p. 175). Crosby's grief at leaving Abercorn Terrace is ironically contrasted with Eleanor's relief.

The long and important section 1914 is given partly from Martin's point of view and partly from Kitty's. During the 'radiant' spring day Martin encounters Sara and takes her to lunch, then to the park to find Maggie and her baby. They pass by Speaker's Corner, and Martin considers its alternative: a world without 'I'. In the evening he goes to Kitty Lasswade's party and feels at once too old and too young for it, like Peter Walsh at Clarissa's. As the party ends he sees the very old Lady Warburton leaving, hung about 'with chains, furs and lace': 'The nineteenth century going to bed, Martin said to himself' (p. 215). Kitty, impatient throughout her party to get away, now hurries to catch the night sleeper to the North. Fleeing the London world, she reaches the timeless country moors. Clocks dominate the section, as in *Mrs Dalloway*. People have to meet at certain times; there is a sense of rush and, at the party, of futility. The moments of stillness by the Round Pond and in the country provide a strong contrast to the pressure of clock time in a world at war. *Jacob's Room* is also called to mind.

The ninth section, 1917, shows Eleanor in the dark of a frosty winter discovering, during an air raid, the life of the next generation: Maggie, her husband René, Sara and her homosexual friend Nicholas. Sara speaks of North, Morris's son, going off to war in 'the Regiment of Ratcatchers'. René speaks of his own country.

Trapped underground, all are struggling to find some vantage point against a brute externality. But when the war ends, in the next section, there is no sense of hope: in a November mist, the disgruntled Crosby, last relic of Abercorn Terrace and the nineteenth century, hears the guns booming.

The long final section, 'Present Day', is set against a background of light and summer and sky. Though it largely consists of Delia's party, at which all the generations are gathered together, it is prefaced by several encounters: Eleanor with North, North with Sara, Eleanor with Peggy. The party is dominated by the viewpoints of North, Peggy and Eleanor. Though Eleanor, up to a point the heroine of the book, has discovered new possibilities and a more hopeful shape to life, the younger adults, North and Peggy, are confused and bitter about the legacy of the past and the suffering of the present.

The summary suggests the book's hazy and disjointed quality, deliberately effected by means of a fragmentary time structure, which replaces the secure sense of regular chronology with the sense of a weight at each end of the book. The first sections, 1880 and 1891, and the last, 'Present Day', are set apart from the central sections, which only cover a period of twelve years, up to and during the war. As a result the long family scenes of 1880 seem to be weighted against the long family party of the last section, and the description of Eleanor's life in the second section is set in balance with the references she makes to that life in 'Present Day'.[1] There is a further avoidance of rigid chronology in the introductory descriptive passages for each 'year'. These were originally intended as 'interchapters', like the interludes in *The Waves*, but she kept to her later idea of 'compacting them in the text'.[2] Though they provide information about the lives of the characters, their historical content is minimal. In the spring of 1910, omnibuses have replaced the hansom cabs and landaus of 1880, and 'Queen Alexandra' is referred to instead of 'the Princess'. But there is no great difference in tone; both seasons have the same

[1] 'This last chapter must equal in length and importance and volume the first book: and must in fact give the other side, the submerged side of all that' (*AWD*, 22 May 1934, p. 219).

[2] *AWD*, 2 February 1933, p. 195.

festive and restless air. There is a far greater difference between the spring of 1910 and the March of 1908. The introductory description of 1908 is grim and cruel. A different mood, rather than a different historical setting, is emphasized in each section by means of the season, the weather, and sometimes a recurrent leitmotif like burning leaves or flowers. It is evident that the sections were thought of in terms of their dominant images by the reference in the diary to the 'wind chapter'. [1]

The use of such images for each section points to the novel's whole method. Like the chronology, the characterization and history of the family are carried on in unexpected ways. We do not have the satisfaction of knowing any person's life completely, nor the excitement produced by love or ambition. The mother's death in the first section is the most dramatic and important event in the novel, which consists mainly of tangential or unfinished conversations, events of little apparent importance, obscure passages of thought and snatches of description. Instead of the domination of action or character, we find the domination of images. *The Years* is thus a development from, rather than a reaction against, *The Waves*. But the images that fill *The Years* aim at diffuseness rather than concentration, and create a random pattern, rather than a dense rhythm. Their function, however, is in part to provide continuity. The caravan procession of shoppers and businessmen in 1880 becomes the caravan procession of market carts in 1907 (pp. 5, 105).[2] The London season is summed up by the sight of flags flying both in 1910 (p. 130) and in 1914 (p. 181). The statues in Parliament Square are for ever carrying 'rods or rolls of paper (pp. 73, 106). Other recurrences are found not in the impersonal narrative voice but within the minds of the characters, linking the passage of time with the processes of memory. But, unlike the earlier novels in which images recur for similar reasons, here the minds of the characters seem impoverished. The images that haunt them, whether an inkstained, walrus-shaped penwiper or 'the song Pippy used to sing as she wiped your ears with a piece of slimy flannel' (pp. 75, 182), are trivial or unpleasant.

[1] *AWD*, 3 November 1936, p. 270.
[2] At one point she thought of calling the novel *The Caravan* (*AWD*, 11 January 1935, p. 237).

The grim beginning – a masterly piece of naturalistic writing – employs a collection of images which encapsulate the oppressiveness of Victorian family life. The most striking of these are the ugliest: the man exposing himself to Rose on the street corner, his face returning in her dream, 'bubbling in and out, grey, white, purplish and pock-marked' (p. 34), Colonel Pargiter's deformed hand fumbling at his mistress's neck or fumbling for coins in his pocket, and Mrs Pargiter on her deathbed, 'the skin [...] stained with brown patches [. . .] soft, decayed but everlasting' (pp. 19, 20). This emphasis on the physically repulsive, which is unprecedented in the novels, continues throughout; at the final party Milly is described in the same terms as the dying Mrs Pargiter (p. 302). But quieter images in the first section have as strong and lasting an effect. In Abercorn Terrace we are inside one of the houses into which Katharine Hilbery glanced

> with curtains on the inside which must, she thought, since you could only see a looking glass gleaming above a sideboard on which a dish of apples was set, keep the room inside very dark.[1]

Abercorn Terrace, heavy with furniture, seems as though it will last for ever, like the dying mother. For Crosby there is a grandeur in its air of permanence:

> Knives and forks rayed out round the table. The whole room, with its carved chairs, oil paintings, the two daggers on the mantlepiece, and the handsome sideboard – all the solid objects that Crosby dusted and polished every day – looked at its best in the evening. Meat-smelling and serge-curtained by day, it looked lit up, semi-transparent in the evening. And they were a handsome family, she thought [. . .] (p. 30)

The house has the same suffocating solidity as Wimpole Street in *Flush*:

> The Barretts never left London. Mr Barrett, the seven brothers, the two sisters, the butler, Wilson and the maids, Catiline, Folly, Miss Barrett and Flush all went on living at 50 Wimpole Street, eating in the dining-room, sleeping in the

[1] *Night and Day*, p. 291.

bedrooms, smoking in the study, cooking in the kitchen, carrying hot-water cans and emptying the slops from January to
December. The chair-covers became slightly soiled; the carpets
slightly worn; coal dust, mud, soot, fog, vapours of cigar smoke
and wine and meat accumulated in crevices, in cracks, in
fabrics, on the tops of picture-frames, in the scrolls of carvings.[1]

The Pargiter children are similarly imprisoned by 'solid objects',
'the jugs, the tumblers, the covered bowls' of the sick room (p. 16),
the 'heavy frame' of the picture and the rim of the dog's bowl
(p. 36) which Eleanor sees on her way down from the nursery, the
kettle which always takes so long to boil, the 'ink-corroded walrus'
at which Eleanor stares while she is doing the house-keeping
accounts:

> That solid object might survive them all [. . .] It was part of
> other things – her mother for example . . . She drew on her
> blotting-paper; a dot with strokes raying out round it. (pp. 74–
> 75)

The image from *Night and Day* suggests Eleanor's intuition of a
possible alternative to the Victorian world of 'solid objects' – the
housekeeping accounts and the family furniture. But although at
the end of her life she feels that she has grown up into a more
'quiet, spacious world', it is clear that no simple escape from materialism can be made. The Pargiter children who do leave Abercorn
Terrace do not, like Elizabeth Barrett, vanish into romantic,
colourful Italy. *Flush* presents a simplified alternative, a little like
Forster's opposition of Sawston and Monteriano in *Where Angels
Fear to Tread* (1905). But in *The Years* escape from the Victorian
home does not mean escape from solid objects. They are found again
in the satirical descriptions of twentieth-century public life, as
seen through unsympathetic eyes. The men in the Law Courts 'all
looked like pictures [. . .] like eighteenth-century portraits hung
upon a wall' (p. 89). Trafalgar Square consists of 'A man [. . .]
joined to a pillar; a lion [. . .] joined to a man; they seemed
stilled, connected, as though they would never move again (p. 92).

[1] *Flush* (1933), p. 58.

The statues at Temple Bar are 'as ridiculous as usual – something between a serpent and a fowl' (p. 189). The boss of the newspaper office is 'the mahogany man, the clean-shaven, rosy-gilled, mutton-fed man' (p. 275), and the 'fat man brandishing his arm at Speaker's Corner' (p. 195) is for ever saying 'I, I, I', 'like a vulture's beak pecking, or a vacuum-cleaner sucking, or a telephone bell ringing' (p. 290). The aggression, humbug, self-aggrandizement and self-deception which the Pargiter children suffered from in their father's home are more widely and more dangerously practised in the public, male-dominated, warmongering world of the twentieth century. But this argument is not stated, only contained within impressionistic, fictional terms. The analogy between paternalism and fascism is drawn undisguisedly in *Three Guineas* (1938), which is valuable if only as a non-fictional appendix to *The Years*. Virginia Woolf herself thought of them as 'one book'.[1]

The relationship between the two works is exemplified by their use of Sophocles' *Antigone*. In *Three Guineas* the *Antigone* is described as the best literary analysis of the corrupting 'effect of power and wealth upon the soul'.[2] Creon is compared to Hitler or Mussolini. Antigone's line (quoted by Edward Pargiter in *The Years*) – ''Tis not my nature to join in hating, but in loving' – is said in *Three Guineas* to be 'worth all the sermons of all the archbishops',[3] and her elevation of personal judgement over the laws of the city is used as an illustration of the moral obligation on women to retain, on entering the predominantly masculine professional world, the peace-loving rational attitudes they have acquired from 'poverty, chastity, derision, and freedom from unreal loyalties'. In *The Years*, Sara, as a young girl, recounts to herself the story of the *Antigone*, and identifies with the heroine:

> The man in the loincloth gave three sharp taps with his mallet on the brick. She was buried alive. (p. 111)

The 'three sharp taps' echo through the novel; they have already been heard at Mrs Pargiter's funeral:

> Earth dropped on the coffin; three pebbles fell on the hard shiny surface; and as they dropped she [Delia] was possessed

[1] *AWD*, 3 June 1938, p. 295.   [2] *Three Guineas* (1938), p. 148.
[3] Ibid.

by the sense of something everlasting; of life mixing with death; of death becoming life. (p. 72)

Mrs Pargiter has, like Antigone, been the victim of a masculine world; endlessly bearing children, she has been exploited and deceived by the Colonel. Her children, too, feel as though they have been buried alive; their mother's death is the first possibility of escape for them. But 'the three sharp taps' recur in the outside world. Kitty Lasswade (who has been identified with Antigone by Edward Pargiter) goes from a feminist meeting to a performance of Siegfried:

> The dwarf was hammering at the sword. Hammer, hammer, hammer, he went with little short, sharp strokes. (p. 148)

The moment is echoed in the scene which follows between Sara and Maggie. They talk of the afternoon's meeting; outside a drunken man is being thrown out of a pub. Sara is filled with disgust:

> 'In time to come,' she said, [. . .] 'people, looking into this room – this cave, this little antre, scooped out of mud and dung, will [. . .] say "Pah! They stink!"' (p. 153)

Then they hear Upcher, the drunkard, knocking to be let in:

> The hammering stopped. Then it began again – hammer, hammer, hammer. (p. 154)

Siegfried, the drunken man and the hammer strokes on Antigone's coffin contribute to the same idea. Sara's image of cave-dwellers (influenced by Plato's *Republic* as well as by Sophocles) also recurs, in Eleanor's question during the air raid: 'When shall we live adventurously, wholly, not like cripples in a cave?' (p. 239).

That these images should never harden into an explicit discussion of the links between paternalism, professionalism and patriotism is a lesson learned from the *Antigone* itself. Though we may try (Virginia Woolf says in *Three Guineas*) to identify the heroine with Mrs Pankhurst, the play will not let itself be thus reduced:

When the curtain falls we sympathize, it may be noted, even with Creon himself. This result, to the propagandist undesirable, would seem to be due to the fact that Sophocles (even in a translation) uses freely all the faculties that can be possessed by a writer; and suggests, therefore, that if we use art to propagate political opinions, we must force the artist to clip and cabin his gift to do us a cheap and passing service.[1]

Virginia Woolf here propagates her opinion that fiction should have no truck with opinions or propaganda. The form and content of *The Years* celebrate this conviction; but the celebration is not an altogether triumphant one. Her reliance upon images to do the work of argument has led to the criticism that 'a deeply felt . . . indictment of an historical social order' is 'based, quite incongruously, upon fragmentary and trivial details'.[2] Though this complaint does not allow for Virginia Woolf's belief that the technique of the book had to *be* its argument, the 'fragmentary and trivial details' being a necessary form for her indictment of society, it does nevertheless point to the unease we feel at reading a political and historical novel which continually shies away from the factual.

> 'A meeting?' Maggie murmured. 'Where?'
> 'In a room,' Sara answered. 'A pale greenish light. A woman hanging clothes on a line in the back garden; and someone went by rattling a stick on the railings.'
> 'I see,' said Maggie. She stitched on quietly.
> 'I said to myself,' Sara resumed, 'whose heads are those . . .' she paused.
> 'A meeting,' Maggie interrupted her. 'What for? What about?'
> 'There were pigeons cooing,' Sara went on. 'Take two coos, Taffy. Take two coos . . . Tak . . . And then a wing darkened the air, and in came Kitty clothed in starlight; and sat on a chair.' (pp. 151–2)

It is in accordance with the novel's aesthetic and ethical principles,

[1] *Three Guineas*, p. 302, note 39.
[2] A. D. Moody, *Virginia Woolf* (Edinburgh and London, Oliver and Boyd, 1963), p. 73.

as well as with Sara's character, that she should reply thus; but the reader may well want to reiterate Maggie's questions. The characters' reluctance to state anything other than impressions becomes, at length, frustrating. All are tongue-tied.

> 'I know,' she said guiltily. 'I haven't been to Papa lately. But then there's always something – ' She hesitated.
> 'Naturally,' said Mrs Malone, 'with a man in your father's position . . .' Kitty sat silent. They both sat silent. (p. 67)

> 'And now,' she said, leaning back comfortably, 'tell me all your news.'
> The Colonel, too, lay back in his chair. He pondered for a moment. What was his news? Nothing occurred to him on the spur of the moment. [. . .] While he hesitated, she began. (p. 99)

> Eleanor turned. The others were still arguing.
> 'You'll agree with me one of these days,' Martin was saying.
> 'Never! Never!' said Kitty, slapping her gloves on the table. She looked very handsome [. . .]
> 'Why didn't you speak, Nell?' she said, turning on her.
> 'Because –' Eleanor began, 'I don't know, she added, rather feebly. (pp. 144–5)

> 'My life . . .' she said aloud, but half to herself.
> 'Yes?' said Sara, looking up.
> Eleanor stopped. She had forgotten her. But there was somebody listening. Then she must put her thoughts into order; then she must find words. But no, she thought, I can't find words; I can't tell anybody. (p. 295)

Their difficulty (culminating in Nicholas's repeatedly incompleted speech at the final party) in answering questions, finishing sentences, stating beliefs or opinions or giving information, manifests the unsatisfactory conditions of social intercourse. This realistic insistence on the characters' ineffectuality gives the novel a negative, uncertain quality, arising in part from there not being very much to set against the tentative, unsatisfactory social relationships. There are a few powerful moments of stillness or solitude, such as Kitty's Orlando-like communion with the country, and there is an idea of harmony and enfranchisement in the 'Present Day' party scene, particularly in Eleanor's consciousness. But the main emphasis is on difficulty rather than on achievement, on unease rather than on contentment. The lack of balance is made more noticeable by the very length of the book.[1] Accumulated inconclusiveness has a wearisome effect. Individually, however, there are moving moments of pathos and uncertainty, as here in the air-raid scene, where the wistful, romantic, tentative idealism has a markedly Chekhovian tone:

> 'About the new world . . .' she said aloud. 'D'you think we're going to improve?' she asked.
>
> 'Yes, yes,' he said, nodding his head.
>
> He spoke quietly as if he did not wish to rouse Renny who was reading, or Maggie who was darning, or Sara who was lying back in her chair half asleep. They seemed to be talking, privately, together.
>
> 'But how . . .' she began, '. . . how can we improve our-selves . . . live more . . .' – she dropped her voice as if she were afraid of waking sleepers – '. . . live more naturally . . . better . . . How can we?'
>
> 'It is only a question,' he said – he stopped. He drew himself closer to her – 'of learning. The soul . . .' Again he stopped.
>
> 'Yes – the soul?' she prompted him.
>
> 'The soul – the whole being,' he explained. He hollowed his hand as if to enclose a circle. 'It wishes to expand; to adventure; to form – new combinations?' (p. 238)

> MASHA: Isn't there some meaning?
>
> TOOZENBACH: Meaning? . . . Look out there, it's snowing. What's the meaning of that?' (*A pause.*)

[1] Virginia Woolf expresses repeated concern in the diary about the novel's 'immense length' (*AWD*, 2 August 1934, p. 221); her revisions are an agonizing process of 'perpetual compressing' (*AWD*, 4 March 1936, p. 266), and when the proofs are at last corrected, after great suffering and uncertainty, her dominant feeling is that she will 'never write a long book' again (*AWD*, 10 November 1936, p. 273).

MASHA: I think a human being has got to have some
          faith, or at least he's got to seek faith. Other-
          wise his life will be empty, empty ... How
          can you live and not know why the cranes
          fly, why the stars shine in the sky! You must
          either know why you live, or else ... nothing
          matters ... everything's just wild grass ...
          (*A pause.*)[1]

TROFIMOV: I can see happiness, Ania, I can see it
          coming ...
ANIA: (*pensively*): The moon's coming up.
          (*YEPIHODOV can be heard playing his guitar,
          the same melancholy tune as before. The moon
          rises. Somewhere in the vicinity of the poplars
          VARIA is looking for ANIA and calling:
          'Ania! Where are you?'*)
TROFIMOV: Yes, the moon is rising. (*A pause.*) There it
          is – happiness – it's coming nearer and nearer,
          I seem to hear its footsteps. And if we don't
          see it, if we don't know when it comes, what
          does it matter? Other people will see it!'[2]

The resemblance to Chekhov is more than merely atmospheric.
The characters in *The Years* are struggling towards some concept
of general happiness, however remote. Their language is uncertain
because they have no secure basis of faith. It is the common predicament of an unsettled generation. Elizaveta Fen, in her introduction to her translation of Chekhov's plays, points out

> the affinity between the disenchanted Russian of 1880–1900
> and the frustrated Englishman of 1919–1939. The two
> periods – unhappy interludes between wars and revolutions –
> are stamped with spiritual discouragement: the men and
> women who lived through them are haunted by the same emo-
> tions and thoughts.[3]

---

[1] *Three Sisters* (1901), *Plays of Anton Chekhov*, translated Elizaveta Fen (Harmondsworth, Penguin, 1959), p. 282.
[2] *The Cherry Orchard* (1904), ibid. p. 369.   [3] Ibid. p. 9.

And Virginia Woolf in her essay 'The Russian Point of View' quotes Chekhov in explanation of the peculiar and unexpected emphases she finds in his stories:

> '... such a conversation as this between us,' he says, 'would have been unthinkable for our parents. At night they did not talk, but slept sound; we, our generation, sleep badly, are restless, but talk a great deal, and are always trying to settle whether we are right or not.'[1]

Chekhov's stories and plays sprang from 'that restless sleep, that incessant talking'; but his main interest is not, she says, really in society nor in psychology:

> Is it that he is primarily interested not in the soul's relation with other souls, but with the soul's relation to health – with the soul's relation to goodness? [...] The soul is ill; the soul is cured; the soul is not cured. These are the emphatic points in his stories.[2]

Chekhov, she suggests, expresses the spiritual predicament of his generation in terms verging on the abstract. There is a close analogy with *The Years*, where the younger generations struggle to heal or liberate their souls in a social environment conducive neither to faith nor to happiness. Though there are considerable numbers of what she refers to as 'upper-air scenes',[3] in which the social environment of the characters is portrayed, the true emphasis of the novel is, as in Chekhov, more abstract; it is on 'the soul's relation to goodness'.

But the soul and society cannot be simply divided. The search for goodness necessitates the search for a *modus vivendi* with other people, not in solitude. The enemy to goodness, both in the Victorian home and in the public world, is the voice of egotism that says 'I, I, I'. Eleanor, Sara and Nicholas, Martin, Maggie and Renny, Martin, Norris and Peggy, all want to combat that

---

[1] 'The Russian Point of View' (*CE* I, p. 241), published in *The Common Reader* (London, Hogarth Press, 1925).

[2] Ibid.

[3] *AWD*, 16 October 1935, p. 258; 21 November 1935, p. 259.

enemy, but have no ready-made defences. Possibly the only alternative to the domineering 'I' is 'the world without a self', contemplated by many of Virginia Woolf's narrators from the speaker in 'The Mark on the Wall' to Bernard in *The Waves*. The characters in *The Years* wistfully ask themselves: 'What would the world be [. . .] – he was still thinking of the fat man brandishing his arm – without 'I' in it?' (p. 195). But, as in *The Waves*, an entire loss of identity – the ultimate simplification – is rejected because it is feeble. It is not enough for the soul to merge with the impersonal world, be lost, and be at peace. The fact that tyranny and injustice exist implies a need for the personality to express itself as a positive part of society. But such exercise need not be the aggressive 'quack, quack!'[1] of opinion or tyranny. The soul need not deceive itself or impose its will, but should mix with others without losing its own identity, giving and receiving freely as part of society. Thus Eleanor's chance reading of Dante's lines

> For by so many the more there are who say 'ours'
> So much the more of good doth each possess. (p. 171)

is at the philosophical centre of the book. 'Ours' is the alternative to 'I': egotism is combated, not with the loss of self, but with the interdependence of souls. The quotation from Dante embodies the political belief in *The Years* that the activity of sharing increases the worth – and indeed the amount – of what is shared. The novel's main drawback is that this, its central idea, is not enacted; what is enacted is the *difficulty* of saying 'ours' instead of 'I'. But the idea does grow in strength and urgency towards the end of the book, and dominates the last section.

'Present Day' is not in the least idyllic. The sense of fragmentation and inadequacy in social relationships persists. The encounters before the party are unsatisfactory; North eats a squalid meal with Sara and is puzzled by her emotions and her way of life; Peggy is irritated by Eleanor and cannot understand her past. Running through the scenes like an erratic tune are the rival claims of society and solitude. North, that afternoon, has heard Eleanor's friends having 'Serious talk on abstract subjects'. 'Was solitude good; was

---

[1] *Quack, Quack!* is the title of Leonard Woolf's attack on the political and intellectual barbarisms of the 1930s (London, Hogarth Press, 1935).

society bad?' (p. 249). At Sara's, he picks up a book, but it is too dark to read; instead he quotes Marvell by heart:

> Society is all but rude –
> To this delicious solitude. (p. 272)

The party indeed seems to show that solitude is the only good. The generations do not understand each other, and no one can describe or sum up their own lives and memories to anyone else. Nicholas will not finish his speech of thanks: 'This is not a time for making speeches' (p. 337). When the caretaker's children come in to eat cake, they will say nothing – 'The younger generation [. . .] don't mean to speak' (p. 344) – but instead burst into a discordant, unintelligible song:

> Etho passo tanno hai,
> Fai donk to tu do,
> Mai to, kai to, lai to see
> Toh dom to tuh do –

That was what it sounded like. Not a word was recognizable. The distorted sounds rose and sank as if they followed a tune. They stopped. (p. 345)

The moment is at once grotesque and sinister, emphasizing to the point of parody the lack of kinship between the isolated members of the family. The assumption made by Molly and Hugh Gibbs of a family bond is ridiculous and oppressive. Familial emotions seem only to be conducive to saying 'I' rather than 'ours', as North feels with Maggie:

> He looked down at her hands. They were strong hands; fine hands; but if it were a question, he thought, of watching the fingers curl slightly, of 'my' children, of 'my' possessions, it would be one rip down the belly; or teeth in the soft fur of the throat. We cannot help each other, he thought, we are all deformed. (p. 305)

The family intercourse of the last section seems to reiterate the novel's earlier despondency about social relationships. And the frail alternative to despondency that was found in the lines from

Dante is now reconsidered in ironic terms by North's sister Peggy, a doctor, whose bitterness at the suffering that surrounds her leads her to think of 'sharing' in terms of pain, not of good:

> Pleasure is increased by sharing it. Does the same hold good of pain? she mused. Is that the reason why we all talk so much of ill-health — because sharing things lessens things? Give pain, give pleasure an outer body, and by increasing the surface diminish them . . . But the thought slipped. He was off telling his old stories [. . .]
> How many people, she wondered, listen? This 'sharing', then, is a bit of a farce. (p. 283)

Peggy, deciding that the sharing of suffering in 'a world bursting with misery' is the only possible kind of sharing, longs for the peace that comes from not thinking: 'she would force her mind to become a blank' (p. 312). But a moment later she is drawn back from 'the world without a self' through laughter. The others have made a cartoon of society from a game of pictorial consequences:

> On top there was a woman's head like Queen Alexandra, with a fuzz of little curls; then a bird's neck; the body of a tiger; and stout elephant's legs dressed in child's drawers completed the picture. (p. 313)

The absurdity of this is different in kind to the absurdity of the children's song. The latter is a mystery, something unmanageable; it suggests that the youngest generation at the party (of a different class from the Pargiters) are 'moving about in words not realized'; they hold some secret and untranslatable clue to the future. The cartoon is, by contrast, reassuring. It takes the recognizable emblems of 'pride, pomp, and circumstance' and renders them powerless through a liberating ridicule, which is activated and enjoyed by a group. This sharing process is one of the important antidotes to the continuing sense of suffering and frustration found in the last section. The others are provided by Eleanor and by North.

Eleanor is at times portrayed from the outside, as an endearingly optimistic old lady like Mrs Swithin, and at times internally, as she tries to order her memories into a coherent life. From both vantage points she expresses a tentative idea of happiness drawn from suffering and confusion themselves. If the solid objects to which she was in bondage for most of her life have vanished, then there has been some progress and there will be more, however much the present generation feels at a loss. That very sense of bafflement implies hope.

> She shut her hands on the coins she was holding, and again she was suffused with a feeling of happiness. Was it because this had survived – this keen sensation (she was waking up). and the other thing, the solid object – she saw an ink-corroded walrus – had vanished? She opened her eyes wide. Here she was; alive; in this room, with living people. She saw all the heads in a circle [. . .]
> There must be another life, she thought, sinking back into her chair, exasperated. Not in dreams; but here and now, in this room, with living people [. . .] This is too short, too broken. We know nothing, even about ourselves. We're only just beginning, she thought, to understand, here and there [...]
> She held her hands hollowed; she felt that she wanted to enclose the present moment; to make it stay; to fill it fuller and fuller, with the past, the present and the future, until it shone, whole, bright, deep with understanding. (pp. 342–4)

Eleanor's meliorism is of the haziest, but it is emphatically concerned with an improvement in mutual, not merely individual, experience, and is thus aptly summed up by the image of the two people getting out of a taxi.

These figures are young, and it is a younger member of the Pargiter family who formulates more coherently Eleanor's hopes for 'another life'. True to the shape of the novel, North is a minor character, but his thoughts at the party provide us with the conclusive summing up of the morality of *The Years*:

> For them it's all right, he thought; they've had their day: but not for him, not for his generation. For him a life modelled on the jet (he was watching the bubbles rise), on the spring, of the hard leaping fountain; another life; a different life. Not halls and reverberating megaphones; not marching in step after leaders, in

herds, groups, societies, caparisoned. No; to begin inwardly, and let the devil take the outer form. [. . .] Not black shirts, green shirts, red shirts – always posing in the public eye; that's all poppycock. Why not down barriers and simplify? But a world, he thought, that was all one jelly, one mass, would be a rice pudding world, a white counterpane world. To keep the emblems and tokens of North Pargiter [. . .] but at the same time spread out, make a new ripple in human consciousness, be the bubble and the stream, the stream and the bubble – myself and the world together – he raised his glass. [. . .] But how can I, he thought [. . .] unless I know what's solid, what's true; in my life, in other people's lives? (pp. 329–30)

The uncertain, inconclusive peroration is characteristic, but deceptive. Ineffectuality is in fact rejected in the passage, and in the novel. Being passive, giving in, are as much indicted as the megaphones and black shirts of the aggressors. Another life must be forged from the moral sense that social interdependence, based on understanding, is the only means to right action. The conclusion that is here implied is more explicitly set out in the conclusion of *Three Guineas*, where the voice of the narrator is supported by a diversity of corroborating voices, Coleridge, Rousseau, Whitman and George Sand, all speaking on behalf of 'sharing':

All existences are interdependent, and any human being who was to present his own in isolation, without linking it with that of his fellow creatures, would only be presenting a riddle in need of solving. His individual existence, by itself, has no significance or importance whatsoever. It only takes on some kind of meaning by becoming a fragment of life in general, by merging with the individuality of all of us, and it is only by this means that it becomes a part of history.[1]

[1] George Sand, *Histoire de ma vie* (my translation), quoted *Three Guineas*, pp. 328–9, note 49.

9

Between the Acts

1941

I N *Between the Acts* Virginia Woolf returns to the methods which
suit her. By contrast with *The Years*, her last novel is lyrical,
carefully patterned and highly controlled. But its range, paradoxically, is broader. This time the family in its relation to society
is made part of the history of all England: a history which, 'on a
June day in 1939', may be without a future. Although *Between
the Acts* is in the tradition of the kind of English novel, from
Mansfield Park to *Howards End*, which has a firm sense of English
locality, the members of a family as its main protagonists, and a
humorous tone used for a serious moral purpose, it is an extremely
experimental work. Although it has the air of a delicate social
comedy, it is more disturbing and more inclusive than that description implies.

The novel opens out in a series of concentric rings, englobing
Pointz Hall at its centre. The house, lying in its hollow, contains
the lives of three generations: Old Bartholemew Oliver and his
widowed sister Lucy Swithin; Bart's son Giles and Giles's wife,
Isa; and their two children. On the day of the novel there are two
self-invited visitors to the house, Mrs Manresa, the brash, sed-
uctive 'child of nature', who has in tow an 'unknown young man',
William Dodge, nervous, civilized and repressed. They act as
catalysts to the emotions of the family. Just outside, on the terrace,
is Miss La Trobe's world of the pageant, which involves as actors
and audience the 'gentles and simples' of the village and of surroun-
ding villages. Pointz Hall is only thirty-five miles from the sea;

beyond that lies a continent on the brink of war. Below all social and national boundaries lies the earth, frequently imagined by Mrs Swithin as it was in its inchoate state, before the coming of language or divisions, before, even, the channelling off of England from the continent. The sense of a broadening radius is intensified by contrasts. Giles is tortured by the thought of Europe, 'bristling with guns, poised with planes' (p. 42), while his son George can dwindle the radius of his own world to a flower blazing in the roots of a tree. Local gossip about Miss La Trobe's Russian blood and Mrs Manresa's Tasmanian birth stretch the radius to 'foreign parts'; at the same time Mrs Sands the cook, who 'had never in all her fifty years been over the hill, nor wanted to' (p. 26), contracts it.

The setting of *Between the Acts* reflects the radius of Virginia Woolf's life in the years in which she wrote the novel and completed her biography of Roger Fry. From late 1938 to 1941, because of the war, Leonard and Virginia spent more and more time at Monk's House, living there permanently from October 1939. The last sixty pages of *A Writer's Diary* (and the last chapter of Quentin Bell's biography) show how closely *Between the Acts* (meant to reflect 'the present state of my mind'[1]) was evolved from the two major elements of Virginia Woolf's last years: country life and the war. Though the first was agreeable, at times even 'a long trance of pleasure',[2] the threat and then the actuality of the second dominated it. The stability and pleasant pettiness of the one, the monstrous ruination of the other, provided an ironic, even nonsensical, contrast, brought out both in the diary and the novel:

> Ding dong bell . . . ding dong – why did we settle in a village? And how deliberately we are digging ourselves in! And at any moment the guns may go off and explode us.[3]

At any moment guns could rake that land into furrows. (p. 42)

The feeling of 'pressure, danger, horror'[4] grows in her towards the middle of 1940. She cannot conceive of a future:

[1] *AWD*, 26 April 1938, p. 290. [2] *AWD*, 29 March 1940, p. 330.
[3] *AWD*, 28 August 1938, p. 301. [4] *AWD*, 31 August 1940, p. 345.

We pour to the edge of a precipice . . . and then? I can't conceive that there will be a 27th June 1941.[1]

'The doom of sudden death hanging over us,' he said. (p.82)

The idea of personal and national destruction is linked to her sense as a writer that her audience is being destroyed. The civilization she writes for is ceasing to exist: 'No audience. No echo. That's part of one's death.'[2] The feeling lies behind Miss La Trobe's struggle to master her audience.

But, in the second half of 1940, while *Between the Acts* was being completed, and before the last recurrence of her mental illness in March 1941, Virginia Woolf had what Bell calls 'an euphoric interval'.[3] This sense of pleasure also finds its way into the novel.

A day like this is almost too – I won't say happy: but amenable. The tune varies, from one nice melody to another. All is played (today) in such a theatre. Hills and fields; I can't stop looking; October blooms; brown plough; and the fading and freshening of the marsh [. . .] And one thing's 'pleasant' after another: breakfast, writing, walking, tea, bowls, reading, sweets, bed [. . .] Queer the contraction of life to the village radius.[4]

The view repeated in its own way what the tune was saying. The sun was sinking; the colours were merging; and the view was saying how after toil men rest from their labours; how coolness comes; reason prevails; and having unharnessed the team from the plough, neighbours dig in cottage gardens and lean over cottage gates. (pp. 95–6)

Though *A Writer's Diary* always provides an extremely interesting selfconscious analysis of the writing of each novel, never before has the material and style of the diary been so markedly analogous to the 'work in progress'. Though plurality rather than

[1] *AWD*, 27 June (misdated 22 June) 1940, p. 337.
[2] *AWD*, 9 June 1940, p. 336.
[3] Bell II, p. 221.
[4] *AWD*, 12 October 1940, pp. 354–5.

individuality (" "I" rejected: "We" substituted'[1]) is the keynote of *Between the Acts*, the book is nevertheless very close to Virginia Woolf's own life in her last years.

The new relationship between the diary and *Between the Acts* suggests that the novel is of a different sort from its predecessors. And, though obvious comparisons can be made with the episodic structure of *Jacob's Room*, the use of a single day in *Mrs Dalloway*, the pageant of English history in *Orlando*, and the relationship between a family group and an artist in *To the Lighthouse*, *Between the Acts* is a new departure, in being more concerned with language, history and place than with individuals. It is unprecedented, particularly, in its use of speech.

The characters in Virginia Woolf's novels, with the exception of *The Waves*, speak a language which hovers between the naturalistic and the symbolic. Terence in the jungle with Rachel repeating 'We're so late – so late – so horribly late', or Andrew Ramsay, 'coming up from the beach' saying 'It's almost too dark to see', use phrases which are colloquial and at the same time resonant with suggested, half-felt meanings. It is usually unclear whether the characters are aware of the significance that irradiates their words, or whether they are even speaking out loud. Such ambiguity allows for the fluid interplay between internal and external states which is relinquished in *The Waves* in favour of a formalization of selfconsciousness. The characters in *The Waves*, however colloquial their 'speech' may be at times, are in full possession of the symbolic value of their statements. One is not tempted to read their speeches naturalistically; it is clear that the verb 'said' is a formula which does not indicate actual speech.

In reaction against that linguistic restriction to significant, inner experience, *The Years* provides colloquial speech in a realistic context. As in the novels preceding *The Waves*, the speech frequently suggests a meaning beyond the words. But the methods whereby this is achieved are now more diffuse, as befits a novel which deals with fragmentation and frustration. There is not the economy of dialogue that there was in *To the Lighthouse*. People talk a great deal, but their conversations are tangential and random,

[1] *AWD*, 26 April 1938, p. 289.

they speak at cross-purposes or in unfinished sentences. Their language is thin and conventional, except for Sara, who speaks in a rambling, poetic style as an indication of how different she is from the others and how much at odds with the real world.

Like *The Years*, *Between the Acts* incorporates a longing for a more lyrical and impersonal existence than that provided by the chaotic and destructive reality of the thirties. But the scrappiness of modern life is now embodied in a condensed, unnaturalistic narrative which largely consists of speech. All the characters, but particularly Isa, speak a language which in *The Years* was restricted to Sara, the misfit. Their speech fuses the lyrical and the colloquial; every word and phrase seems to ring with significance. Because the burden of meaning is almost entirely carried by speech – either that of individuals, or of the characters in the play, or of the 'voices' of the audience – *Between the Acts* comes to be a book *about* speech, considering the history of a people as created and sustained by the spoken word, and adducing its present decay through the state of language. But, side by side with the emphasis on speech, words and names, a suggestion is found which is summed up by Bartholemew's question: 'Thoughts without words, [...] Can that be?' (p. 43). As alternatives to the domination of speech, the book enters into domains of speechlessness – fishponds and faith – which undermine the emphasis of the novel's last words, 'They spoke.'

The language of English speech has evolved, through history, from primeval incoherence, like the fishpond in the grounds of Pointz Hall, created where 'water, for hundreds of years, had silted down into the hollow, and lay there four or five feet deep over a black cushion of mud' (p. 35). People are like the fish, silent and uncaught below the surface, in the speechless areas of the personality, but occasionally rising to the surface for bait. At the surface they must communicate; so relationships are summed up by images of fishing (pp. 19, 38), and Isa's bondage to the routine of domesticity, by her ringing up to order the fish.

In the whole structure of the book, language and speech seem to be patterned in ever-widening circles over the surface of silence. The most private, inner speech, nearest to the heart of silence, is Isa's poetry, which, as Daiches points out, provides 'in part, the probability for the lyrical mood of the book'.[1] Isa's poems are escapist in the same vein as Katharine Hilbery's fantasy life and Rhoda's imaginary journeys. They yearn towards another world, of moors and moonlight, where there will be freedom and truth: 'To fly away, from night and day, and issue where – no partings are – but eye meets eye' (p. 62). As the book progresses, Isa's longing for escape becomes increasingly desperate. Her earlier need for water becomes a desire for drowning (pp. 75–6); she imagines herself as a donkey burdened by the past, ordered to go on 'till your heels blister and your hoofs crack' (p. 109). But her world of escape from this bondage itself becomes a place of terror:

> To issue where? In some harvestless dim field where no evening lets fall her mantle; nor sun rises. All's equal there. Unblowing, ungrowing are the roses there. Change is not; nor the mutable and lovable; nor greetings nor partings. (p. 109)

Heaven is changeless, we are told elsewhere in the novel (p. 121). But for the modern consciousness there is nothing to choose between heaven and hell. Isa's longing for a world without change, society or the complications of language seems a dreary, passive form of retreat from the harsh world. Her lyricism is joyless as well as incommunicable. It is symptomatic of the inhibitions and frustrations of the characters that Isa 'writes her poetry in a book bound like an account book lest Giles might suspect' (p. 39), and that she is embarrassed at being overheard by William Dodge. But her sense of isolation is ironic; she is not as alone as she thinks. Her speech is linked with that of the other characters, as well as with the language of the play. Giles, William, Bartholemew, even Cobbet of Cobbs Corner, also voice their inward thoughts in scraps of rhyme. And their conversations, though on such apparently trivial subjects as the weather, the distance of Pointz Hall from the sea, or the two pictures on the dining-room walls, are lyrical and resonant, partly because of a stong sense of rhythm which turns conversations into recurring tunes, partly because of the emphasis given to simple phrases:

---

[1] David Daiches, *Virginia Woolf* (London, Nicholson and Watson, Editions Poetry, 1945), p. 116.

'Are we really,' she said, turning round, 'a hundred miles from the sea?'

'Thirty-five only,' her father-in-law said, as if he had whipped a tape measure from his pocket and measured it exactly.

'It seems more,' said Isa. 'It seems from the terrace as if the land went on for ever and ever.'

'Once there was no sea,' said Mrs Swithin. 'No sea at all between us and the continent.' (p. 25)

At times this lyrical, significant tone is remarked on as though it is consciously created by the speakers.

'The nursery,' said Mrs Swithin.
Words raised themselves and became symbolical. 'The cradle of our race,' she seemed to say. (p. 54)

As Mrs Swithin is aware, everyday speech is significant, even if it dwells on insignificant topics, because it is silted up with the detritus of the past. English people have in common an inherited language of literature and folklore which is, consciously or unconsciously, always on their lips. Old Bart remarks that 'as a race' we do not have the same intimate, unconscious familiarity with our painters as with our poets. His point is ironically illustrated by a series of incompetent misquotations from Shakespeare and Keats by Mrs Manresa, Isa and William. Scraps and fragments are all that come to mind. But there is still truth in Mrs Swithin's reference to the books: 'Here are the poets from whom we descend by way of the mind' (p. 52). Scrappily though the modern English mind may remember, it nevertheless contains something of a literary heritage. Bart, remembering his mother's gift of a Byron, actualizes his inheritance with two quotations. Even Giles, the most unliterary of men, has bits of *Lear* and Cowper in his mind and everyone in the village audience has a rough idea of Miss La Trobe's literary models. English people have a common consciousness which is partly made up of their literary history and partly of the folk traditions which imbue English speech with proverbs, catchphrases, nursery jingles, old tales and legends. The mother of Bart and Lucy (almost the personification of Old England) gave

Byron to her son; to her daughter, old sayings and a consciousness of English words, expressed in her two injunctions: 'Don't stand gaping, Lucy, or the wind'll change' (p. 11) and 'Never play on people's names' (p. 28). Son and daughter argue for facts against faith. Mrs Swithin asks for the origin of 'Touch wood'; Bart replies 'Superstition' (p. 22). He will not hear her when she asks the name of the man who, 'hearing the waves in the middle of the night', 'saddled a horse and rode to the sea' (p. 24), though he nods in approval when she comes up with a 'fact' about lobsters. But though they are irreconcilable on the question of faith, they share a verbal heritage. Though Bart is scathing about the servants' need for a ghost story, and teases Mrs Manresa for rhyming over her cherry stones, it is he who repeats the old stories about the 'great eighteenth-century winter' (p. 10) at Pointz Hall, and who alludes to the fable of 'the donkey who couldn't choose between hay and turnips and so starved' (p. 46). The folk language is general; it may not necessarily be Mrs Swithin who is heard wondering in the audience 'What's the origin [. . .] of the expression "with a flea in his ear"?' (p. 88). Isa incorporates folk legends and nursery rhymes into her stories, Giles and Mrs Manresa find a point of verbal contact in 'Pop goes the Weasel' (p. 100). Folk traditions characterize the smallest details of rural life: 'There was another name in the village for nettle-rash' (p. 49).

But this folk language is in decay. No one can remember whole quotations, the origins of phrases or the characters in the old stories. Through repetition, the old rhymes have become senseless or irritating. It is only Mrs Swithin who tries to sanctify them with understanding, chanting 'an old child's nursery rhyme to help a child' (p. 54). As in *The Waste Land*, the fragmentation of modern consciousness is very largely conveyed by the use of these residual scraps (like the scraps of tunes in *The Years*) from a more dignified and literary past. The play itself incorporates this decay into its subject matter. It is a medley of literary and folk allusions, providing the audience with a parody of English literary history. Incorporated in its crude pastiche are scraps of folk tunes and nursery rhymes ('I'm off with the raggle-taggle gipsies, O!') and fragments of genuine literary material ('Call for the robin redbreast and the wren'), culminating in the final 'uproar', where Stevenson, Tennyson, Dante, Shakespeare and 'Anon' are jangled together with Miss La Trobe's own inventions.

Like the successive historical scenes in *Orlando*, the play shows the development of the language from highly coloured dramatic Elizabethan verse, to the elegance of eighteenth-century lyrics and prose, to the sentimental or bombastic clichés of Victorianism, to the cacophany and incoherence of the present. As each of its styles throws off the last, so each of its scenes shows the younger generation throwing off the older. Within the pastiche there are some striking moments of lyricism:

> What pleasure lies in dreaming
> When blue and green's the day?
> Now cast your cares behind you.
> Night passes: here is Day. (p. 89)

of vitality:

> Yet to think on't – how we hid in the dairy the day the cat jumped. And read romances under the holly tree. La! how I cried when the Duke left poor Polly . . . And my Aunt found me with eyes like red jellies. 'What stung, niece?' says she. And cried 'Quick Deb, the blue bag.' (p. 97)

and of humour:

> My mother with her last breath charged me to give this ring only to one to whom a lifetime in the African desert among the heathens would be – ELEANOR (*taking the ring*) Perfect happiness! (p. 116)

But as a whole the play seems to be exaggeratedly literary, and too long. These failings in the play are necessary, though they weaken the novel. If Miss La Trobe is to communicate the literary history of England to an English audience, she has to exaggerate or they won't understand her. Representation involves distortion, as her last scene with the mirrors makes clear. And, if the play is to communicate a sense of history, it must also communicate a sense of duration. It fills the main part of this short novel, and like the history of England, it seems, until its abrupt closure, to be going on for ever. Any impatience the reader may be tempted to feel is controlled by Mrs Manresa's comically philistine reaction, which the reader will not be willing to share:

> Mrs Manresa looked at her programme. It would take till midnight unless they skipped. Early Briton; Plantagenets; Tudors; Stuarts – she ticked them off, but probably she had forgotten a reign or two. (p. 61)

The long process of history is imaged in the play by the disintegration of historic forms of language into the 'jangle and the din' of the modern age, followed by the 'megaphontic anonymous loudspeaking' voice (p. 130) which tells the audience that it consists of 'scraps, orts and fragments'. A loss of dignity, culminating in the Rev. Streatfield's peroration, has been traced. It is a quality which is carefully made away with in the novel. The heroine makes her first appearence looking like a bolster; romantic emotions – unrequited love, the hatred of war – are rendered absurd; and one has only to compare Mrs Swithin to Mrs Ramsay or Miss La Trobe to Lily Briscoe to see that the characters who embody sympathetic or admirable states of mind have become ridiculous or grotesque.

The breakdown of dignity is neatly summed up by the use of nicknames. Mrs Swithin, Cindy to her brother, is known variously to the servants as 'Batty' (p. 11), 'Old Flimsy' (pp. 23, 107), 'Old Swithin' (p. 23) and 'old Mother Swithin' (p. 28). She knows and accepts this – 'Old Flimsy – that's me' (p. 46) – just as Miss La Trobe knows that the villagers call her 'Bossy' (p. 147). Bartholemew Oliver, Bart to his sister, had his drawing-room name, 'The Master', changed to 'Bartie' downstairs; likewise the cat, Sung-Yen, undergoes 'a kitchen change into Sunny' (p. 27).

The recurrent nicknames partly serve as brilliant illustrations of the novel's social climate. The villagers have a subtle and long-standing attitude to the gentry, which accepts class divisions ('It's all my eye about democracy' (p. 75) Mrs Manresa concludes), resents outsiders (Miss La Trobe is 'an outcast' (p. 147)), and does not spare eccentricities. The attitude, as Virginia Woolf explains, is a kind of snobbery, part of the chauvinism which prevents Mrs Sands from ever going 'over the hill' and makes the servants want to 'have their ghost'.

Snobs they were; long enough stationed that is in that one corner of the world to have taken indelibly the print of some three hundred years of customary behaviour. So they laughed; but respected. (pp. 23–4)

As this passage shows, the servants' use of nicknames makes a historical point as well as a social one. The downgrading of names reflects not only the relationship between gentry and villagers, but also the erosion of the grandeur of the past. This is emphasized in the constant iteration all through the play of the villagers' real names side by side with the characters they represent: '*England am I*, Phyllis Jones continued' (p. 58); 'From behind the bushes issued Queen Elizabeth – Eliza Clark, licenced to sell tobacco' (p. 62). As the play's time span comes within living memory, the absurd dichotomy between the villagers and the characters they represent lessens: Budge (the publican) is the right name for a Victorian policeman. Two points are being made at once. The continuity of English history is established: the figures of the past live again in the local village people. But the village names also seem ridiculous by contrast with the historic figures, suggesting the inferiority of modern times.

A close analogy is drawn between the downgrading of names and the decline in dignity of the house:

> The house before the Reformation, like so many houses in that neighbourhood, had a chapel; and the chapel had become a larder, changing, like the cat's name, as religion changed. (p. 27)

Pointz Hall, like all of England, takes its character from the distant past. The roots of the pear tree go under the flags (p. 109), the garden is said to be 500 years old (p. 106), the view from the garden (as described in 'Figgis's Guide Book, 1833') has not changed. As Mrs Swithin remarks, 'That's what makes a view so sad [. . .] and so beautiful. It'll be there [. . .] when we're not' (p. 41). The house has its accumulated legends and trophies: the concealed passage, the doomed lady's ghost, the watch 'that had stopped a bullet on the field of Waterloo' (p. 10). But Pointz Hall is not what it was. It has been sold to a family which does not reach very far back into the country's history (unlike the Swithin family, Lucy's by marriage, who 'were there before the Conquest' (p. 26)):

> The Olivers, who had bought the place something over a century ago, had no connexion with the Warings, the Elveys, the Mannerings, or the Burnets; the old families who had all intermarried, and lay in their deaths intertwisted, like the ivy roots, beneath the churchyard wall. (p. 9)

The unfinished wing has never been completed; the chapel is now the larder; the bedroom furnishings are ugly mid-Victorian things from Maples, and the library is full of 'shilling shockers that week-enders had dropped' (p. 16).

The change for the meaner is general. The cesspool is to overlay the original Roman road; the festal pageant is for the installation of electric lighting in the church. The communal voice of the villagers harks not only on the war, poised to destroy these fragments of civilization, but also on the new bungalows and the impact of 'the motor bike, the motor bus, and the movies' (p. 57). Family names sum up the decline. Some of the local names are in 'the Doomsday Book' (p. 26):

> Had Figgis been there in person and called a roll call, half the ladies and gentlemen present would have said: '*Adsum*; I'm here, in place of my grandfather or great-grandfather,' as the case might be. (p. 56)

but others had been wiped out, as in the case of

> the great lady in the bath chair, the lady whose marriage with the local peer had obliterated in his trashy title a name that had been a name when there were brambles and briars where the Church now stood. (p. 69)

Names and speech thus reveal the tension of modern life between enduring tradition and impoverishing encroachments. And the encroachments themselves take the form of language. Against the fragmented 'historical' language that remains in old family names, old sayings, old plays and poems, is thrust the language of the modern age, apt for a 'book-shy' (and 'gun-shy') generation. Isa and her contemporaries can, she feels, no longer use their own literary and linguistic heritage:

> For her generation the newspaper was a book; and, as her father-in-law dropped *The Times*, she took it and read: 'A horse with a green tail . . .' which was fantastic. Next, 'The guard at Whitehall . . .' which was romantic and then, building word upon word she read: 'The troopers told her the horse had a green tail; but she found it was just an ordinary horse. And they dragged her up to the barrack room where she was thrown upon a bed. Then one of the troopers removed part of her clothing and she screamed and hit him about the face . . .'
> That was real. (pp. 18–19)

It is not a fairy story after all, but the horrific reality with which each day the newspaper 'obliterates the day before' (p. 150). *Between the Acts* deals with the appallingly destructive impact of war on civilization in a characteristically inhibited and tangential way. Violence is explicitly contained in the few references to the war, in this account of the rape, and in Giles's trampling on the snake and the toad, a gesture all the more brutal for its isolation and its point-lessness. But more usually the idea of destruction is channelled into an emphasis on the destruction of language. It is appropriate, though, that when Isa picks up the newspaper she reads of something horrific: it is all that the modern media has to speak of. When it speaks of hope, it speaks of it in the sterile language of the age. Machines are its Messianic promise:

> Homes will be built. Each flat with its refrigerator, in the crannied wall. Each of us a free man; plates washed by mach-inery; not an aeroplane to vex us; all liberated; made whole . . .
> (p. 127)

The communal voice of the audience, which periodically takes over from individuals or from the narrator, is filled with the arid trivia of modern language, culled from newspapers and radio. Temporarily, the play lures them towards a historic language, particularly during the Victorian scenes, which are close enough for them to remember. Here the communal voice changes: street-cries and old stories seep in. But after the play is over, the language of the time recurs, and any glimpses of the past are immediately overborne:

> Then those voices from the bushes ... Oracles? You're referring to the Greeks? Were the Oracles, if I'm not being irreverent, a foretaste of our own religion? Which is what? ... Crepe soles? That's so sensible ... They last much longer and protect the feet ... (p. 138)

But the scraps and fragments of modern speech are not the outermost ring in the linguistic structure of the novel. Encircling all is the language of the narrator, whose speech is by turns decorative, witty and lyrical. It abounds in crisp, formal figures of speech – the birds singing 'like so many choir boys attacking an iced cake' (p. 10), the nurses rolling words 'like sweets on their tongues' (p. 11), the pigeons 'as ornate as ladies in ball dresses' (p. 53) – which (rather like the language of the interludes in *The Waves*) humanize the natural world and impose a sense of order and decorum on experience. These decorations are part of the humour of the narrative frame, which constantly deflects the book's intense sadness into an ironic tone, very largely created by the narrator's fluid participation in her characters' trains of thought and turns of phrase. It is the technique of *To the Lighthouse*, abandoned in *The Waves* and now masterfully reinstating the humour which that novel lacked.

> Mrs Manresa was nettled. What for had she squatted on the floor then? Were her charms fading? Both were gone. But, woman of action as she was, deserted by the male sex, she was not going to suffer tortures of boredom from the refeened old lady. Up she scrambled, putting her hands to hair as if it were high time that she went too, though it was perfectly tidy. Cobbet in his corner saw through her little game. He had known human nature in the East. It was the same in the West. (pp. 79–80)

The man was an ancestor. He had a name. He held the rein in his hand. He had said to the painter:
> 'If you want my likeness, dang it sir, take it when the leaves are on the trees.' There were leaves on the trees. He had said:

'Ain't there room for Colin as well as Buster?' Colin was his famous hound. But there was only room for Buster. It was, he seemed to say, addressing the company not the painter, a damned shame to leave out Colin whom he wished buried at his feet, in the same grave, about 1750; but that skunk the Reverend Whatshisname wouldn't allow it. (pp. 29–30)

The passage leads on to a change in the narrator's diction for the lyrical evocation of the empty room where the pictures hang.

> The room was a shell, singing of what was before time was; a vase stood in the heart of the house, alabaster, smooth, cold, holding the still, distilled essence of emptiness, silence. (p. 30)

Every so often the squalor, indignity or frustration of the protagonists is encircled by such passages of narrative, which are pointedly evocative and romantic, as though standing in defiance of the fragmentation of language which the rest of the novel describes. By contrast with Miss La Trobe's cumbersome pastiche and Isa's affected, inhibited rhymings, the narrator's lyricism is fluent and masterful. It operates in direct contrast to the language of the media, of, for example, the weather forecast:

> 'The forecast,' said Mr Oliver [. . .] 'says: Variable winds; fair average temperature; rain at times.' [. . .] Certainly the weather was variable. It was green in the garden; grey the next. Here came the sun – an illimitable rapture of joy, embracing every flower, every leaf. Then in compassion it withdrew, covering its face, as if it forebore to look on human suffering. (p. 20)

> And then a breeze blew and all the muslin blinds fluttered out, as if some majestic goddess, rising from her throne among her peers, had tossed her amber-coloured raiment, and the other gods, seeing her rise and go, laughed, and their laughter floated her on. (p. 55)

> No one had seen the cloud coming. There it was, black, swollen, on top of them. Down it poured like all the people in the world weeping. Tears. Tears. Tears. (p. 125)

Such passages are characterized by their sanctification of the universe with mystical presences. The lyrical language of the narrator, which comes so hard to the characters within the novel, is used to evoke a sense of faith. Thus the outer ring of language acts as an implied antidote to the sense of dereliction which is central to the book, and which is found most intensely in Isa's poems.

The word that characterizes Isa to herself is 'abortive', and it is a word which echoes through the book, imaged by the 'monstrous inversion' of birth (p. 72), the snake with the toad in its mouth. Relationships, social intercourse, art, all are abortive. Miss La Trobe's sense of failure, which almost always stays with her, is analogous to the failure that accompanies all attempts to communicate or harmonize. The action of the book is itself abortive. There are no developments in relationships; any perceptions aroused by the play are lost and dispersed by the day's end; Giles and Isa go on re-enacting their conflict of love and hate. Such pointless repetition is the condition of modern man; individual unhappiness is descriptive of a general experience. (Hence the peculiar fact that, though the relationships are powerfully presented, the characterization of individuals is rather sketchy.) The social and familial organization of the novel suggests a destructive tension between over-closeness and lack of communication. The unhappy married pair are 'pegged down' and 'pressed flat' by their situation, Giles tied to work for which he has no love or aptitude, Isa to a domesticity which she resents. They are only alone at nightfall, spending their days exposed to the family group, which in its turn has continually to accommodate to social intrusions. Individuals are given up to the group, and have to struggle for some sort of private integrity and sense of meaning within a press of people, which seems to increase in oppressiveness as the family group is merged with the larger, more formalized group of the village audience.[1]

---

[1] Virginia Woolf had been reading 'Freud on Groups' (*AWD*, 18 December 1939, p. 322), where it is pointed out that the origins of the group personality are to be found in the more circumscribed family circle (*Group Psychology and the Analysis of the Ego*, translated James Strachey (London and Vienna, International Psycho-Analytical Library, 1922), p. 3).

The characters struggle constantly but ineffectually to find free and private ways to communicate. William Dodge is taken by Mrs Swithin to look at the house and by Isa to look at the greenhouse, but they do not find words for what they want to say to each other. Giles unsuccessfully tries to vindicate his manhood to himself by disappearing with Mrs Manresa. But for most of the time they are imprisoned in the social sphere which prevents their passions from finding release through expression:

> He said (without words) 'I'm damnably unhappy.'
> 'So am I,' Dodge echoed.
> 'And I too,' Isa thought.
> They were all caught and caged; prisoners; watching a spectacle. Nothing happened. (p. 123)

Their situation is none the less desperate because it exists within a pleasantly rural, genteel, traditional social occasion. As in Jane Austen's novels, personal submission to the small social round can be horrific. And, in Jane Austen's words, it is the 'little zigzags of embarrassment'[1] which characterize the horror of social bondage.

The hostility of the social world to its misfits colours the existence of the novel's two homosexuals, Miss La Trobe and William Dodge, who deal with their pariahdom in opposite ways, the first by aggression and activity, the second by retreat into a nervous reserve. But all the characters, not only the obvious cases of unadaptability, are struggling with the necessities of social behaviour. This is why Mrs Manresa, though predatory and not quite honest, still shows up well for her calculated defiance of conventions. However much of an affectation, it is still a virtue in her because of its liberating effect:

> for everybody felt, directly she spoke, 'She's said it, she's done it, not I,' and could take advantage of the breach of decorum, of the fresh air that blew in, to follow like leaping dolphins in the wake of an ice-breaking vessel. (p. 33)

Mrs Manresa 'feels free' because she is in fact the most well-adjusted character in the novel. She can afford to flout conventions,

---

[1] Jane Austen, *Emma* (1816), Ch. 15.

not being threatened by them. Her counterpart in this respect is Mrs Swithin, whose mind is not tied down by social forms. But the other characters are painfully imprisoned. As a result, there are frequent moments in which some form of social embarrassment acts as an indication of inner suffering or unwillingness to adapt. The first scene, in which all the themes of the novel are densely woven, contains one such uncomfortable moment. Mrs Haines, aware of the emotion 'circling' her husband and Isa, rises to leave, extending her hand.

> But Isa, though she should have risen at the same moment that Mrs Haines rose, sat on. Mrs Haines glared at her out of goose-like eyes, gobbling, 'Please, Mrs Giles Oliver, do me the kindness to recognize my existence . . . ' which she was forced to do, rising at last from her chair [. . .] (p. 9)

Isa refuses here to embark on the kind of social rescue operation with which, the next day after lunch, she covers up for her husband, whose horror at his situation is beginning to show itself. To distract attention, Isa 'half purposely' knocks over a coffee cup (p. 46), an acceptable, manageable social blunder. (William Dodge, delicately 'managing', catches the cup.) But social embarrassment can take less obvious forms. A case in point is Bartholemew's game with George. The old man means to amuse, not to frighten; the boy, startled, his private world destroyed by the intrusion, refuses to 'play along'. It is analogous to Isa's refusal to 'play along' with Mrs Haines. Mother and child both cause dismay by their refusal to share the other person's terms of reference. Such inopportune misunderstandings are frequent. Isa asks William to look at the greenhouse, but not when he wants her to; Mrs Swithin's failure to communicate with Miss La Trobe is embarrassing until Mrs Swithin breaks through the impasse; Miss La Trobe is not there when she should be being thanked by the vicar. Only Mrs Manresa is oblivious and unembarrassed when her attempts to communicate misfire:

> 'Scenes from English history,' Mrs Manresa explained to Mrs Swithin. She spoke in a loud cheerful voice, as if the old lady were deaf. 'Merry England.' (p. 61)

The discomfort of social bondage is at its height in the extraordinarily horrifying scene in the garden after lunch, which includes Isa's knocking over of the cup. The conversation touches lightly on the pageant; but the real, inexpressible conversation concerns Giles's racked preoccupation with the war, his resentment of William Dodge, and Isa's awareness of all his feelings. The view is the same as it has always been, the weather is hot, and there is nothing for them to do but to look at the view and wait for the pageant:

> They stared at the view, as if something might happen in one of those fields to relieve them of the intolerable burden of sitting silent, doing nothing, in company. Their minds and bodies were too close, yet not close enough. We aren't free, each one of them felt separately to feel or think separately, nor yet to fall asleep. We're too close; but not close enough. So they fidgeted.
> [. . .] The flat fields glared green yellow, blue yellow, red yellow, then blue again. The repetition was senseless, hideous, stupefying. (pp. 50–1)

It is hell on earth: no escape, no end, no privacy and no communication. Mrs Swithin can escape, taking William with her; Bartholomew, his intoxication with Mrs Manresa wearing off, retreats into sleep. The scene does end, but it is stupefying while it lasts, a powerful example of the way in which this novel builds a complex pattern of relationships, and the sense of duration and intensity, out of short, fragmented scenes.

The imprisoned group watching the view and drinking coffee anticipates the predicament of Miss La Trobe's audience. A theatrical experience is the perfect means of exhibiting extreme forms of social embarrassment. The discomfort which is limited to individuals when one person refuses to shake hands with another is kin to that felt by a large group when something goes wrong on stage, or when nothing happens at all and 'Illusion fails'. It is a grotesque version of the many delicate shades of misunderstanding and embarrassment in social life: grotesque, because the spectators, instead of acting naturally and unconsciously as social beings, are artificially made to participate as a group. As long as the illusion works, they lose their selfconsciousness and are passive and willingly convinced: 'The audience sat gazing; and beheld gently and approvingly, [. . .] for it seemed inevitable, a box tree in a green tub [. . .]' (p. 96). But as soon as things don't 'seem inevitable' they are made aware of themselves, and embarrassed. 'All their nerves were on edge. They sat exposed [. . .] They were suspended, without being, in limbo' (p. 124). Miss La Trobe is herself embarrassed — it is like death for her — by her failure to convince, which is an extreme form of a social failure to communicate. She wants to discomfort her audience, not through the inadequacy of her art, but through the triumph of illusion. This she finally succeeds in doing by 'holding the mirror up to nature' and forcing the audience to recognize its own hapless participation in what it has been watching — a play about the history and character of England. The spectators (apart from Mrs Manresa) are embarrassed at having to stare at themselves in public. The experience is horrible; reality seems grotesque. But their embarrassment at this point is useful, unlike that which resulted from the failure of illusion. Miss La Trobe's efforts to make them see the truth have succeeded — though only by the crudest and most haphazard of means.

All Miss La Trobe's moments of theatrical success are fortuitous, and due to nature and music rather than to speech. It is the bellowing of cows and the downpour of rain which 'take her part' in moving the audience and concentrating its wandering attention, and the tunes of the gramophone which determine the spectators' moods, lamenting for their dispersal, but also lulling them, keeping them together, unifying them to be 'all comprehending; all enlisted' (p. 131).

The comparative ineffectuality of language is of central importance, not only in the context of the play. So far two areas of the novel's concern with language have appeared: the dereliction of the modern age, where language is in decay, and the bondage of social intercourse, where language is necessary but inadequate. But there are areas of human experience in which language is redundant. In the novel's subtly organized short sections, an alternation is noticeable between scenes of communication and scenes of silence. Midway through the lunch party, for example, the scullery maid communes in silence with the ghost of the lady in the lilypond.

Once the play takes over the main part of the book, the alternation is between the acts and the intervals. After the play, the pattern is to some extent continued (Miss La Trobe's solitary musings contrasting with the leavetakings of the audience) until the final scene, which impressively welds silence and communication together.

Some of the silent scenes show places without people, lovely but sad (like the deserted house in *To the Lighthouse*) because unseen. They suggest a world lying just behind the populated world we know, like the 'other play which always lay behind the play she had just written' (p. 48). The empty dining-room with its two pictures, 'a shell, singing of what was before time was' (p. 30); the nursery, 'a ship deserted by its crew' (p. 54); the barn, 'empty', but pullulating with animal life (p. 73): all conserve a secret tranquillity which the entrance of people destroys. The dining-room's two pictures sum up the two worlds of speech and silence: the 'talk producing' ancestor is contrasted with the 'picture', the lady who 'led them down green glades into the heart of silence' (p. 39).

But people are necessary, however attractive the heart of silence is made to seem.

> The fire greyed, then glowed, and the tortoiseshell butterfly beat on the lower pane of the window; beat, beat, beat; repeating that if no human being ever came, never, never, never, the books would be mouldy, the fire out and the tortoiseshell butterfly dead on the pane. (p. 16)

The uninhabited world behind the world of speech and personality is fearsome. Its presence presses in on the characters so that they are felt to be threatened with the potential return of a prehistoric condition in which the earth would be given back to swamp and jungle and the animals. The effect is partly produced by the prehistoric images which fill Mrs Swithin's mind from her reading, and partly by the constant use of animal metaphors for the characters, particularly noticeable in the sinister identification of Bartholemew with his dog Sohrab. In no case are these comfortable images: on Mrs Swithin's forehead is 'a blue vein wriggling like a blue worm' (p. 55); the lady married to a local peer 'resembled an uncouth, nocturnal animal, now nearly extinct' (p. 69). By the end, when the family is seen as a circle of insects, and Giles and Isa's relationship is compared to the dog-fox fighting with the vixen in the fields of night – 'the night before roads were made, or houses' (p. 152) – the effect has become terrifying. The destruction of England is imminent; perhaps this is the only future imaginable, a return to prehistory with all civilization wiped out. But, though civilization as it stands is oppressive, trivial and decaying, the alternative of a speechless animal life is not altogether enticing. Some creative and harmonizing personality is still required; as ever, human attempts to find momentary order over chaos must still continue

> and now,
> Under conditions that seem unpropitious.[1]

They are made by the narrator in her establishing of a lyric frame around a story of dereliction; they are made by Miss La Trobe in her painful and ungainly struggle to be true to the fragmentary nature of life, while giving it coherence; and they are made, ridiculously, but with tenderness and grace, by Mrs Swithin.

Mrs Swithin's unifying vision of life is not at the centre of the novel; it is one of many fragments. Nor is it presented with any grandeur or dignity. She is laughed at because she is a ridiculously eccentric figure, she has her weaknesses (her insensitivity to Miss La Trobe after the play, for example), and she has weighed herself down with an allegiance to crucifixes and clergymen which the other characters find difficult to understand. Her vision is at every point undermined by her brother's elevation of reason and fact: their conflict is irreconcilable, yet it is the conflict of lovers, following the mould of the Ramsays' relationship (even to their conversation about the weather). Rather like Mrs Ramsay, Mrs Swithin is at times a sinister character. Her appetite for the prehistoric world is alarming; she enters 'carrying a hammer' (p. 19) while Isa is reading about the rape; she lures William Dodge into the bedrooms of the house almost like a siren; at the end, after staring eerily into the picture of Venice in search of 'a little figure – woman, veiled; or a man?' 'in the hood of the gondola' she returns into the room 'like a tragic figure from another play' (p. 149). She is partly a figure of doom, the prophetess of the destruction of civilization and

[1] T. S. Eliot, 'East Coker', V (1940), *Four Quartets*.

its return to 'a swamp'. For all this, she is heroic, particularly in her resistance to Bart, and her vision of unity is presented in a sympathetic tone, all the more convincing because it stems from characters within the novel.

> She was off, they guessed, on a circular tour of the imagination
> – one-making. Sheep, cows, grass, trees, ourselves – all are one.
> If discordant, producing harmony – if not to us, to a gigantic
> ear attached to a gigantic head. And thus – she was smiling
> benignly – the agony of the particular sheep, cow, or human
> being is necessary; and so – she was beaming seraphically at the
> gilt vane in the distance – we reach the conclusion that *all* is
> harmony, could we hear it. And we shall. Her eyes rested on
> the white summit of a cloud. Well, if the thought gave her
> comfort, William and Isa smiled across her, let her think it.
> (p. 122)

The tone does not lend much credence to this Emersonian vision, but makes its enthusiasm attractive. Its good effect, too, is emphasized: Mrs Swithin *is* creating harmony at this moment between Isa and William. Faith in organized religion has not been given charitable treatment in the novels, but here it coexists with kindness and integrity. And Mrs Swithin's faith, though official, and in some ways risible, is familiar to us in its ingredients. In an exaggerated and simplistic version it restates the tentative consolations for suffering and death found in *Jacob's Room*, *Mrs Dalloway* and *To the Lighthouse*. The self may free itself from the bondage of personality, and be merged in an impersonal world. Mrs Swithin, like Clarissa, hopes that this is the meaning of death: an immortality of speechlessness. But, appropriately in a novel which describes the conflicting claims of language and silence, her hope also suggests the impersonal achievement of the writer, whose immortality is words.

> 'But we have other lives, I think, I hope,' she murmured.
> 'We live in others, Mr ... We live in things.' (p. 53)

Select bibliography

ANNAN, NOEL. *Leslie Stephen: His Thought and Character in Relation to his Time.* London, MacGibbon and Kee, 1951.

AUERBACH, ERICH. *Mimesis: The Representation of Reality in Western Literature.* Berne, Francke, 1946. Translated Willard Trask. Princeton, NJ, Princeton University Press, 1953; New York, Anchor Books, 1957. Chapter 20.

BASHAM, C. '*Between the Acts*'. *Durham University Journal*, Vol. 52 (1959), pp. 87–94.

BAYLEY, JOHN. *The Romantic Survival: A Study in Poetic Evolution.* London, Constable, 1957; Chatto and Windus, 1969.

BAZIN, NANCY TOPPING. *Virginia Woolf and the Androgynous Vision.* New Brunswick, NJ, Rutgers University Press, 1973.

BEACH, J. W. 'Virginia Woolf'. *The English Journal*, Vol. 26 (October 1937), pp. 603–12.

BELL, QUENTIN. *Virginia Woolf: A Biography.* Vol. I: *Virginia Stephen, 1882–1912.* Vol. II: *Mrs Woolf, 1912–1941.* London, Hogarth Press, 1972.

—— *Bloomsbury.* London, Weidenfeld and Nicolson, 1968; Omega edition, Futura, 1974.

BENNETT, JOAN. *Virginia Woolf: Her Art as a Novelist.* Cambridge University Press, 1945; 2nd ed. 1964.

BLACKSTONE, BERNARD. *Virginia Woolf: A Commentary.* London, Hogarth Press, 1949.

BRADBROOK, MURIEL. 'Notes on the Style of Mrs Woolf'. *Scrutiny*, Vol. I (May 1932), pp. 33–8.

BREWSTER, DOROTHY. *Virginia Woolf*. London, Allen and Unwin, 1963.

CHAMBERS, R. L. *The Novels of Virginia Woolf*. Edinburgh and London, Oliver and Boyd, 1947.

DAICHES, DAVID. *Virginia Woolf*. Norfolk, Conn., New Directions, 1942; London, Nicholson and Watson, Editions Poetry 1945; rev. ed. New York, New Directions, 1963.

—— *The Novel and the Modern World*. Chicago, University of Chicago Press, 1960.

FORSTER, E. M. 'Virginia Woolf'. *The Rede Lecture*. Cambridge University Press, 1941. Collected in *Two Cheers for Democracy*. London, Edward Arnold, 1951; Harmondsworth, Penguin, 1965.

FREEDMAN, RALPH. *The Lyrical Novel: Studies in Hermann Hesse, André Gide, and Virginia Woolf*. Princeton, NJ, Princeton University Press, 1963.

GREENE, GRAHAM. 'François Mauriac'. *Collected Essays*, pp. 115–16. London, Bodley Head, 1969.

GUIGUET, JEAN. *Virginia Woolf and Her Works*. Translated Jean Stewart. London, Hogarth Press, 1965.

HAFLEY, JAMES. *The Glass Roof: Virginia Woolf as Novelist*. Berkeley and Los Angeles, University of California Press, 1954.

HOLMS, J. F. '*Mrs Dalloway*'. Review in *Calendar of Modern Letters* (July 1925), pp. 404–5.

HOLROYD, MICHAEL. *Lytton Strachey: A Critical Biography*. 2 vols. London, Heinemann, 1967–8. Reissued as *Lytton Strachey and the Bloomsbury Group: His Work, Their Influence* and *Lytton Strachey: A Biography*. Harmondsworth, Penguin, 1971.

HOLTBY, WINIFRED. *Virginia Woolf*. London, Wishart, 1932.

JOHNSTONE, J. K. *The Bloomsbury Group: A Study of E. M. Forster, Lytton Strachey, Virginia Woolf, and Their Circle*. London, Secker and Warburg, 1954.

KELLEY, ALICE VAN BUREN. *The Novels of Virginia Woolf: Fact and Vision*. Chicago and London, University of Chicago Press, 1973.

KETTLE, ARNOLD. *An Introduction to the English Novel*. Vol. II. London, Hutchinson University Library, 1953; reprinted 1969.

KIRKPATRICK, B. J. *A Bibliography of Virginia Woolf*. London, Hart-Davis, 1957.

KUMAR, SHIV. *Bergson and the Stream of Consciousness Novel*. London and Glasgow, Blackie, 1962.

LATHAM, JACQUELINE E. M. (ed.) *Critics on Virginia Woolf: Readings in Literary Criticism*. London, Allen and Unwin, 1970.

LEAVIS, F. R. 'After *To the Lighthouse*'. *Scrutiny*, Vol. X (1942), pp. 295–8.

LODGE, DAVID. *Language of Fiction: Essays in Criticism and Verbal Analysis of the English Novel*. London, Routledge and Kegan Paul, 1966.

MAJUMDAR, ROBIN, and MCLAURIN, ALLEN (eds.) *Virginia Woolf: The Critical Heritage*. London and Boston, Routledge and Kegan Paul, 1975.

MARDER, HERBERT. *Feminism and Art: A Study of Virginia Woolf*. Chicago and London, University of Chicago Press, 1968.

MCLAURIN, ALLEN. *Virginia Woolf: The Echoes Enslaved*. Cambridge University Press, 1973.

MELLERS, W. H. 'Mrs Woolf and Life'. *Scrutiny*, Vol. VI (1937), pp. 71–5. Reprinted in Eric Bentley (ed.), *The Importance of Scrutiny*. New York, G. W. Stewart, 1948.

MOODY, A. D. *Virginia Woolf*. Edinburgh and London, Oliver and Boyd, 1963.

NAREMORE, JAMES. *The World Without a Self: Virginia Woolf and the Novel*. New Haven and London, Yale University Press, 1973.

RICHTER, HARVENA. *Virginia Woolf: The Inward Voyage*. Princeton, NJ, Princeton Universtity Press, 1970.

SAVAGE, D. S. *The Withered Branch: Six Studies in the Modern Novel*. London, Eyre and Spottiswoode, 1950.

SPRAGUE, CLAIRE (ed.) *Virginia Woolf: A Collection of Critical Essays*. Twentieth Century Views. Englewood Cliffs, NJ, Prentice-Hall, 1971.

TROY, WILLIAM. 'Virginia Woolf: The Novel of Sensibility'. In Morton Zabel (ed.), *Literary Opinion in America*, New York, Harper and Row, 1937, pp. 324–37.

WOOLF, LEONARD *Sowing: An Autobiography of the Years 1880–1904.* London, Hogarth Press, 1960.

—— *Growing: An Autobiography of the Years 1904–1911.* London, Hogarth Press, 1961.

—— *Beginning Again: An Autobiography of the Years 1911–1918.* London, Hogarth Press, 1964.

—— *Downhill All the Way: An Autobiography of the Years 1919–1939.* London, Hogarth Press, 1967.

—— *The Journey not the Arrival Matters: An Autogiography of the Years 1939–1969.* London, Hogarth Press, 1969.

VIRGINIA WOOLF: TEXTS

The Voyage Out. London, Duckworth, 1915; Harmondsworth, Penguin, 1970.

Night and Day. Duckworth, 1919; Penguin, 1969.

Jacob's Room. London, Hogarth Press, 1922; Penguin, 1965.

Mrs Dalloway. Hogarth Press, 1925; Penguin, 1964.

To the Lighthouse. Hogarth Press, 1927; Penguin, 1964.

Orlando. Hogarth Press, 1928; Penguin, 1942.

A Room of One's Own. Hogarth Press, 1929; Penguin, 1945, 1963.

The Waves. Hogarth Press, 1931; Penguin, 1951.

Flush: A Biography. Hogarth Press, 1933.

The Years. Hogarth Press, 1937; Penguin, 1968.

Three Guineas. Hogarth Press, 1938.

Roger Fry: A Biography. Hogarth Press, 1940.

Between the Acts. Hogarth Press, 1941; Penguin, 1953.

A Haunted House and Other Short Stories. Hogarth Press, 1944; Penguin, 1973.

A Writer's Diary: Being Extracts from the Diary of Virginia Woolf. Ed. Leonard Woolf. Hogarth Press, 1953.

Virginia Woolf and Lytton Strachey: Letters. Ed. Leonard Woolf and James Strachey. Hogarth Press, 1956.

Contemporary Writers. Hogarth Press, 1965.

Collected Essays. Ed. Leonard Woolf. 4 vols. London, Chatto and Windus, 1966, 1967.

Mrs Dalloway's Party. A short story sequence. Ed. Stella McNichol. Hogarth Press, 1973.

INDEX

Index

Index 235

Errata to original text